A. DALE TUSSING

Poverty in a Dual Economy

ST. MARTIN'S PRESS · NEW YORK

1981

Poverty in a
Dual Economy

Contents

Introduction

This is not a book solely about the "economics of poverty." I am an economist and am proud of the analytic power, depth, and achievements of my discipline, which I hope are to some extent represented in this volume. But the concept of an "economics of poverty" is, by itself, too narrow to be of use to the general student, to the serious scholar, or to the legislator or policy-maker. In writing this book, therefore, I have drawn on the literature, methods, and perspectives of many fields.

This is also not, primarily, a book about poor people. Studies of the poor, of which there is an abundance, have important functions. The stereotyped images of poor people are frequently inconsistent with the facts, and such studies help "demythologize" the poor. They sensitize us to the enormous burdens of poverty, many of which are socially imposed. And, by clarifying the nature of the pathology of poverty, these studies help us to learn what kinds of policies can overcome the effects of poverty. A concentration on the characteristics of the poor can, however, leave the inaccurate impression that these characteristics are the *cause* of poverty.

Basically, this book was motivated by a desire to make three major points. The first is that most of the causes of poverty lie in the social and economic system as a whole, and not in the characteristics of the poor. The second is that an economy or a society with a dominant majority of nonpoor persons and a minority of poor people has special characteristics, which are not perceived when one focuses only on the poor. The third point is that such economies in general, and the U.S. economy in particular, exhibit a fundamental duality. Such economies adjust to the needs and behavior of the nonpoor majority, with subtle but harmful consequences for the poor. Moreover, the U.S. economy has developed dual sets of institutions—including a dual labor market (discussed in Chapter 2), a dual welfare system (discussed in Chapter 4), a dual housing system (discussed in Chapter 5), and others.

There are certain risks in adding another work to the literature on poverty. The attention given to poverty in the past decade has in many ways been useful, but it has contributed to a change in public focus that has had certain harmful effects. In the 1940s and before, and even to an extent during the 1950s, economic discontent in America focused on the excesses of the rich and on the power wielded by large corporations. Although the rhetoric of this discontent was sometimes exaggerated, on the whole the emphasis was a healthy one. There was—and is—a built-in tendency toward the concentration of economic wealth and power in the American economic system, and it is wise to keep the rich and powerful under continual scrutiny. If the notion of society as consisting of the rich and nonrich (the latter including the poor, the working class, and the middle class) was an oversimplification, it was a better oversimplification than the more recent notion of society as consisting of the poor and nonpoor.

Since the mid-1960s, public economic discontent has focused increasingly on the imagined excesses of the poor. Somehow, the impression has grown that the poor are a privileged leisure class, who can live comfortably—even luxuriously—without working and can, moreover, live the amoral lives of promiscuity and recklessness once attributed to the very rich. This erroneous picture of the poor is not, to be sure, solely a result of the rediscovery of poverty; it has other sources as well. But the abundant literature on poverty, by speaking of "poor" and "nonpoor" as distinct categories, has indirectly fostered the stereotype. For this reason one hesitates to enlarge the number of studies unless something useful and productive can come of it. I hope that this book, far from reinforcing a distorted conception of American poverty, will contribute to correcting it.

A widespread change has also occurred in the image the poor have of themselves. Before the 1960s, and particularly before World War II, it was possible for the poor to view themselves (as many did) as *exploited*. They could argue, with justice, that it was they who did the real, backbreaking work with which the wealth of the rich and powerful, and of the nation, was built. Today, although a few groups (like the farm workers) remain so clearly exploited that the old rhetoric still applies, most poor people are made to feel that they are *not needed*, and that they are a *burden* on society. (Of course this crushing feeling is something the poor share with other groups in American society—particularly old people, youth, and many women.) Although, obviously, no normal person would want to be either exploited or useless, presumably self-respect would lead most of us to prefer the former.

The poor have been made to carry a heavy burden of guilt. They begin with guilt that is based on their apparent "failure" in a success-oriented society. This guilt is compounded by the focus on the poor as the modern equivalent of the privileged rich. It is further aggravated by the apparent social uselessness of most poor people. Finally, the structure of many public programs, including antipoverty programs, implicitly attributes poverty to personal defects and solidifies this feeling of guilt.

In the late 1960s, in an effort to analyze this guilt, I wrote a series of articles in the *Home Town News*, a militant black newspaper in Syracuse, New York, edited by the late Chris Powell, whose powerful and brilliant personality will always remain a major influence on my life. Though I did not know it at the time, those articles were the genesis of this book. The series of articles continued in another Syracuse publication, *The Nickel Review*, whose editor, Walt Shepperd, learned much, as I did, from Powell.

Others from whom I learned much—though they may not have known it—include Jane Whitney, Clarissa Nichol, Ken Stokes, Lillian Mohr, and Wretha Wiley. In addition, two graduate students of mine, Gorden Allen and Thomas Carroll (who are also good friends), made a great many suggestions that improved my perceptions and understanding. Tom also did some of the research for this book. My colleague Jesse Burkhead is one more who made many helpful suggestions. Useful comments on the manuscript were supplied by another colleague, Louis Kriesberg, and by Dr. Robert Seidenberg of Syracuse.

An earlier version of part of Chapter 1 appeared as "Poverty, Education, and the Dual Economy" in the *Journal of Consumer Affairs*, 4 (Winter 1970), published by the American Council on Consumer Interests. Permission to reprint this material is gratefully acknowledged. An earlier version of Chapter 4 appeared in *Society* (January/February 1974), under the same title, "The Dual Welfare System." Chapter 3 is based on a paper, *A Social Model of Poverty and the Progress of the Welfare State* (1969), distributed in mimeograph form by the Educational Policy Research Center, Syracuse, New York. Parts of Chapters 2 and 6 have been adapted from another paper, *The Education Strategy* (1972), also distributed by the EPRC. The Center is not responsible for the views presented in those chapters or, for that matter, in the papers themselves. However, their support of my research was invaluable and is gratefully acknowledged.

1

The Problem
of Poverty

The subject of this book is poverty in a "dual economy"—a particular
type of dual economy in which the large majority are nonpoor and a
minority are chronically poor. It is the poverty of a minority subgroup,
not the poverty of a nation. Yet to understand it we must study not only
poor people but the economy *as a whole* and the poor's position in it.
Many "poverty studies" consist largely of studies of the poor. An
unfortunate, though no doubt unintended, consequence of this approach
is that it leaves the impression that poverty is a consequence of the
characteristics of the poor. In reality, however, one does not necessarily
come to understand the causes and implications of poverty by studying
poor people. In fact, it may even be more fruitful to study the rich,
although that is not the approach we shall use here.

Our purpose in this book is to examine (1) what poverty is and who is
poor, (2) the effects and implications of the existence of poverty in a dual
economy, (3) the fundamental causes of poverty, and (4) ways of ending
poverty.

The purpose of this chapter is to introduce the concept of poverty
(which is less self-explanatory than one might think) and the type of dual
economy with which we are concerned. Chapter 2 will examine a number
of the major characteristics of poverty, particularly those which are both
its causes and its effects, thereby forming a vicious circle. Chapter 3 will
develop a theoretical model to explain the existence or absence of poverty
under given conditions and the forms it may take. Chapters 4 and 5 will
examine the role of the welfare system in sustaining the poor and in
preventing, alleviating, and perhaps perpetuating poverty. Finally,
Chapter 6 will examine some nonwelfare approaches to combating poverty.

WHAT IS POVERTY?

Let us not confuse the *meaning* of poverty with the way it is measured. These are related but separable issues. Poverty has meant a great many different things to different people. Some aspects of it are easily measurable; others are not. Of the possible definitions of poverty, the most crucial for our purposes are those most closely related to our reasons for being concerned with it. When, and only when, we have ascertained what these definitions are should we attempt to determine whether and how well poverty in these terms is measurable.

It is common to define poverty as an insufficiency of means relative to needs, or as a condition of *moneylessness*. There is also a broader, though less concrete, concept of poverty as an aspect of social pathology that includes not only moneylessness but dependency, helplessness, lack of political influence, and the like. Poverty in this sense is a condition of *powerlessness*. This type of poverty is less easily measured.

Poverty as Moneylessness

Poverty in the sense of moneylessness means not having enough of the basic medium of exchange to satisfy elementary human needs and to function economically and socially. Elementary human needs exist in any society. And although standards of living vary from place to place and over time, there are still some common minimums: nutritious food, rest, and shelter; clothing in cold areas; medical care and sanitation in civilized nations; and recreation and entertainment in affluent ones. Poverty is a lack of sufficient resources, or money, to obtain these things.

The *way* in which various human needs are satisfied is determined socially and will, like standards of living, differ from society to society. In some cultures, each person may grow his own food. In others, food may be purchased daily in town markets or small neighborhood shops. In still others, food, some of it canned or frozen, may be purchased in larger quantities in shopping centers; buyers will use automobiles to transport it, and refrigerators and freezers to store it. Poverty will be defined differently in each of these societies. In one, the lack of a refrigerator may indicate indigence; in others it may not. There is no universally applicable standard of poverty, either in terms of dollars or in terms of goods and services.

Conceptually, the most direct way to determine who is poor in a society is to draw up a list of the basic goods and services needed to function in that society and place a money value on them. Persons whose incomes are below this value (that is, persons whose means are insufficient to meet basic needs) are classified as poor. This is a rather crude definition of who is impoverished, but it can be improved by excluding all those whose incomes are only temporarily low (such as graduate students and persons temporarily between jobs), whose lifelong incomes are expected to be fairly high, for whom low incomes are not a chronic problem to be passed on to the next generation, and whose low incomes do not constitute a social problem.

It can also be improved by taking into account *economic vulnerability*. A person who has a job that pays him precisely the minimum needed to function according to current standards, but who cannot be certain that he will have enough to get by tomorrow if his income falls or his needs increase, is in a highly vulnerable position. He may become poor at any moment. This limits his range of choices and affects his behavior. Economic vulnerability can be avoided, and economic security achieved, in four ways: by the ownership of wealth, or assets; by access to credit (the ability to borrow); by insurance; and by income-maintenance programs. With no welfare programs and no insurance, the only way to provide for such economic hazards as sickness, unemployment, and business failure is by saving (accumulating wealth) or by maintaining a good credit rating (which often depends on wealth). Welfare and insurance programs are substitutes for wealth. A person can have no assets, and no credit, and yet be fairly invulnerable to economic hazards if he is protected by medical insurance, workmen's compensation, retirement pensions, and the like. A person who has income security, insurance, and some assets may be less poor than a person with a higher income but with none of these protections.

POVERTY AS POWERLESSNESS

The poor do not differ from their fellow men (or women) merely in the size of their paychecks. Many are dependent psychologically as well as economically. Poor people have higher than average rates of criminality, suicide, narcotics addiction, physical and mental illness, and alcoholism. They are more likely to live in unhealthy surroundings in physically unsafe structures. Social and family disorganization are endemic to them. These problems are compounded by a pathological feeling of powerlessness. The poor lead lives that are, or seem to them to be, ordered largely by forces outside their control—by people in positions of authority, by perceived evil forces, or by "hard luck." To quote Professor Warren Haggstrom, the poor are faced with "a particularly difficult variety of situational dependency, a helplessness to affect many important social factors in their lives, the functioning or purpose of which they do not understand, and which are essentially unpredictable to them." In the United States, where material success is important and where commonly accepted mythology holds it to be within the reach of all, the poor are considered, by a definition even they seem to accept, failures. Their survival often depends on others, and their apathy in social matters is heightened by their economic vulnerability.

What people refer to, then, as "the problem of poverty" is not identical with an insufficiency of means relative to needs. Poverty is measured in terms of a lack of power as well as money. This power, moreover, is that of the most essential sort, control over one's own destiny. There are people who are poor in terms of income, savings, and the ability to meet future needs who are not poor in the pathological sense associated with powerlessness. And there are some who are poor in a pathological sense but who are not moneyless. (This group is probably not very large, however, since moneylessness is an important part of powerlessness.)

The equation of poverty with powerlessness has some important implications. One is that many of the most effective solutions to the problem of poverty must come from the poor themselves. Such movements as the National Welfare Rights Organization (NWRO) and The Woodlawn Organization (TWO), which aim not only at better economic conditions for welfare recipients and people in poor neighborhoods but also at a greater voice for them in matters that affect them, constitute a two-pronged attack on poverty. On the other hand, some ostensibly "antipoverty" programs that reinforce dependency and powerlessness by taking away from the poor control over their own lives may actually increase their sense of psychological dependency, stultify their personal development, and perpetuate their poverty.

THE RELATIONSHIP OF MONEYLESSNESS TO POWERLESSNESS

The opposite of powerlessness, of course, is power; but in what sense? We are talking about power not in the sense of authority over others but in the sense of *freedom*, the ability to make choices vitally affecting one's own life. Those with high incomes have many more choices than those with low incomes. They can choose where they will live, what forms of entertainment and recreation they will take, how they will dress, and often where they will work. Moneylessness is a vital aspect of powerlessness.

The concept of poverty as powerlessness underlines the importance of economic vulnerability. The poor are separated from the nonpoor not only by their current standard of living, but by their greater vulnerability to economic catastrophe, a vulnerability that limits their choices and hence their freedom. In short, moneylessness and economic vulnerability are forms of powerlessness.

MEASURES OF POVERTY

When American poverty was first "rediscovered" in the early 1960s, no detailed analysis of the incidence of the problem was available. Since some guidelines were needed, the government decided to use a family income of $3,000 as a rule-of-thumb "poverty line," regardless of the family's size, the age of its members, or their place of residence. The poverty line for unrelated individuals living alone was set at $1,500. A fixed poverty line is still used for some purposes (e.g., to determine eligibility for certain public programs), but it is hardly an ideal yardstick.

In 1964, scholars in the Social Security Administration developed a formula for a new, variable poverty line that has come into standard use in measuring the incidence of poverty. This new formula, still obviously crude, takes into account family size, the sex of the family head, the age of family members, and the family's place of residence. Department of Agriculture nutrition studies are used to determine the food budget necessary for families of each type. Since poor people tend to spend about one-third of their budget on food (somewhat less if the family is small), this figure is multiplied by three (slightly more in the case of smaller families) to obtain the minimum income, or poverty line, in each case. The poverty line for farm families is adjusted downward on the assumption that their basic living costs are 85 percent of those of urban families.

Average poverty lines for 1972, as indicated by government data, are given in Table 1-1. The most frequently quoted figure is the average poverty line for a family of four, $4,247, a figure which allows 32¢ per person per meal.

Most government data on poverty are gathered with the definitions and

TABLE 1 – 1

The Poverty Line for U.S. Families and Unrelated Individuals, 1972

Family Status	Total	NONFARM RESIDENCE			FARM RESIDENCE		
		Total	Male Head[a]	Female Head[a]	Total	Male Head[a]	Female Head[a]
Unrelated individuals (weighted average)	$2,101	$2,109	$2,207	$2,046	$1,774	$1,824	$1,723
Under 65	2,163	2,168	2,254	2,085	1,861	1,916	1,772
65 or over	1,994	2,005	2,025	2,000	1,708	1,722	1,698
All families (weighted average)	3,788	3,813	3,854	3,524	3,277	3,287	3,072
With 2 members	2,703	2,724	2,734	2,670	2,296	2,302	2,197
Head under 65	2,790	2,808	2,823	2,729	2,393	2,399	2,258
Head 65 or over	2,505	2,530	2,532	2,516	2,153	2,154	2,141
With 3 members	3,319	3,339	3,356	3,234	2,830	2,838	2,702
With 4 members	4,247	4,275	4,277	4,254	3,643	3,644	3,598
With 5 members	5,011	5,044	5,048	4,994	4,302	4,301	4,355
With 6 members	5,633	5,673	5,679	5,617	4,851	4,849	4,900
With 7 or more members	6,917	6,983	7,000	6,841	5,947	5,963	5,771

SOURCE: U.S. Bureau of the Census, *Current Population Reports*, Series P-60, No. 88 (June 1973).

[a] As used by the Bureau of the Census, "male head" means that the father is present and the mother may or may not be present, and "female head" means that the mother is present and the father is not. Thus, the Bureau of the Census seems to be assuming that whenever both mother and father are present, the father is the "head" of the family.

measures reflected in Table 1-1 in mind. The data in Figure 1-1 and in Tables 1-2, 1-3, 1-4, for example, all reflect the variable poverty line of the Social Security Administration. According to this measure, there were about 24.5 million poor persons in 1972, compared to just under 40 million in 1959. Most of the improvement occurred among white male individuals and families headed by white males, and, to a lesser extent, among nonwhite males and their families. Poverty among single women and families headed by women actually increased between 1959 and 1972. Total measured poverty increased slightly during the 1959-1960 recession, and by 1.2 million persons during the 1969-1970 recessions. Had there been no recession from 1969 to 1971, and had poverty decreased at the same rate between 1969 and 1972 as it did between 1959 and 1968, it would have fallen to approximately 19.5, or by an additional 5 million persons, by 1972.

Some idea of who the poor are is provided by the breakdown of data in Tables 1-2, 1-3, and 1-4. Table 1-2 shows, for example, that only 9 percent of the white population was classed as poor in 1972, whereas almost 32 percent of the nonwhite population was. Almost 41 percent of the nonwhite families living outside the metropolitan areas were poor, and almost 42 percent of the nonwhite persons classed as poor were children.

The *aggregate income deficit* referred to in Table 1-3 is the difference between the actual income of the family or person and the poverty line income for that family or person. Note that the entire poverty gap in 1972 amounted to just over $12 billion. By comparison, the Gross National Product in 1972 was $1,152 billion; the defense budget was $78 billion, and the interest on the federal debt was $21 billion. (However, because of uncertain negative effects on incentives, positive effects on health and nutrition, and other unpredictable consequences, it does not necessarily follow that $12 billion more in government transfers to the poor would have eradicated measured poverty in that year.)

Of particular interest are the work and labor force data in Table 1-4. As many as 36.8 percent of poor families had no earners in 1972, but only 5.4 percent of the heads of these families were unemployed; a far larger number (50.1 percent) were not in the labor force at all. Low earnings from employment (because of low wages and part-time or irregular employment) and the inability to seek work at all seemed to be more strongly associated with poverty than actual unemployment. Only 53.6 percent of the family heads had *any* job at all during the year. (This figure

FIGURE 1 - 1

Persons Below the Poverty Level, 1959-1972

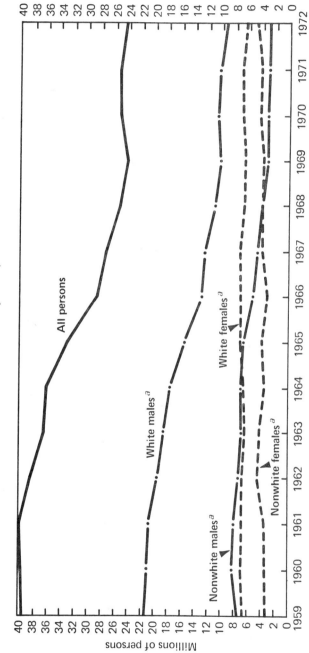

SOURCE: U.S. Bureau of the Census, *Current Population Reports*, Series P-60, No. 86 (December 1972) and No. 88 (June 1973).

NOTE: Because of revisions in government information-gathering methodology in 1966, the 1966-1972 data are not strictly comparable with the 1959-1965 data. The revisions alone accounted for a decline of 1.9 million in the number of poor persons reported in 1966. In addition, because the 1970-1972 data are based on 1970 census population controls, they are not strictly comparable to data for 1959-1969.

[a] For persons in families, sex of head of family; for unrelated individuals, sex of individual.

TABLE 1 – 2

Persons Below the Poverty Line, by Family Status and Race, and Families Below the Poverty Line, by Type of Residence, 1972

	NUMBER (IN THOUSANDS)			PERCENTAGE OF TOTAL POPULATION BELOW POVERTY LINE			PERCENTAGE DISTRIBUTION OF POOR FAMILIES BY RACE		
	Total	White	Non-white	Total	White	Non-white	Total	White	Non-white
All Poor Persons	24,460	16,203	8,257	11.9	9.0	31.9	100.0	100.0	100.0
Persons in families	19,577	12,268	7,309	10.3	7.4	31.0	80.0	75.8	88.6
Head of family	5,075	3,441	1,634	9.3	7.1	27.7	20.7	21.3	19.8
Children under 18	10,082	5,784	4,298	14.9	10.1	41.2	41.2	35.7	52.1
Other family members	4,420	3,043	1,377	6.6	5.1	18.9	18.1	18.8	16.7
Unrelated individuals	4,883	3,935	948	29.0	27.1	40.9	20.0	24.3	11.5
All Poor Families	5,075	3,441	1,634	9.3	7.1	27.8	100.0	100.0	100.0
In metropolitan areas	2,938	1,819	1,119	8.0	5.6	24.1	57.9	52.9	68.5
In central cities	1,828	901	927	11.3	7.2	26.0	36.0	26.2	56.7
In suburbs & fringe areas	1,110	918	192	5.3	4.7	17.9	21.9	26.7	11.8
Outside metropolitan areas	2,137	1,622	515	12.3	10.0	40.9	42.1	47.1	31.5
Farm residents	323	270	53	12.8	11.3	41.1	6.4	7.8	3.2
Nonfarm residents	4,753	3,171	1,582	9.2	6.9	27.4	93.7	92.2	96.8

SOURCE: U.S. Bureau of the Census, *Current Population Reports,* Series P-60, No. 88 (June 1973).

NOTE: Details may not add to totals because of rounding.

TABLE 1 – 3

The Aggregate Income Deficit of Families and Unrelated Individuals Below the Poverty Line, 1972

	Number Below Poverty Line (in thousands)	Percentage Distribution	Aggregate Income Deficit (in millions)	Percentage Distribution
Total	9,958	100.0	$12,035	100.0
Families	5,075	51.0	7,618	63.3
Male head	2,917	29.3	4,130	34.3
Female head	2,158	21.7	3,487	29.0
Unrelated individuals	4,883	49.0	4,417	36.7
Male	1,410	14.2	1,437	11.9
Female	3,473	34.9	2,980	24.8

SOURCE: U.S. Bureau of the Census, *Current Population Reports*, Series P-60, No. 88 (June 1973).

NOTE: Details may not add to totals because of rounding.

includes those who were self-employed, and even those who worked without pay on a family farm.)

Unlike Figure 1-1, the tables do not show trends over time. However, it is worth noting that, between 1959 and 1972, the proportion of poor families with a female head rose from 14 to 22 percent; the number of poor families without an earner rose from 24 to 37 percent; the number of poor families whose head was not in the labor force increased from 39 to 50 percent; and the number of heads of poor families with any work experience at all during the year dropped from 68 to 55 percent. Finally, as we have already noted, the absolute number of poor nonwhite women and persons in poor families headed by nonwhite women actually rose during that period, in spite of the fairly impressive overall decline in officially measured poverty. There is other evidence as well that during the general economic expansion of the 1960s, many persons escaped poverty in the traditional way, by obtaining more and better employment. Those who remained poor were increasingly a hard core corresponding more closely to the pathologically powerless poor discussed earlier.

Table 1-4 shows that there were 878,000 poor families headed by a person aged 65 or over in 1972. These families represented 11.6 percent of all families headed by persons of that age, and 17.3 percent of all poor people. However, as we shall see later, these figures may exaggerate somewhat the extent of poverty among the elderly.

There are other income-based estimates of a "poverty line," in addition to the official measure reflected in Table 1-1. In 1969, after a major study of living costs, the Department of Labor released its figures for "lower," "moderate," and "higher" budgets in 39 areas in the United States. These budgets are updated annually, to reflect changes in living costs. The "lower" budget, sufficient for a "nutritionally adequate diet" and "healthful housing," was a national average of $7,386 per year in autumn 1972 for a typical family of four (consisting of an employed 38-year-old father, a nonworking mother, a 13-year-old son, and an 8-year-old daughter).

Of the 8,257,000 nonwhite persons classed as poor in 1972, 7,710,000 were black. Between 1959 and 1972, black Americans escaped poverty at a somewhat slower pace than whites. Forty-eight percent of black families were classed as poor in 1959, as opposed to 29 percent in 1971. Similarly, 53 percent of all black persons were classed as poor in 1959, and 33 percent in 1971. By comparison, the incidence of poverty declined from 15 percent to 8 percent among white families and from 18 percent to 10 percent among white persons over the same period.

TABLE 1 – 4

Families Below the Poverty Line, by Selected Characteristics, 1972

	Number (in thousands)	Percentage of All Similar Families	Percentage Distribution
Total	5,075	9.3	100.0
Age of head			
Under 25	684	16.3	13.5
25 – 44	2,153	9.5	42.4
45 – 64	1,360	6.8	26.8
65 or over	878	11.6	17.3
Size of family			
2 persons	1,803	9.0	35.6
3 persons	867	7.5	17.1
4 persons	793	7.5	15.7
5 persons	547	8.6	10.8
6 persons	456	14.3	9.0
7 or more persons	607	22.3	12.0
Number of related children under 18			
None	1,454	6.2	28.7
1 – 2	1,818	8.8	35.9
3 – 4	1,181	14.7	23.3
5 or more	620	30.3	12.3
Number of earners			
None	1,868	34.7	36.8
1	2,169	10.7	42.8
2	845	4.0	16.7
3	192	2.6	3.8
Employment status of head			
Employed	2,234	5.4	44.1
Unemployed	272	20.5	5.4
In armed forces	29	3.4	0.6
Not in labor force	2,539	24.2	50.1

TABLE 1 – 4 (Continued)

Occupational classification of head (longest job) [a]	Number (in thousands)	Percentage of All Similar Families	Percentage Distribution
Professional or managerial worker	315	2.5	6.2
Clerical or sales worker	280	4.4	5.6
Craftsman or foreman	376	3.9	7.4
Operative or kindred worker	540	6.6	10.7
Service worker (incl. in private households)	549	14.5	10.9
Nonfarm laborer	249	10.8	4.9
Farmer or farm laborer	407	19.0	8.1
Did not work	2,328	27.3	46.2
Educational Attainment of head [b]			
8 years or less	2,026	17.0	40.0
1 – 3 years high school	1,010	12.3	19.9
4 years high school	959	5.8	18.9
1 – 3 years college	230	3.9	4.6
4 or more years college	166	2.2	3.3

SOURCE: U.S. Bureau of the Census, *Current Population Reports*, Series P-60, No. 88 (June 1973).

NOTE: Details may not add to totals because of rounding.

[a] Of the 2,716 heads of families who worked in 1972, only 1,006 (37 percent) worked 50 or more weeks at a full-time job.

[b] Head 25 years or over.

Again over the same period, the median income of black families as a percentage of that of white families rose from 51 to 59 percent. (Actually, it rose to 61 percent in 1969, but it had fallen back to 59 percent by 1972.) Part of the increase was explained by a more rapid increase in black earnings than in white earnings, and part by the fact that the percentage of families in which both husband and wife worked rose faster among blacks than whites.

In 1972, 26 percent of the persons in the United States of Spanish origin (mainly of Mexican, Puerto Rican, and Cuban extraction) were poor. The poverty rate for Puerto Ricans was the same as for blacks (32 percent), and the median family incomes of the two groups were nearly the same (about $6,200). The median family income of American Indians was about $5,800, but incomes were much lower than that on reservations. The first Americans had the lowest median income, the highest unemployment rate, and the highest poverty rate of any racial or ethnic group of significant size.

The preceding discussion of poverty statistics is based on income measures, which have several defects. They do not, by definition, take into account wealth (assets), which can contribute to spending power as well as to economic security. Moreover, they measure only *money* income (wages, salaries, social security, public assistance, pensions, etc.) and not such nonmoney income aids as surplus food or subsidized public housing. As we shall see in Chapter 5, these benefits are very unevenly distributed among the poor. Finally, income measures do not take into account government services, which can have a great effect on the poverty or well-being of citizens. In some countries, recreational facilities, health care, water, garbage collection, and other services are provided free of charge, whereas in others they are marketed at a price. There seems to be a strong trend in the United States toward the privatization of such services. This can reduce the well-being not only of the poor but of the working class as well if, for example, public parks and playgrounds are allowed to deteriorate while sales of backyard play equipment, swimming pools, and vacation homes burgeon.

THE EFFECT OF WEALTH: ECONOMIC POSITION

The detailed information needed to combine income measures with all indicators of economic security or vulnerability is not yet available, but data do exist that link income and *net wealth* (a person's assets minus his liabilities). There is no simple way to combine these two phenomena.

Income is what economists call a *flow* (a rate over time, such as money received per week or month), whereas wealth is a *stock* (an amount of money or other assets owned at a given time). Stocks and flows, like apples and pears, cannot be added. If your income is $5,000 per year and you have $5,000 in assets, you cannot say that you have total resources of $10,000, since (unless you never spend anything) you will never have that much at any one time. Furthermore, if you spend $10,000 in a year's time, you will no longer have $5,000 in assets.

Burton A. Weisbrod and W. Lee Hansen of the University of Wisconsin's Institute for Research on Poverty have suggested a new indicator of economic status, which they call *economic position* and which they define as the sum of a person's annual income plus the *annual lifetime annuity value* of his current net worth. To find this value, we must first know about how many more years an individual will live. (We may not actually know this for any given individual, but the life-expectancy tables prepared by statisticians do tell us how many persons of a certain age are likely to live another 25 years, another 20 years, and so on.) If a man's net wealth were to be put in an interest-paying account and interest compounded annually, the annual lifetime annuity value of his current net worth would be the equal annual payment to him out of this account that would leave a balance of zero at his death, taking into account the interest to be paid on the account.

A person's economic position depends, then, on his age, his net wealth, and the interest rate used to calculate its annual lifetime annuity value.

Because of data problems, Weisbrod and Hansen use the old, fixed poverty line of $3,000 in their calculations. They found that combining income and net worth in a measure of economic position had the following effects.

1. Assuming that the poverty line is kept at $3,000, measuring economic position rather than income alone means that fewer people are categorized as poor. In 1962, 20 percent of the nation's families received less than $3,000 in current income. Only 18 percent, however, had an economic position below that figure, assuming an interest rate of 4 percent. Assuming an interest rate of 10 percent, only 17 percent of all families were below the poverty line. (These two interest rates, 4 and 10 percent, appear to be the minimum and maximum appropriate, with the best estimate somewhere in between.)
2. As Table 1-4 showed, 17.3 percent of all families classified as poor in

1972 (using income measures alone) were headed by an aged person, and 11.6 percent of all such families were poor. Using 1962 figures and a fixed poverty line of $3,000, 34 percent of all poor families were headed by an aged person, and 47 percent of such families were poor. But when economic position rather than current income is considered, only 29 percent of all poor families had aged heads, and only 36 percent of such families were poor when annuities were calculated on the basis of a 4-percent interest rate. When 10 percent was used as the interest rate, the percentages fell to 27.5 percent and 32 percent respectively. The reason is simple. Older people have relatively little current income and a relatively large amount of wealth. On his retirement day, the typical head of a household has more wealth than he has had at any other time in his life. As he begins to live on this wealth, it will gradually decline; but retired people still tend to have more wealth, on the average, than younger people. Thus figures that rely solely on current income exaggerate the poverty of old people (and of anyone else whose current income is low relative to his wealth).

3. Comparing the distribution of income in America with the distribution of economic position shows the latter to be significantly less equal. In other words, when the definition of economic equality is made more comprehensive, and more accurate, more inequality is revealed. This is because the distribution of net wealth is vastly more unequal than that of current income.

THE DUAL ECONOMY IN THE UNITED STATES

Let us turn now from the definition of poverty to an exploration of the environment in which American poverty exists. As we noted earlier, we have in this country not an underdeveloped economy but a dual economy. Only a minority of people are poor; and they are poor not because of an inadequate total output or Gross National Product, but because of inequalities in the distribution of income and wealth. There is no real break in the distribution of income curve in the United States. Families can be found in every economic condition from indigence to opulence. Nevertheless, it does no violence to reality to perceive a division between the poor and the nonpoor. As we move down the income scale past the poverty line, the difference in how people live ceases to be a difference in degree and becomes a difference in kind.

The fact that the poor and the nonpoor are inhabitants of a dual economy manifests itself in various ways. *The most salient characteristic of the dual economy is that it adjusts to and accommodates the state of development of the larger, dominant, nonpoor element, to the absolute as well as the relative disadvantage of the poor.* This is the main point of this section, and one of the main points of this book. Some of its implications are discussed below.

CONSUMPTION TECHNOLOGY

The concept of *technology*, which most people conceive of as applying only to production, applies to consumption as well. Like production technology, consumption technology changes over time. The techniques used by families to feed, house, transport, and amuse themselves and otherwise satisfy their needs change in response to changes in relative prices (reflecting changes in production technology), to higher incomes, and to the introduction of new or changed products.

Poor families, being in the minority, are forced in many instances to adopt consumption technologies appropriate to the nonpoor. As a result, they are made even poorer. For example, consider the oft-heard proposition that the American poor are really quite well off, from both a worldwide and a historical standpoint. Those who claim that American poverty is only relative argue either that the money incomes of the American poor are high or (more commonly) that many of them have consumer goods which none but the elite in truly poor nations have —telephones, automobiles, television sets, and even a basic education.

Education is not directly related to consumption technology, and will be dealt with separately. But the other three "goods" are.

Cars, telephones, and TVs are the items most frequently cited as evidence of the relative affluence of the American poor. For example, Clair Wilcox, in *Toward Social Welfare*, notes that

the American poor enjoy many things that would have been regarded as luxuries by their forebears and that would mark them as belonging to the middle class in Europe or to the upper class in much of Latin America, in Asia, or in Africa. Among the fifth of the people who fell below the CEA (fixed) poverty line in 1962, 14 percent had bought an automobile within the previous year, 19 percent had a home freezer, 73 percent had a washing machine, and 78 percent owned a television set.

But are these products really symbols of affluence? In a generally poor, underdeveloped country, having a telephone would be pointless for most people. Most personal communications are made face to face. Since no one whom the average person might call is likely to have a telephone, there is no real value in having one. In a society that has not adjusted to the telephone, the lack of one does not constitute poverty. But in the United States, where much of the daily business of production and consumption is conducted by telephone, and where the telephone is the major way of dealing with all kinds of emergencies, not to have one is a form of deprivation.

The same point can be made about the automobile. As Americans have become richer, they have acquired more, larger, and more luxurious automobiles; public transportation has accordingly declined in quantity and in quality, and those who have suffered have been those too poor to have cars. The example of Watts, California, which is not only poor, but remote from the job market and ill-served by public transportation, suggests itself. Throughout America, the development of suburban shopping centers, remote from most of the poor, has depended on and assumed widespread ownership of automobiles, and those without them have suffered. Before World War II, there was hardly a household need that could not be supplied either by delivery men or by some kind of mobile store. The vegetable wagon, the egg man, the bread man, and the like represented an extremely inefficient product-distribution system, and for the most part it is good that it has been replaced. But for those whose incomes do not permit them to have cars, the prewar consumption technology is still more appropriate. One virtually certain indicator of a poor neighborhood is the shopping carts, "borrowed" from supermarkets, parked near the homes of the carless poor.

As another consequence, the urban slum dweller is far more reliant on small "ma-and-pa" type neighborhood stores than is his nonpoor neighbor, and even if slum chain stores have the same prices as non-slum chain stores, and if slum neighborhood stores have the same prices as non-slum neighborhood stores, the slum dweller must pay more for his groceries.

The family television set, a symbol of affluence to critics of public assistance, also represents the dominant consumption technology, in this case in the area of amusement. Every society has *some* type of popular entertainment. In our own culture, television is the dominant form of amusement. In other societies, where the state of amusement technology is different, the movies, local "opera houses," or singing and dancing (live) on the nearest street corner are more important. Whether Americans are richer or poorer for having substituted television for less polished but more intimate forms of entertainment is beside the point; television has taken over, and other forms of popular entertainment do not exist as alternatives for the poor. Where live entertainment still exists, in the form of plays and concerts, it is beyond the reach of the poor and is beginning to be beyond the reach of all but a wealthy elite. Even motion pictures, the dominant mass entertainment medium of only a few years ago, are becoming too costly for the poor. Take away the telephone, the car, and the television set from Americans and they are cut off from important means of participation in the economy and interaction with their fellow men.

A study of American poverty leads to various conclusions. One is that, in some ways, it is better to be poor in a poor society than in a rich one. In poor societies, the structure of the economy and of major institutions has adjusted to poverty, and the poor can at least function. The significance of individual products—whether they be automobiles or horses—cannot be assumed to be constant across societies. Our idea of what constitutes "luxury" goods does not fit our own society when we view telephones, television sets, and cars as in that category. We tend to underestimate the poverty of our own people. Of course, poor Americans need shelter, medical care, nutritious food, and other things that satisfy universal human needs. But because they also need other goods such as automobiles, telephones, and television sets to function in our society, they have even less money left for these biological necessities.

Changes in consumption technology also affect the distribution of income in a society. Suppose a person's income is lower than average and remains unchanged while the average income rises. Obviously, then his *relative* position has declined. What is less obvious, but probably more important, is that, almost inevitably, his *absolute* position will have declined as well. Even though his income has not changed, he is likely to be absolutely worse off as the result of the progress of others *and* the adaptation of society to that progress.

EDUCATION

In a dual economy, society adjusts to the level of *educational* attainment as well as the consumption patterns of the dominant, nonpoor element, with similar results. It is widely believed that an education confers advantages on the recipient but that, as more and more others are educated, these advantages lessen. For instance, it is often said that the widespread possession of a high school education in the United States has lowered the value of a high school diploma and that the value of a college (bachelor's) degree is declining because so many are receiving degrees. Sometimes, it is argued, a master's degree is needed to obtain the position once virtually ensured by a bachelor's degree.

These propositions contain elements of both truth and falsity. This is because they can be interpreted in either a relative or an absolute sense. Clearly, the education of others weakens the *relative* position of an educated person in society. But does it really make him worse off in an *absolute* sense? To find the answer to this question, suppose we look at an extreme case.

If a person is among a handful of educated people in an otherwise uneducated society, he will almost certainly have an important position in that society—as a government official, a lawyer, a doctor, or whatever. His income and manner of living will probably be well above those of the rest of the community. However, he will also be at a disadvantage in some ways. He will probably have little access to books, newspapers, or magazines, except possibly from foreign sources. Even signposts will be rare, and those that exist are likely to have pictures, conferring no advantage on the literate. In many areas, he will have "no one to talk to." If he attempts to pass on his knowledge, he may not be believed. If he is a doctor, he may lose out to competition from faith healers; if he is a lawyer, he may find the law ignored; if he is a scientist, he may find that myth and superstition are too powerful to permit the spread of new ideas. At worst, the educated person in an uneducated community runs the risk of being executed for his knowledge and the threat it poses.

As more people are educated, and as a society adjusts to a higher level of education, the advantages of an education increase. More books and periodicals become available. If production techniques are reorganized to take advantage of human expertise, those having that expertise can exploit it. In a thousand ways, the accommodation of society to a high level of education—which produces not only literacy and the ability to manipulate numbers, but an understanding of cause and effect, a greater ability to deal with new situations without fear, and a greater tolerance of ambiguity—confers advantages on those already educated. Having an education in an uneducated society is almost the same as having a telephone in a society without a telephone system; it creates a potential benefit *that does not become active* until a significant part of society shares it.

In most cases then, and for most people, the widely held proposition that the value of high school diplomas and college degrees is declining since so many are receiving them is incorrect. Actually, the *more* people who have these things, the more valuable they become. In a dual economy, where the poor are also the less educated (see Table 1-4), those who lack a diploma or a degree and the education they imply suffer in an absolute sense as the general level of education rises. As society increasingly adapts to a high educational level, the uneducated person becomes less and less able to function. Even unskilled jobs require attitudes shared by the educated but not by him; he is bewildered by access codes, area codes, and direct dialing; afraid to fly; distrustful of banks; lost a few blocks from home; and generally left behind and set adrift by the educational progress of his society. He is alienated in a very basic sense.

It is not true, then, that educating *anyone* makes everyone better off. Educating more people more thoroughly makes those being educated better off; it makes those already educated also better off in an absolute sense, and it makes those left uneducated worse off in an absolute and relative sense. On the other hand, an educational policy that concentrates on raising the educational level of those who are presently less educated *will* tend to benefit everyone, so long as it is comprehensive.

THE PRICE STRUCTURE

The *price structure* of an economy (the relationship among an economy's prices, wage rates, interest rates, and the like) reflects a society's priorities and preferences, as well as the scarcity or abundance of products and resources. It is a powerful determinant of what people buy and how things are produced.

To understand the price-structure problems in a dual economy such as that in the United States, let us imagine, for a moment, that the two components of the economy, the poor and the nonpoor, have separate economies, each with its own currency and price structure. How will the price structure in the poor economy differ from that in the nonpoor economy?

Presumably, there will be a severe capital shortage among the poor, reflecting their weak net worth. Consequently, interest rates will be higher than in the nonpoor economy. And if the poor have (as it is sometimes alleged) a greater preference for immediate consumption and less inclination to save, there will be a further upward pressure on interest rates. However, just as capital is relatively scarce, so labor will be relatively abundant, and presumably cheap. With cheap (and generally unskilled) labor and scarce and expensive capital, the poor economy will have a *comparative advantage* in, and presumably will specialize in, the production of different products from those produced in the nonpoor economy—small handicrafts, possibly, which require large amounts of labor relative to capital. The theory of *comparative advantage* is a concept commonly offered as a rationale for specialization in international trade.

According to this theory, an economy should (and in the event of free trade will) specialize in the production of those goods which it can produce at a lower cost than other goods, where "cost" is defined in terms of lost opportunities to produce other goods rather than in terms of resource used or money. Hence economies with abundant labor relative to capital should specialize in the production of goods that require large amounts of labor relative to capital, even if they must use more units of labor per unit of output than economies where labor is relatively scarce.

The nonpoor economy, on the other hand, will have a comparative advantage in, and presumably will specialize in, industries that economize on labor, that use skills and talents which do not exist or are dormant in the poor economy, and that are relatively capital-intensive. Wage rates will tend to be high relative to interest rates. Of course, the dual economy in the United States is not really two separate economies. It is one economy, and its price structure is appropriate to the dominant, nonpoor element. At the same time, it is inconsistent with the state of development of the poor sector.

It would be far easier for indigenous "black capitalism" to develop in central cities if the price structure of 50 years ago, rather than that of today, were to prevail. Poor people may even be handicapped by high wages: If the socially determined minimum wage (which may or may not be the legal minimum) exceeds the value of the expected contribution of the unskilled poor person, he will not be employed at all. A person with low-wage skills in a high-wage economy suffers from the advanced state of economic development around him.

Additional problems are created if the poor are concentrated in industries in which rapid technological change is occurring, but where they themselves do not share in that progress. For instance, much rural poverty (and, through migration and inheritance, much urban poverty) is attributable to the failure of the smallest farmers, usually tenant farmers, to participate in the agricultural revolution, both because they lack the wealth or the credit to finance fertilizers and equipment and because their landholdings are too small to farm efficiently with the new methods. Failing to share in technological change, these farmers have nonetheless shared in its consequences—that is, in the long-run decline in farm commodity prices relative to other prices in the economic system. To the large individual or corporate farmer, the decline in farm prices relative to other prices was tolerable (though of course not welcome) since it was offset by the increase in productivity that was its cause. One can accept lower prices per unit of product sold if one can get more output per unit of input. And, in fact, well-to-do farmers' incomes generally continued to rise over the years. As for those unfortunate enough to share in the effects of the price decline but not in the productivity increase, their incomes continued to decline. Once again, those who stood still found themselves worse off, not only relatively but absolutely.

Some Implications of a Dual Economy

An analysis of the dual economy in the United States indicates that, whatever one's level of income, one is better off in many ways if the majority of one's fellow citizens have approximately the same income. There is an added burden, in short, in being either far ahead of or far behind the rest of society. There are disadvantages to being rich, just as there are to being poor. However, the disadvantages of being rich are so amply compensated for as to generate little sympathy. The same cannot be said of the problems of being poor.

Decentralization and community control are so attractive to the poor precisely because the nonpoor have constructed, and continue to reconstruct, American society for their own convenience. They are not even conscious that in doing so they make it still more difficult for the poor and uneducated to function. The fact that this behavior is not malicious and represents merely ordinary self-interest does not help.

Demonstration Effect

What is the reaction of poor people to life in a dual economy? One response is related to the *demonstration effect*, a concept important in the study of economically underdeveloped areas.

The consumption patterns of poorer people reflect, to some extent, emulation of the rich. It is hard for people in underdeveloped countries to resist high consumption expenditures and to devote resources to capital formation because, having the example of developed countries before them, they demand rapid improvements in their level of living. On the other hand the demonstration effect also creates incentives to speed up the development process. People in underdeveloped nations may work harder to obtain the things rich societies have.

In a dual economy, the demonstration effect takes a somewhat different twist. Suppose a family has the income to buy adequate food, health care, and so on *or* a good automobile, but not both. Will it sacrifice the former for the latter? We have already seen that it is difficult to function in America in the 1970s without an automobile. But that is not the end of the story. In a success-oriented economy, many poor people will concentrate their limited resources on the *external manifestations* of success. If they cannot be affluent, they can at least look affluent; then, at least, people will not look down on them. For a variety of reasons (an inability to get mortgage loans, discrimination, etc.), poor people are unlikely to make houses into status symbols. As a result, they tend to spend a larger fraction of their incomes on clothing and automobiles than the nonpoor. This makes their poverty more ''invisible'' and their problems easier to ignore.

There are also poor people who respond to life in a dual economy by refusing to take menial, low-wage, low-status jobs, even if that refusal means unemployment, because these jobs are considered a badge of inferiority or failure. This reaction is by no means universal among the poor, but it is widely observed among men from poor families. It is less common among poor women, perhaps because the general employment status of *all* women is lower than that of men. The disparity between the jobs available to poor and nonpoor men is much greater than that between the jobs available to poor and nonpoor women, especially when the poor are also members of a racial or ethnic minority.

POVERTY AND INEQUALITY

It is sometimes argued that the problem of poverty and the problem of inequality are the same—that ''poverty'' is simply the term applied to the condition of the lowest economic group in any society. According to this view, poverty is only relative, not absolute. And from this standpoint, there will always be poverty; as the general income level in a society rises, so will the poverty line. This argument is related to another argument discussed earlier, that America's poor are only poor in the context of our present affluence, and that from a worldwide or a historical standpoint they are really quite rich.

There is no simple answer to the question of whether poverty is *absolute* or *relative*. As one goes from a poor country to a rich one (or from a poor era to a rich one) three things will be apparent. First, some basic goods—public health care, clothing (depending on the climate), nutrition, and a few others—will be needed in about equal quantities in both nations. This is because basic human needs *are* absolute. Second, the minimum level of living considered acceptable by the vast majority will be different in the richer economy. What is acceptable in India is not acceptable in the United States. And what was acceptable for an American workingman in 1874 will not suffice in 1974. Acceptable minimums of certain goods, then, are relative. And third, more income is needed just to function in a high-income society. A person without an automobile is poorer in an auto-oriented rich society than in a poorer one. (However, a person with an automobile in a rich, auto-oriented society is probably richer than one *without* a car in a poorer society that depends upon mass transit.)

It is impossible to have poverty without inequality. An insufficiency of means relative to needs is meaningful only if there is a standard of sufficiency which is set either by richer persons in one's own society (in which case there is *intraeconomy* inequality) or by a richer society (in which case there is *intereconomy* inequality). Poverty implies inequality, but is it possible to have inequality without poverty? In order to abolish poverty, everyone must receive enough income to buy the minimum amount of goods and services considered acceptable by society *and* to function normally. Everyone must also have a minimum level of income security. There is more than one way of achieving these goals. In the United States' dual economy, for instance, abolishing poverty would require (among other things) that everyone have a car *or* that mass transit be improved *or* that residential, employment, and commercial patterns be reoriented to make travel by foot or bicycle a feasible alternative for everyone.

There is no reason to believe that the elimination of poverty is necessarily incompatible with some degree of inequality in the distribution of income, of economic position, or even of power in general. It is, how-

ever, incompatible with extreme inequality at the lower end. The aboli-
tion of poverty would require, in effect, lopping off the bottom "tail" of
the income distribution.

We say that it is "probably" possible to have inequality without
poverty because there are no clearcut examples of societies where such a
situation prevails. Of course, if inequality *is* possible without poverty,
then the two are not the same thing. That this may be so is no particular
comfort in present-day America, which experiences them both.

REFERENCES

The quotation from Warren Haggstrom is from his article "[Poverty] Perspec-
tives from . . . [a] Psychologist," in Herman P. Miller, ed., *Poverty—American
Style* (Belmont, Calif.: Wadsworth, 1966). The Social Security Administration's
variable poverty line is due mainly to Mollie Orshansky. See her "Counting the
Poor: Another Look at the Poverty Profile," *Social Security Bulletin*, 28 (January
1965). For a criticism of the use of a constant food-to-needs ratio, see David M.
Gordon, "Trends in Poverty," in Gordon, ed., *Problems in Political Economy:
An Urban Perspective* (Lexington, Mass.: Heath, 1971).

For poverty data, see the U.S. Bureau of the Census, *Current Population
Reports*, Series P-60, No. 86 (December 1972) and No. 88 (June 1973). For
information on the social and economic status of the black population, see Series
P-23, No. 42 (July 1972). For data on persons of Puerto Rican, Mexican, and
other Spanish origins, see Series P-20, No. 238 (July 1972). The study of
"economic position" appears in Burton A. Weisbrod and W. Lee Hansen, "An
Income-Net Worth Approach to Measuring Economic Welfare," *American
Economic Review*, 58 (December 1968).

An earlier version of the section entitled "The Dual Economy" originally
appeared under the title "Poverty, Education, and the Dual Economy" in *The
Journal of Consumer Affairs*, 4 (Winter 1970), copyright 1970 by the American
Council on Consumer Interests. (Permission to reprint this material is gratefully
acknowledged.)

The Wilcox quotation is from Clair Wilcox, *Toward Social Welfare*
(Homewood, Ill.: Irwin, 1969).

2

Vicious Circles and the Role of Welfare

Those who are poor manifest a number of characteristics that are both a *result* of their poverty and a *cause* of continued poverty. These characteristics create a large number of *vicious circles* in the lives of the poor. Because they are poor, their nutrition and health are poor; because of this, they are less productive; because they are less productive, they are poor. Because they are poor, they can afford less time for education; because they are less educated, they earn less and remain poor. In this chapter, we shall document a number of important examples of this pathology of poverty. The various vicious circles we will describe are mutually reinforcing, and are often referred to collectively as *the* vicious circle of poverty.

A discussion of the vicious circle of poverty is really an extension of our previous discussion of the definition of poverty. The vicious circle is really *part of* poverty—at least, of the chronic, pathological poverty that is our main concern in this book. Antipoverty policy must consist, then, of *prevention* techniques, to keep vicious circles from coming into existence, and of *curative* techniques, to interrupt and correct existing vicious circles. A full discussion of curative techniques will be postponed to the last chapter. In this chapter, after treating the concept of vicious circles in detail, we will examine poverty prevention. The first social line of defense against poverty is the welfare system. (As will be seen, our interpretation of the expression *welfare system* is a broad one, including *all* social devices for income protection and maintenance, whatever form they take.)

THE VICIOUS CIRCLES OF POVERTY

The concept of vicious circles has been used to describe a variety of chronic problems, from racism to economic underdevelopment. Vicious circles are a special case of cycles of cumulative causation, which can be benign as well as vicious. For example, the ability to save grows more than proportionately as a person's income rises; thus those with high incomes save a larger percentage of their income than those with low incomes. A poor person may be altogether unable to save, and because he cannot accumulate any savings, unable to build a cushion to make him less vulnerable to economic reverses, unable easily to continue his schooling, and unable to move to another place that might provide a better choice of jobs. He may, in a number of ways, be unable to take advantage of opportunities that could make him less poor. If his income were suddenly to jump, enough so that he could begin to save, he could then begin to accumulate wealth, which might someday facilitate a move out of poverty. In both cases the *cycle of causation* is the *same* (from income to saving to income); but in the first case it is vicious, and in the second, benign.

In general, then, benign and vicious circles follow the same pattern. They resemble, in a sense, the phenomena affected by Newton's law of inertia: An object in motion tends to stay in motion, and an object at rest tends to say at rest, until and unless they are acted upon by an outside force.

One of the most elegant statements concerning vicious circles of poverty appeared in the 1964 Economic Report of the President, shortly after the rediscovery of American poverty.

A poor individual or family has a high probability of staying poor. Low incomes carry with them high risks of illness; limitations on mobility; limited access to education, information, and training. Poor parents cannot give their children the opportunities for better health and education needed to improve their lot. Lack of motivation, hope, and incentive is a more subtle but no less powerful barrier than lack of financial means. Thus the cruel legacy of poverty is passed from parents to children.

One must be careful not to oversimplify the problem. Although our discussion of vicious circles necessarily focuses on one variable—such as employment, education, or health—at a time, these circles are in fact a multivariable system in which the ultimate patterns of causation are complex, interdependent, and often unknown.

In this section, we will elaborate upon the vicious circles that are characteristic of poverty in present-day America. We shall continue the task, begun in Chapter 1, of laying out the characteristics of poverty and the poor, before going on in Chapter 3 to a discussion of the causes of poverty.

UNEMPLOYMENT

Poor people have difficulty getting jobs, and the jobs they do get are often only part-time or temporary. Those that are full-time or "permanent" often provide no opportunity for advancement. It is clear that poverty can be a *result* of unemployment and other employment problems. But these problems are part of a vicious circle of poverty; that is, they can be the *result* of poverty as well. Sometimes characteristics associated with poverty handicap persons in such a way that they are (in the eyes of employers) "unemployable." Sometimes unemployment is caused by other factors, completely external to the poor, as in the case of a recession or depression; but even in these cases, the characteristics of the poor may place them at the end of the job line. In short, the characteristics of the poor sometimes *cause* their unemployment, whereas at other times they only determine the *distribution* of unemployment caused by other factors. In practice, at the individual level, it is virtually impossible to tell which is the case.

Poor people have difficulty getting jobs for a variety of reasons. They are less educated, regardless of whether education is measured in years of schooling or diplomas acquired. Sometimes a given level of education is a practical necessity. The job cannot be done by someone without a particular type of knowledge; sometimes educational requirements are merely a job-rationing device, used to simplify hiring when the number of applicants exceeds the number of openings. In any event, whether such requirements are real or nominal, they do exclude a great many poor people from millions of jobs.

Another factor that excludes many of the poor from employment is their arrest record. It is unfortunately true that poor people tend to commit crimes more frequently than nonpoor people; they are also more likely to be apprehended when they do commit a crime, and they are more likely to be convicted. Moreover, the crimes that so often appear on their records—theft, assault, robbery—are precisely those which worry potential employers most. The poor people who have the greatest difficulty getting worthwhile jobs are, of course, ex-convicts, almost regardless of the nature of their crimes. Much is made of the high rate of recidivism (the tendency of ex-convicts to return to crime) in America, and it is often alleged that our prisons are "schools of crime" which teach those who make a single mistake to become chronic criminals. Although there is doubtless some truth in this argument, the *main* reason for high recidivism is that most ex-convicts simply cannot find a job.

Both the subject of education and the subject of crime are so important to understanding the vicious circles of poverty that they will be discussed separately below.

Some of the poor who pass the educational and other tests for employment (perhaps because in a given case they are not applied) fail a physical examination, formal or informal, because of chronic illness or malnutrition. Physical problems are also a reason the poor often lose jobs.

Many poor people do not get jobs because they do not apply for them. Either they do not know how to find jobs, or they are afraid of being embarrassed or humiliated by interviews, application forms, reference checks, and the like. It should not be surprising that poor people do not know how to find jobs. A 1951 study by labor economist Lloyd Reynolds showed that most people, in those days, did not.

> Most youngsters (and their parents) approached the choice of a first job with no clear conception of where they were going; the great majority of first jobs were found in a very informal way, preponderately through relatives and friends; the great majority of youngsters took the *first* job they found and did not make comparisons with any other job; their knowledge of the job before they took it was in most cases extremely meager; and in most cases the job turned out to be a blind alley.

It is probably still true that most first jobs are found through "connections"—relatives or friends. Most relatives and friends of poor people are themselves poor and not of much value in finding good jobs. And for poor people today, the situation is worse than in 1951. There has been a considerable expansion of school placement services since then, and these offices are rarely of much use to dropouts.

Another reason poor people have difficulty getting and keeping jobs is that places of employment are frequently long distances from the homes of the poor, and public transportation has become increasingly inadequate. Transportation problems are a fact of daily life for most poor persons.

Finally, there is the very special problem of poor youths raised in fatherless homes in which the mother, because of Social Security, public assistance, alimony, or other transfer payments, is able to stay home and care for the children rather than having to work. Since work motives are partly learned, if there is no example of a working parent for the children to copy, those motives will be less well-developed. Instead, the child may learn an entirely different lifestyle, one involving a variety of public agencies. The fact that the welfare system can foster dependency and in a variety of ways become *part of*, rather than interrupt, vicious circles of poverty is an important point, and one that will be developed at greater length in Chapters 4 and 5.

As we have noted, poor people lose jobs more readily than the non-poor. One reason is that, as the business cycle turns down, poor people are more likely to be fired or laid off. A study by economist Lawrence DeWitt showed that those with incomes less than $3,000 had considerably higher than average unemployment rates. According to DeWitt,

$$U_{phf} = 2.22 + 1.78U_{ahf}$$

and

$$U_{pp} = 3.80 + 1.61U_{ap}$$

where

U_{phf} is the unemployment rate of poor heads of families,

U_{ahf} is the unemployment rate of average heads of families,

U_{pp} is the unemployment rate of all poor persons, and

U_{ap} is the unemployment rate of all persons.

His first equation tells us that to find the unemployment rate of poor heads of families we must first multiply the overall average unemployment rate of heads of families by 1.78 and then add 2.22 percentage points. For instance, if the unemployment rate of heads of families were 4 percent, that of poor heads of families would be 9.34 percent (2.22 + 7.12). According to his second equation, if the national unemployment rate were 4 percent (a level often regarded as "full employment"), that for poor people would be 11.85 percent—a rate which, if it prevailed throughout the entire economy, would mean depression, and a rate which has not been seen in the United States since before World War II.

One way to combat inflation is to reduce the amount of spending in the economy (for instance, by raising taxes). Unfortunately, such antiinflationary policies also increase unemployment. There are indications, as we shall see in Chapter 6, that the U.S. economy achieves price stability only with an average unemployment rate of 5 1/2 percent or more. It is primarily poor people who pay the price of anti-inflation policies: When the average unemployment rate is 5 1/2 percent, that of poor people (according to DeWitt's second equation) is 12.76 percent.

If anything, these unemployment figures understate the problem. When those who are chronically unemployed give up hope of finding employment and adopt a lifestyle more consistent with reality (that is, one of dependency, crime, or intermittent employment), if they stop looking for work, they are no longer counted as "unemployed." The number of discouraged job-seekers who have left the labor force is probably greater among the chronic poor than the number of persons counted as unemployed. (See Table 1-4 in Chapter 1, "Employment status of head.")

OTHER EMPLOYMENT PROBLEMS

Besides unemployment, poor people face the prospect of employment at low wages, unsteady employment, lack of promotion opportunities, and the like. Two recent theoretical contributions help explain the special employment problems of the poor. These are the concept of the *dual labor market* and the theory of *job competition*.

A Dual Labor Market. A number of economists have concluded that there is a "dual labor market" in the United States. There is a "primary," or regular, labor market, where employment is stable, labor productivity is fairly high, and workers receive above-poverty-level wages. And there is a "secondary" labor market where employment is irregular and intermittent, labor productivity is low, and workers receive poverty-level wages.

The two markets are quite distinct, and each represents an internally consistent system. For instance, the intermittent character of employment in the secondary labor market seems to serve the needs of both employers and employees. Workers in this market seem to have less interest in keeping a permanent job, they quit as often as they are fired, and they hold many different jobs during their working lives. The jobs themselves do not require a great deal of skill and can be learned very quickly. Consequently, wages are low and neither the employer nor the employee invests much in training. Because workers are unskilled and the employer has no motive to hold onto them, it is in his interest to release them during slack periods when they are not actually needed. Because employment is so irregular at the lowest level, there is little or no tendency to promote people from the ranks.

By contrast, jobs in the primary labor market require a certain amount of skill. Assuming that much of this skill is acquired on the job and that it is costly to train workers, employers have good reason to keep turnover rates low. The workers who enter this labor market, who are by and large nonpoor, themselves seek stable employment. Because of the skills acquired, worker productivity is high, as are wages. Moreover, it is easier for these workers to organize into unions, not only because the worker group is stable but also because it is too difficult or costly for the company to fire people and bring in strikebreakers during work stoppages.

An interesting footnote to the concept of a dual labor market is provided by economist Bennett Harrison, who notes that the unstable character of the secondary labor market is shared by other aspects of the economic environment of the poor. For instance, research seems to indicate that the large majority of public assistance recipients move on and off the welfare rolls. Manpower training programs frequently have a high dropout rate. "Enrollees in such programs," Harrison notes, "typically earned no higher wages after graduation than before undertaking training. Many refused to take the programs seriously at all, remaining in them for short periods of time, earning small training stipends and then dropping out. . . . Many enrollees told evaluators frankly that they thought of the manpower training system in the same way they thought of any other form of low wage, marginal activity: as a temporary source of income." Finally, there is evidence that urban ghettos have more or less systematic "markets" for criminal and other "irregular" activities. "When the structure of this 'market' was explored," Harrison writes, "it was found to be characterized by high turnover, unstable participation, and (after accounting for the high risks involved) relatively low average 'wages.' '' Thus the secondary labor market, manpower training, public assistance, and what Harrison calls the "irregular economy" have remarkable similarities. (Harrison does not note that there may also be a "primary" counterpart to each of these—not only a primary labor market but a welfare system for the nonpoor, characterized by higher transfer payments and greater stability, a primary educational and manpower training system, and even a primary market for criminal activities that provides higher incomes and more stable "employment" to some persons.)

Job Competition. Economist Lester Thurow has developed an interesting and important theory of the operation of labor markets which he calls the *job competition model.* Although the theory is still controversial, it seems to explain much recent American experience.

According to Thurow, there is a certain distribution of job opportunities in the economy at any time. There are high-wage jobs and low-wage jobs, each with certain characteristics. Workers hired for any jobs will be trained, formally or informally, to give them the skills they need. Thus workers are not paid for the productive capability they bring to the job (since what they have learned at school is rarely of immediate, practical relevance), but rather for the productive capability they acquire from the job. Thus it is vital to get a good job in the first place.

Employers give the best jobs to those with the most education, those who graduate with the best grades, those from the "best" schools, or those who perform best on personnel examinations—not because these things mean that they have the most skills but because such persons are likely to be the most easily *trainable* at the lowest cost.

Thurow's theory fits in nicely with the concept of a dual labor market. It suggests that workers are not assigned by society to primary or secondary markets because of their productivity; rather, differences in productivity arise out of the nature of these markets and hence are determined by the assignment society makes.

Thurow's theory also suggests, as we will see in Chapter 6, that there are limits to how useful education can be in combating poverty. If we give enough additional education to the poor (assuming that that is actually a plausible alternative, which it may not be), they may be able to move ahead of other people in what Thurow calls the "labor queue," and get better jobs. But that would mean simply that other people would be moved back in the labor queue and get the low-wage jobs. Poverty would be redistributed, not reduced.

EDUCATION AND SCHOOLING

As Table 1-4 in Chapter 1 showed, poor people attend school for fewer years than the nonpoor. As of 1970, 90 percent of poor males 25 or over had not finished high school, compared to 40 percent of those above the poverty line. The situation for women was similar. Seventy-one percent of the poor women in this country had not finished high school, compared to 49 percent of the nonpoor women. Sixty percent of the poor men and 42 percent of the women had only a grade-school (eighth-grade) education, whereas only 24 percent of the nonpoor men and 30 percent of the nonpoor women were similarly disadvantaged.

Poor children tend to leave school at an earlier age than nonpoor children for a variety of reasons. They are not actively seeking careers that require higher education. They do not do well in school, and seek more rewarding ways of using their time. They and their families need incomes, and they are forced to seek employment. Frustrated, they often become troublemakers and are expelled or suspended.

As more and more of the population completes high school—or college—the costs of not doing so mount. An assumption of higher and higher educational attainment gets built into jobs, into the economy's consumption technology, and into other aspects of nonvocational life. This assumption is built in, for example, by the fact that there are fewer and fewer legitimate ways of spending one's youth other than being in school. In the days when large numbers of people left school during their teens, it was possible to begin a career at a low level—as a clerk or messenger—and advance to a position of greater responsibility. Today, those who climb the executive ladder are more likely to begin as "management trainees" after high school or college. The jobs generally available to dropouts are dead-end jobs, such as washing cars or dishes, in the secondary labor market.

Poor children not only leave school earlier, but they do more poorly while they are there. In a study of poverty and inequality in the schools of an unidentified midwestern city, Patricia Cayo Sexton found that 10.9 percent of the pupils from poor families (in this case, those with up to $3,500 in income) failed to be promoted in a given year, compared to 5.5 percent of those whose families earned between $3,500 and $7,000, 2.6 percent of those whose families earned more than $7,000, and 0.8 percent of those from families with more than $11,000 in income. She also found that 34.4 percent of the children from families with incomes above $7,000 were chosen for programs for "gifted children," whereas only 3.7 percent of those from families with incomes below $7,000, and absolutely no children from families in the below-$5,000 group, were selected for these programs.

In most schools, there is some form of "ability tracking." The typical secondary school has a college-preparatory curriculum, a business and vocational curriculum, and a "general" curriculum that prepares pupils neither for college nor for a career. Often, the curricula pupils take are determined not by ability and interest but by race and socioeconomic class. For instance, a white boy from a "good," middle-class home who fails to make outstanding marks in the seventh and eighth grades may nonetheless be urged to go into a college-preparatory program; nonwhite or poor boys or girls who do similarly unimpressive work in the seventh and eighth grades are less likely to get this kind of encouragement.

Poorer children (those from families with incomes up to $5,000) in Sexton's study tended to enroll not in business and vocational courses, as might be expected, but in the general curriculum, whose main purpose, one would guess, was to satisfy state attendance requirements. Forty-eight percent of the poorer children were enrolled in this program; 46 percent of those from families with incomes of $6,000-$7,000 took the business and vocational course, which was primarily a lower-middle- and middle-middle-class curriculum; those from families with higher incomes concentrated on the college preparatory program.

None of these statistics shows the extent to which schools teach poor children to fail. If teachers expect poor children to do poorly, that expectation will be transmitted to and learned by the children. This is true regardless of whether the teachers love the children and are seeking to protect them from frustration by not challenging them or whether they hate and fear their poor pupils.

Nor do these statistics show the different perceptions of the school held by the poor child on the one hand and by the nonpoor child on the other. The poor child may see the school as an extension of an oppressive authority system from which he and all his friends and relatives are alienated. The nonpoor child, on the other hand, may find the teachers, the principal, and even the characters in his schoolbooks little different from the people he meets and deals with every day, at home and elsewhere. The poor child does poorly partly because his preschool experience and at-home environment do not prepare him for life in school. In the homes of most poor people, there are few books. Reading is not encouraged, and complex sentences and symbolic abstractions are rarely used. Since out-of-school learning is probably as important as (or more important than) in-school learning for all purposes except obtaining the degrees and diplomas required by potential employers, the poor child is doubly deprived. And as such children reach adulthood, they not only find it harder to get jobs or to rise in the jobs they get, but they are more easily victimized and manipulated in their nonworking lives as well.

HEALTH, NUTRITION, AND PERSONAL SAFETY

The poor have less nourishing diets than the nonpoor, more congenital defects, more accidents, more disease, and a higher rate of mental illness. Consequently, they have higher absentee rates at school and work, lower energy levels, and lower productivity. They also have lower IQs, a higher incidence of mental retardation, and shorter lives. Poor diets, poor health, and poor productivity form one of the most potent of the vicious circles of poverty.

It is not known how many people in the United States have inadequate diets, although the figure is certainly in the millions. Poor diet is associated with a number of physical problems. The poorly fed individual is less resistant to most diseases, and he is more likely to be slow and listless or short-tempered and irritable. Well-fed people, as a rule, make better marriage partners, better friends, and better fellow workers.

Poor children and adults live surrounded by a variety of physical hazards that increase their disease and accident rates. For example, until its dangers were fully appreciated, leaded paint was commonly used for houses and furniture. As that old paint now peels from walls and woodwork in ghetto apartments, it is often eaten by small children, some of whom die, and many of whom suffer permanent brain damage.

It is doubtful whether there is or has been a disease with the virulence and incidence of lead poisoning that has attracted as little public notice—and such a meager federal response. It is estimated that as many as 225,000 children in America have high lead levels in their blood. Lead poisoning may have killed and crippled more children than polio did before the Salk vaccine was discovered.

The incidence of many chronic conditions, including cardiovascular disorders, high blood pressure, rheumatic fever, arthritis and rheumatism, heart disease, cancer in all its forms, visual impairments, orthopedic impairments, and diabetes, is inversely related to income. Poor people also have a higher incidence of premature delivery in childbirth, a higher infant mortality rate, and a higher maternal mortality rate.

Finally, there are health problems particularly prevalent among the poor which are treated as social rather than medical problems —alcoholism and narcotics addiction. Whether addiction is a medical or a criminal matter, the fact is that, for all but the richest addicts, the high cost of a "habit" makes crime the only possible source of income to feed it. This makes crime the addict's constant companion.

There are many other environmental hazards in a poor community. Kenneth Clark, in *Dark Ghetto*, describes some of the risks faced by children growing up in Harlem, a primarily poor black neighborhood:

> Multiple use of toilet and water facilities, inadequate heating and ventilation, and crowded sleeping quarters increase the rate of acute respiratory infections and infectious childhood diseases. Poor facilities for the storage of food and inadequate washing facilities cause enteritis and skin and digestive disease. Crowded, poorly equipped kitchens, poor electrical connections, and badly lighted and unstable stairs increase the rate of home accidents and fire. Nor is the street any safer. Harlem's fourteen parks, playgrounds, and recreational areas are inadequate and ugly, and many of the children play in the streets where heavy truck traffic flows through the community all day. Far more children and young adults are killed by cars in Harlem than in the rest of the city.

Some poor children also face the physical hazard of beatings from those to whom the nonpoor look for protection—teachers, police, and even parents. The "battered child syndrome" is much more common (although there are no accurate statistics) among poor families than among nonpoor.

Another special hazard facing the poor is the danger of fire. Daniel P. Moynihan, former counselor to President Nixon, considers this problem to be comparable to that of crime. In a memorandum to the President that was better known for its advocacy of a policy of "benign neglect" on the issue of race, Moynihan wrote,

> Unless I mistake the trends, we are heading for a genuinely serious fire problem in American cities. In New York, for example, between 1956

and 1969 the overall fire alarm rate more than tripled. These alarms are concentrated in slum neighborhoods, primarily black. In 1968, one slum area had an alarm rate per square mile 13 times that of the city as a whole. In another the number of alarms has, on an average, increased 44% per year for seven years. Many of these fires are the result of population density. But a great many are more or less deliberately set. Fires are in fact a "leading indicator" of social pathology for a neighborhood. They come first. Crime, and the rest, follows. The psychiatric interpretation of fire-setting is complex, but it relates to the types of personalities which slums produce.

Most of the physical hazards of the ghetto are faced by adults as well as children. A National Health Survey studied showed that, over a two-year period ending in June 1961, for every 1,000 currently employed persons, 1,250 working days were, on the average, lost because of injuries. Workers with family incomes under $2,000 lost 1,760 workdays, 40 percent more than the average; those with family incomes between $2,000 and $3,000 lost 1,370 workdays. Those with incomes of $4,000 to $6,999 lost 1,220 workdays, and those with incomes of $7,000 and above lost only 960 workdays.

Emotional problems are popularly thought of as a high-income disease associated with the tensions of the executive ratrace, suburban living, and the like. In reality, mental problems seem to be more heavily concentrated among the poor. Nor is this surprising. The poor in a dual economy live in a world designed for and by others, and moreover one in which their inability to cope tends to be attributed to their own failings.

INTELLIGENCE

An impressive and growing body of literature suggests that low intelligence—including what may be defined as mental retardation—is one consequence of poverty.

The causes of low intelligence may be (1) genetic (inherited); (2) organic, but not genetic (brain damage, etc.); or (3) "cultural" or "environmental." The weight of scholarly opinion has shifted, over the years, from attributing most retardation to genetic causes to attributing it to the other two, both of which are strongly related to poverty.

Organic Retardation. The main poverty-related, nongenetic causes of organic retardation are illness, malnutrition, lead poisoning, inadequate prenatal care, and injury. As we have seen, each of these problems is linked with poverty. Poor mothers tend to have a high incidence of chronic diseases and of infections during pregnancy associated with premature delivery. The chances of a premature birth are also great if mothers are unusually young or unusually old—as poor mothers more often are.

Probably, half of the poor mothers in this country either get prenatal care too late or get no prenatal care at all. More than 10 percent of all nonwhite mothers in the United States who gave birth in 1964 did so with no physician in attendance. The risk of brain damage to the infant from inadequate care is very great in such cases.

The association between malnutrition and intelligence is a relatively new discovery; our understanding of the problem is based almost entirely on research published since 1965. Some of the main conclusions of this research are

1. that malnutrition during the early years—particularly after the first six months and up until the child is two-to-four years old—can impair intelligence, probably permanently.
2. that the mature brain can be rehabilitated after starvation. (The effects of malnutrition on adults, then, are not so likely to be permanent.)
3. that children with a certain kind of malnutrition (*kwashiorkor*) often appear lazy and apathetic. Thus teachers, employers, and others may mistake an attitude caused by malnutrition for one of deliberate provocation, and may even give punishment for it.
4. that malnutrition in pregnancy causes mental retardation in children. Caloric deficiencies are associated specifically with prematurity and retardation, and protein deficiencies with low vitality. A vitamin E deficiency is associated with encephaly, vitamin B-2 and B-12 deficiencies with hydrocephalus, and a niacin deficiency with psychosis and apathy.

The connection between lead poisoning and brain damage is well established. Moreover, for every confirmed case of significant damage, there must be several cases of unobserved damage due to eating smaller amounts of lead—cases in which intelligence is lowered but is still within the normal range, and no external causes are suspected. Some analysts have suggested that a significant amount of the poor scholastic performance of America's ghetto children can be explained by lead poisoning *alone*. All these nongenetic, but still organic, sources of low intelligence are preventable; and their prevention may well be more crucial for poor children than the expenditure of additional dollars on schools.

Cultural Deprivation. Cultural, or environmental, deprivation is also associated with retardation, or pseudo-retardation, as it is sometimes called when there are no organic problems. Although the damage to intelligence in such cases may be reversible, in most cases the effort and resources needed to accomplish this reversal are not available.

Infants and small children need sensory stimulation for their physical and mental abilities to develop. Without adequate stimulation, interest, curiosity, and even the ability to learn will remain undeveloped.

There seem to be five major poverty-related causes of sensory and intellectual deprivation.

1. The child is left to himself, or to the care of older children, either because the mother works or because she is distracted by the pressures of poverty. The most important source of environmental deprivation is an inadequate mother-child relationship.
2. A large family can mean too little parental time for each child. There is a negative correlation between IQ and family size among poor children.
3. The absence of the father, a frequent problem in poor families, is also statistically associated with low intelligence.
4. Since poor parents themselves generally have little education, do not read aloud, and do not address each other in complex sentences, the child's abstract reasoning abilities are not developed.
5. The general concomitants of life in poor areas—overcrowding, noise, peer group disdain for intellectual activities and so on—work together to stultify mental development.

U.S. schools in general have not succeeded in reversing the effects of cultural deprivation. This has, however, been a major objective of Operation Head Start, a program we shall review in Chapter 6.

CRIME AND THE JUSTICE SYSTEM

The fact that proportionately more crimes, particularly violent and street crimes, are committed by poor persons than by nonpoor persons is a prominent feature of most discussion of law and order. Less conspicuous in these discussions is the fact that proportionately more crime is committed *against* poor persons as well.

How do we know that poor people are more frequently the victims of violent crime, such as armed robbery, aggravated assault, rape, and murder?

First, there is a limited amount of survey data relating the frequency with which people with different incomes are victims of crime. The data in Table 2-1, for example, indicate the incidence of crime per 100,000 persons in various income groups. The most total crimes, as well as the largest number of rapes, robberies, and burglaries, are committed against those with family incomes under $3,000.

Second, we can judge that most crime is committed against the poor from our information on *where* crime is committed. "Crime is heavily concentrated," writes former Attorney General Ramsey Clark in *Crime in America*, "in small geographic areas of the inner city and pockets of rural poverty. Here, where fewer than one-fourth of the people live, more than three-fourths of all arrests occur." Even crimes against business are concentrated in poor areas. Ghetto businesses are twice as likely to be burglarized, 4 1/2 times as likely to be robbed, and 2 1/2 times as likely to be vandalized. They are 60 percent more likely to be victimized by shoplifters and 35 percent more likely to suffer employee theft, although they are 25 percent less likely to take bad checks. Most ghetto businesses may not be owned by poor people, to be sure; but it is poor people who pay the price of these crimes, through higher prices, lower quality, and higher credit costs.

Third, there is a great deal of information on crimes committed by and against persons according to race. Because of the greater incidence of poverty among nonwhites, and particularly among blacks, these data are a good proxy for income data. As Ramsey Clark writes:

The brutalization of poverty, racism and discrimination in the United States is graphically demonstrated by the dimension of violent crime reported among Negroes. Violent crime in the black ghetto is probably reported less frequently than anywhere else in America. Even so,

TABLE 2 – 1

Victims of Crime, by Income, 1965

(Number per 100,000)

Income of Victims	Total Crimes	Forcible Rape	Robbery	Aggravated Assault	Burglary	Larceny ($50 and Over)	Motor Vehicle Theft
Under $3,000	2,369	76	172	229	1,319	420	153
$ 3,000 – $5,999	2,331	49	121	316	1,020	619	206
$ 6,000 – $9,999	1,820	10	48	144	867	549	202
$10,000 and over	2,237	17	34	252	790	925	219

SOURCE: Executive Office of the President, President's Commission on Law Enforcement and the Administration of Justice. *Report, The Challenge of Crime in a Free Society*, 1967. Cited in *Statistical Abstract of the United States* (1970), Table 217.

Negroes, composing 14 percent of the total population, were involved in 59 percent of the arrests for murder in 1967. This does not mean that Negroes in fact committed 59 percent of all murders. Negroes are arrested more frequently and on less evidence than whites and are more often victims of sweep arrests. But 54 percent of all known murder victims were black in both 1967 and 1968—this is a body count, mathematically precise excepting human error. Blacks are nearly always victims of black violence and suffer some white violence as well.

Nearly one-half of all persons arrested for aggravated assault during 1968 were black—and, again, blacks were the primary victims of the assaults. Sixty-one percent of all persons arrested for robbery were black, with black victims bearing most of the burden. Forty-seven percent of those arrested for rape were black, while approximately one-third of all arrested for serious property crime were black. Blacks were their principal victims. The most tragic and dangerous risk of racism in America today is that it may cause us to misconstrue the meaning of crime among poor blacks. That crime flows clearly and directly from the brutalization and dehumanism of racism, poverty, and injustice. Black America has shown itself to be far gentler and more humane than white America. There is nothing inherent in black character that causes black crime. On the contrary, the slow destruction of human dignity caused by white racism in responsible. This is the most pitiable result of this huge wrong of the American people.

One does not have to agree with the Black Panther argument that all the blacks in America's jails and prisons are political prisoners to find attractive Clark's judgment that even the criminals among blacks and other poor people are, in a sense, victims. The high incidence of black and other nonwhite faces in our penal institutions is explained by the conditions of life for minority groups in the United States. These conditions are conducive to crimes of frustration and hostility. They are also conducive to a life of professional crime. The 1971 *Manpower Report of the President* makes the following observations:

Under present conditions, many people in the slums, especially young black men, see illegal activity as an alternative to menial jobs paying low wages and offering no hope of advancement. A recent study in

Harlem estimates that roughly 2 out of every 5 of the adult inhabitants had some illegal income in 1966 and that 1 out of 5 appeared to exist entirely on money derived from illegal sources.

Part of the study consisted of a series of intensive interviews conducted in 1968 with unemployed young people aged 18 to 24 in Harlem. Many of these black youths subscribed to such generally accepted values as education and training, employment in meaningful and responsible work, and dependence on one's own resources. Furthermore, they were interested in goals such as having a successful career, accumulating money, and achieving status and prestige through possessions. But in many instances, they found the accepted means of realizing these goals too ridden with frustration or out of their reach and viewed illegitimate activities as a much easier way of achieving some measure of economic success and status in the immediate community.

The absence of employment opportunities which could lead to a radical improvement in life styles and movement out of the slums seemed to be the basic reason why jobs, even those which pay above the minimum wages, were sometimes regarded disdainfully. . . . Hustling was often regarded as a logical and rational option. The market for gambling, numbers, prostitution, and narcotics is large and highly profitable, and the possibility of "being on one's own" competes powerfully with the opportunities available in the regulated middle-class world.

The large number of poor people in jails and prisons is also explained by the failings of America's criminal justice system. These failings are chiefly in four areas: arrests, bail, trial, and sentencing.

Arrests. Poor people are more likely to be arrested, both when they are innocent and when they are guilty. This is especially true of ex-convicts, alcoholics, and addicts, whose guilt tends to be presumed, with or without trial. Even though arrest and conviction are not identical, arrest is important because (the Bill of Rights to the contrary) most people, including those who sit on juries, tend to believe that a person would not have been arrested if he were not guilty. Moreover, even poor people who are subsequently acquitted have an arrest record that is held against them by employers.

Bail. The bail system obviously works against poor people; it favors not only those of middle and high incomes but also members of organized crime. Being held in jail pending trial makes it hard for the accused to prepare his defense and cuts off his family's income. Moreover, because of clogged court calendars, the accused may wait months or more than a year for trial. At times, an innocent person may spend less time in jail if he pleads guilty and accepts his sentence than if he waits for a trial and is acquitted.

Trial. The poor person is often at a disadvantage in a trial because of his appearance, his inarticulateness, or his race. And in spite of a series of Supreme Court decisions which require that even paupers be represented by attorneys, poor people receive poorer-quality legal counsel than the nonpoor.

Sentencing. Poor people tend to receive stiffer sentences, particularly prison sentences, than the nonpoor for the same offenses. Over the years they also have received far more death sentences than the nonpoor.

RACE AND RACISM

Racism, like poverty, tends to be propagated by vicious circles. And whenever there is a markedly high incidence of poverty among a particular ethnic or racial group, the vicious circles of poverty and of racism will tend to amplify and reinforce each other. As Myrdal wrote in *An American Dilemma*, "white prejudice and discrimination keep the Negro low in standards of living, health, education, manners and morals. This, in turn, gives support to white prejudice. White prejudice and Negro standards thus mutually 'cause' each other."

The concept of vicious circles helps explain how a problem, such as racism or poverty, is perpetuated once it comes into being. Racism tends to be founded on a number of self-fulfilling propositions. Whenever a minority group is discriminated against, segregated, ostracized, hated, feared, or deprived, it tends to develop characteristics and attributes which in turn tend, in the minds of the majority, to justify their initial racism.

Let us take a specific example: the continuous effort of white American society to emasculate the black man. Whatever the reason, and whether by conscious or unconscious design, there has been a continuing history of efforts, in this country, to deprive black men of their manhood. Under slavery, black fathers were not recognized as parents. Men and women who had lived together as husband and wife for years could be broken up simply by the sale of one or the other. (*Uncle Tom's Cabin*, often thought to be a protest against slavery, is more aptly interpreted as a protest against the American slave laws' destruction of black family life.) A black mother was regarded not merely as the head of the family but as the *only* parent. Thus a child born of a black mother and a white father was a slave, the chattel of the owner of the mother; but a child born of a white mother and a black father was technically born free. The destruction of black families and the removal of black fathers' family responsibilities seemed systematic and intentional.

The assault on black manhood continued after the end of slavery. Lynching, for instance, was almost exclusively reserved for men, who, moreover, were often castrated or otherwise mutilated as part of the ritual.

Calling black men ''boy'' was clearly part of the same pattern. So too was the 20th-century image of the black man as fearful, superstitious, and wide-eyed propagated in books, motion pictures, and animated cartoons.

Today, the pattern is continued by discrimination in employment. The accepted way in which American men prove their manhood is through gainful employment, by which they support their wives and families. They continue to prove it by being promoted to positions of responsibility, often supervising other workers. But black men, more than black women, have been barred from employment by reason of race. And while both black men *and* women have been kept from positions of responsibility as leaders or supervisors, the effects are different, simply because men are expected to prove themselves by leadership, whereas women (because of sex discrimination) are not.

The public assistance system also contributes to the destruction of the black man's role as head of the family by often making assistance available only to families where there is no employable person. Families with a mother, children, *and* an unemployed father are generally ineligible for assistance. In order for the family to become eligible, the father must desert.

Many people who are aware that the public assistance program tends to break up families have a false picture of the process. They envision the father and mother carefully planning their alternatives—conspiring, as it were. Although this may happen occasionally, what seems more common is that the welfare department lurks in the background, as a substitute father—a better provider than the real father, who cannot find a job, or, at any rate, cannot find an adequate job. Since friends and neighbors on public assistance live better, great tensions develop in the household—tensions that culminate in desertion and abandonment. Often, the deserted mother must swear out a desertion warrant against her departed husband; many do so gladly.

The pattern of black emasculation, then, did not end with the Emancipation Proclamation, the 13th Amendment, the Supreme Court desegregation decision, or the Civil Rights Act of 1964. What are its effects?

Family disorganization, the tendency of blacks to have broken homes and illegitimate children, is named in the controversial "Moynihan Report" as the central problem of American race relations. It leads to lower family incomes and a continuing cycle of malnutrition, poor educational performance, and so on, not only because many mothers cannot or will not leave their children to take jobs or because day-care facilities are not available but also because women in American society are still given lower-status and lower-paying jobs than men. It also discourages a continuing, responsible paternal role on the part of black men, it affects their incentive to work, and it feeds the stereotype of black people held by whites.

The unemployment, sporadic employment, and employment in low-paying jobs of black men not only perpetuates their poverty but substantiates the racist picture of blacks as lazy and incompetent. Moreover, deprived of legitimate avenues for proving their manhood, many black men are forced to find other means. Thus they may emphasize the external manifestations of success, as we noted in Chapter 1, through forms of conspicuous consumption that emphasize sexuality and masculinity. Or, they may turn to violence and a life of crime. These patterns reinforce both white contempt and white fear of black men.

The effects of these vicious circles on minority groups are clear: Discrimination vastly increases the chances that one will be poor, and poverty creates or amplifies many of the characteristics which, to the rest of society, seem to justify discrimination. Ironically, however, the non-minority (primarily white) poor *also* suffer as a result of the reinforcement of poverty by racism and vice versa. Poor whites tend to be at least as racist as nonpoor whites, partly, one supposes, because of a need to feel superior to *someone* and partly because they often seem to be competing for the same jobs and benefits. The poor are thus divided against one another, which helps to dissipate what little political and moral power they have.

THE POOR PAY MORE

The four words heading this section form the title of David Caplowitz's important book on consumer practices and costs among the poor in New York City. A fuller title might be *The Poor Pay More, Get Less, and Sometimes Get Nothing at All*. Caplowitz describes the low-income consumer as lacking both money and sophistication. As a buyer, his chances of avoiding manipulation and exploitation by merchants are poor.

Anthony Downs, summarizing the consumption problems of the poor in *Who Are the Urban Poor?*, notes that

1. Retail prices for food and other staples paid by residents of big-city, low-income neighborhoods are often higher than those paid by residents of higher-income areas. This occurs mainly because poor people tend to shop in small local stores, rather than because of price differentials in larger chain stores.
2. Poor residents in big cities pay much higher prices and interest rates for merchandise purchased on credit than wealthier residents pay for exactly the same goods. A Federal Trade Commission study showed that prices of such goods averaged 50 percent more in low-income areas.
3. Housing in low-income areas is far more expensive in relation to the quality of service received—especially in Negro areas—than in middle-income neighborhoods. For comparable or only slightly lower rents, poor households receive smaller units in worse physical condition with poor services and neighborhood amenities.

Consumer protection laws tend to protect primarily sophisticated shoppers, because they operate most often on the principle of disclosure—listing ingredients, truth-in-lending, and truth-in-packaging. The disclosure principle, notes Los Angeles poverty lawyer Florence Bernstein, means that it is all right to do anything to the buyer, so long as you tell him first that you are going to do it. It means little to those lacking the education or background to understand the significance of the information disclosed.

The fact that the poor pay more for the same goods adds to the vicious circle of poverty by reducing still further the real value of their meager incomes. The treatment poor people get from door-to-door salesmen, ghetto merchants, loan companies, landlords, and others from whom they buy, and from the legal system when they cannot or do not pay, also increases the sense of powerlessness that is such an important part of poverty.

THE POOR AND THE GOVERNMENT

One aspect of the powerlessness of poor people in America is their lack of political muscle. They vote in much smaller numbers than the rest of society. And when they do vote, their votes are often wasted by being uninformed and purposeless. They are easily swayed by bids for party loyalty or by hard-sell campaigning. Apart from voting, they rarely follow the standard operating procedure for effecting wanted and blocking unwanted legislation, namely organizing into interest and pressure groups. There are exceptions—most notably, the black organizations such as the National Association for the Advancement of Colored People (NAACP), the Congress of Racial Equality (CORE), and the Urban League; welfare groups such as the National Welfare Rights Organization (NWRO); and community action organizations such as The Woodlawn Organization (TWO) in Chicago and FIGHT in Rochester, N.Y. However, the numbers, strength, and effectiveness of these groups are limited both by the apathy, inexperience, and ignorance of poor people and by an understandable (considering their clientele) lack of resources.

In many instances, when a poor person shakes off his apathy and fear and engages in organized political or pressure action, the long odds against him mean failure—confirming his apathy or cynicism and setting an object lesson for others. Thus the apathy of many poor people may reflect not pathology, but realism. A single vote so rarely makes any difference in an election that some analysts take the position that it is the behavior of those who go to the trouble of keeping informed and voting which requires an explanation, and it is nonparticipation and inactivity which is rational—not only for the poor but for everyone.

Since poor people are politically weaker than most other groups, even when they are organized and active, and since they typically are neither organized nor active, it is hardly surprising that they get poorer social services from government than do the nonpoor. As Anthony Downs notes,

Poor neighborhoods in large cities normally receive the lowest quality of city services (such as garbage collection and police protection). . . . Schools of the lowest quality, with the least qualified teachers and often the oldest buildings and equipment, are usually concentrated in poor neighborhoods, especially in the big cities. Furthermore, wealthy suburbs spend far more per student on all aspects of education. . . . Urban highways are often deliberately routed directly through low-income areas, especially Negro neighborhoods, but bypass wealthier residential districts.

The welfare system, broadly conceived so as to include not only public assistance and other forms of "poor people's welfare," but all the institutions of the welfare state, strongly favors the nonpoor and in many instances acts as a barrier, keeping the poor from escaping poverty. This effect of America's "dual welfare system" is the subject of Chapter 4.

Controversial Vicious Circles

Some of the vicious circles of poverty derive from the way society deals with the poor, some derive from the effects of limited resources, and some derive from the behavior of the poor themselves. In this last category are the vicious circles associated with crime, illegitimacy, and family disorganization, already referred to, as well as those associated with large family size. The prevalence of these (and other) problems among the poor has led to the premise that poverty breeds a set of characteristic attitudes, an outlook, a lifestyle, even a "culture of poverty," that in turn keeps poor people poor.

The sharpest and most extreme statements of this point of view are found in Oscar Lewis's anthropological studies of poor families, such as *The Children of Sanchez*, and in Edward C. Banfield's *The Unheavenly City*.

It was Lewis who popularized the expression "culture of poverty." Poor people generally, he argued, live in crowded homes without privacy, a situation that encourages

gregariousness, a high incidence of alcoholism, frequent use of physical violence in the training of children, wife beating, early initiation into sex, free unions or consensual marriages, a relatively high incidence of the abandonment of mothers and children, a trend toward mother-centered families and a much greater knowledge of maternal relatives, the predominance of the nuclear family, a strong predisposition to authoritarianism, . . . a sense of resignation and fatalism based upon the realities of their difficult life situation, a belief in male superiority which reaches its crystallization in *machismo* or the cult of masculinity, a corresponding martyr complex among women, and finally, a high tolerance for psychological pathology of all sorts.

Banfield's observations, less empirically based, are similar; and Banfield is more quick to draw conclusions. "The lower-class forms of all problems," he writes, "are at bottom a single problem: the existence of an outlook and style of life which is radically present-oriented and which therefore attaches no value to work, sacrifice, self-improvement, or service to family, friends, or community." To Banfield, this places the poor in an inescapable trap: "With the exception of the autobiographical accounts of a few very gifted individuals—Frederick Douglass, Malcolm X, and Claude Brown, for example—there is no direct evidence of there *ever* having been *any* upward mobility from the lower class." [Italics added.]

These statements have produced considerable controversy among students of poverty. There is little question that the behavior mentioned is most prevalent among the poor, particularly the urban poor. The question is whether this behavior represents a "culture" or only a rational set of techniques for adapting to an environment characterized by poverty, sickness, malnutrition, crime, and powerlessness. Some studies indicate a unique set of attitudes among poor people; others indicate values, ambitions, and attitudes similar to those of the nonpoor. Although the returns are divided, that fact alone suggests that poverty does not necessarily create a special culture and psychopathology.

In the following paragraphs, we shall take another look at some of the problems of the poor—family disorganization, promiscuity, crime, violence, and the poor's supposed antipathy toward work—this time to see if they are indeed evidence of a separate culture of poverty or merely "normal" reactions to environmental stress.

Family Disorganization. We have already looked at some of the ways in which society has undermined the role of black men and, as a consequence, white men who find themselves in the same circumstances as the majority of black men. It would be improper, at the very least, to attribute family disorganization to a particular "culture" or "style of life" until public policy, at least, no longer encourages fatherless families among the poor.

Promiscuity. It is widely believed, even by defenders of the poor, that their sexual mores are looser, and their sexual lives more promiscuous, than those of nonpoor. Banfield says that the "lower-class style of life involves an unremitting search for sex...," though he does not say on what he bases this opinion. The evidence most commonly cited is the high illegitimacy and high venereal disease rates among the poor and their large families. (We discount as hopelessly biased the impressionistic evidence of those who claim to know, from their own observation, about the promiscuity of various groups. At best, casual observation can only tell one how discreet or public people are about their promiscuity.) Studies and surveys have shown that poor families want smaller families than the nonpoor; they do not have the information or resources needed to obtain birth control—or abortions, which, legal or illegal, tend to be a technique used primarily by nonpoor women. These same comments apply to illegitimacy rates, which, as far as can be determined, do not indicate either general approval of illegitimate children or a higher incidence of extramarital sexual relations among the poor. Venereal disease is more likely to be evidence of differences in health care and of hygiene-consciousness than of differences in sexual behavior.

Crime. Do higher crime rates among poor people indicate less respect for the law? We have already mentioned a study of youth in Harlem indicating that the attitudes of poor blacks are similar to those of the rest of society, though their behavior may be different. Poor people, who are often victims of discrimination at the hands of law enforcement agencies, may be more cynical about and have less respect for the police and legal systems, but this does not necessarily mean that they accept crime as legitimate.

Banfield, on the other hand, argues that poor people do not have consciences: "The [lower-class] individual's actions are influenced not by conscience but only by a sense of what he can get away with." As evidence, he cites a study in which lower-class and middle-class children, all black, were asked why it is wrong to steal and cheat. The largest group of lower-class children said that it is wrong to cheat because "someone will find it out," whereas the largest number of middle-class children said that it is wrong to steal because "your friends won't like you" and it is wrong to cheat because "children will not want to play with you." Whether this shows a difference in *conscience*, or simply the varying effectiveness of different sanctions, is a question for the reader to decide.

Violence. There is no gainsaying that poor people live in an environment of violence. Crime statistics surely understate the violence among peers, between lovers, and within families among the poor. The incidence of violence is a powerful indicator of the pressures of living in chronic poverty. But even so, violence is not a prerogative only of the poor. The world wars of this century were not started by poor people. It was not the poor who split the atoms that led to Hiroshima. Nor was it the poor who manufactured the napalm and fragmentation bombs used in Vietnam. There is a great deal of violence in the world, some of which is deemed illegitimate and is called "crime," and some of which is deemed legitimate and is called "war" or "punishment." There is a disproportionate concentration of poor people among those whose violence is illegitimate, but it is not necessarily true that there is a disproportionate concentration of poor people among those who commit violence in general.

Attitudes Toward Work.   It is widely believed that a great many poor people do not share the goals of the rest of us, that they see no intrinsic merit in being independent and self-supporting, and that they do not want to work. The poor work records and adjustment to dependency of many poor persons may seem to support this view, but recent research shows it to be false. Leonard Goodwin, reporting on a long-term social-psychological study of work orientations of the poor in which more than 4,000 persons were surveyed, concludes that

> poor people—males and females, blacks and whites, youths and adults—identify their self-esteem with work as strongly as do the nonpoor. They express as much willingness to take job training if unable to earn a living and to work even if they were to have an adequate income. They have, moreover, as high life aspirations as do the nonpoor and want the same things, among them a good education and a nice place to live. This study reveals no differences between poor and nonpoor when it comes to life goals and wanting to work.

Goodwin's monograph, *Do the Poor Want to Work?* (published by the Brookings Institution, for whom the study was conducted), attributes the "plight of the poor" not to their having "deviant goals or a deviant psychology," but to their "different experiences of success and failure in the world."

CAUSAL CHAINS

Early in this chapter, readers were warned not to oversimplify the problem of vicious circles, since patterns of causation may be manifold and complex. To illustrate this point, let us return for a moment to the role of education in creating vicious circles. Briefly, poverty causes educational shortcomings, or deficits; and those educational deficits in turn cause poverty. But the specific connections between poverty and education are by no means clear from such a facile and simplistic statement. It is important to know *how* poverty causes educational deficits and *how* educational deficits cause poverty.

The main links in the chain of causation are given in Figure 2-1. The poor, partly because they lack political power, have unequal access to schooling. Poor mothers and their children have poor health and poor diets. Poor physical condition lowers the intelligence of poor children and reduces their energy. Poverty, partly because of these factors, is associated with low motivation and a lack of effort in school. If, as some claim, poor people have shorter time horizons and less concern about the future than the nonpoor, that will also reduce their motivation to perform well in school. Cultural or environmental deprivation may also reduce learning ability.

The educational deficits that result from these problems in turn cause poverty, primarily through employment problems. Poorly educated persons get worse jobs, partly because their value to employers is less (because of their low productivity), partly because they do not have the required diplomas and degrees, and partly because they do not have school placement services, administrators and teachers, or even old fraternity brothers and the like to find jobs for them.

Figure 2-1 also has some short-circuits. Poor health and diet are directly responsible for some productivity problems. Some of the problems of poverty that are well known to school children directly reduce their motivation to work hard in school. These are only examples. Many more short-circuits, and, for that matter, many more links in the

FIGURE 2 - 1

One Vicious Circle: Education and Poverty

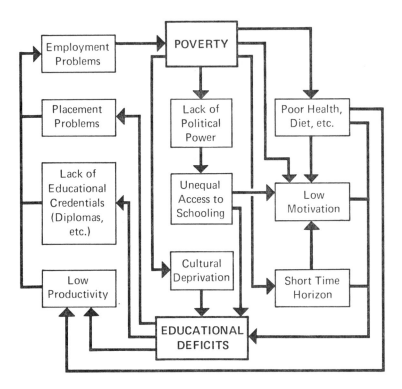

NOTE: Arrows indicate the probable direction of causation.

education-poverty circle could have been shown. Not shown, for instance, is the role played by in-school violence in creating educational problems in poor neighborhoods. Educational deficits may cause or aggravate poverty in ways other than by creating employment problems: Inadequate consumer education may result in wasteful spending; inadequate health education may increase nutrition problems, and so forth.

Figure 2-1 deals specifically with education, but similar figures could easily be drawn for other vicious circles, such as crime, health problems, and unemployment.

THE ROLE OF THE WELFARE SYSTEM

The existence of vicious circles of poverty has important implications for antipoverty policy. As we mentioned earlier, antipoverty policy consists, in general, of techniques for keeping people from becoming poor (preventative policies) and techniques for moving already-poor people out of poverty (curative policies). Preventative policies have as an objective keeping vicious circles from coming into existence, and curative policies have as an objective interrupting and correcting existing ones.

CURING POVERTY

There is a time dimension to vicious circles. In general, the longer one is poor, the more difficult it is to escape from poverty. Those whose ordinarily satisfactory incomes are temporarily interrupted by a business failure, layoffs, or the like may be forced into bad housing and have to subsist on inadequate diets; but unless these conditions continue for long periods of time, they are unlikely to influence such things as a person's skills, connections, general health, intelligence, propensity to commit crime, and role in the family. On the other hand, those who have lived in these conditions for a long time, and in particular those families that have lived this way for more than a generation, will find it particularly difficult to change their circumstances. Thus reliance on a laissez-faire, or "bootstrap," approach to help those affected by chronic poverty probably condemns them to continued poverty.

Small or intermittent and undependable doses of intervention will probably be equally ineffective. There are instances in which making small changes and comparing the increment in costs with the increment in benefits in order to determine whether additional small steps ought to be taken is an appropriate method. This approach, which is a trademark of the discipline of economics, may be valid, for instance, in finding out the optimum scale of operations of a business. But it is not appropriate in evaluating antipoverty policy. (One may compare the problem of antipoverty policy to the problem of pushing a large stone up a hill; suppose one pushes the stone up 10 percent of the way, only to find that it rolls back again. Would it be proper to conclude that because the incremental effort exceeded the incremental benefits that pushing the stone was the wrong way to get it to the top of the hill?)

Even major antipoverty efforts may fail when they focus on only one element of a vicious circle. For instance, even if the per-pupil expenditure in schools serving poor children was raised substantially, the results might be relatively meager if the children still had inadequate diets and poor health, if racial and other barriers still prevented them from getting good jobs even if they did well in school, if their home environments remained nonconducive to learning, and if the schools they attended were still dominated either by peers who terrorized students and faculty alike or by teachers and administrators who represented an authority structure from which they (the poor children) were alienated—in short, if the rest of the vicious circle remained intact. Curative antipoverty policy requires a simultaneous, major attack on a large number of fronts.

Antipoverty policy-makers also consider the possibility that the causes of poverty lie entirely outside the poor and their characteristics. For instance, the economy may provide only a given number of nonpoverty job opportunities, so that a given number of people will always be poor. The vicious circles we have discussed may explain *who* (but not *how many*) are poor. That is, they may influence and be influenced by the distribution of poverty, but they may not cause poverty in an aggregate or social sense. To the extent that this is true, a number of kinds of antipoverty policy, such as compensatory education, may redistribute but not reduce poverty. This issue will be discussed at greater length in Chapter 3, and curative antipoverty policy will be discussed more extensively in Chapter 6.

PREVENTING POVERTY

When most people use the term *antipoverty policy*, it is curative rather than preventative techniques to which they refer. They do not think of devices for keeping the nonpoor from becoming poor.

As we noted at the start of this chapter, vicious circles are a special case of cycles of cumulative causation, which can also be benign. Just as it is the manifold consequences of poverty that are most important in keeping people poor, so too is it the results of having adequate means, or of being affluent, that help keep one comfortable, or even rich. Preventative antipoverty policy is aided by these benign cycles of causation. The elements that make up these benign cycles—good health and nutrition, greater education and job opportunities, better protection against crime and violence (including the ability to move to low-crime suburban areas), fairer treatment by the criminal justice system, fairer treatment of consumers, and political power—make the prevention of poverty much easier.

Preventative antipoverty policy techniques are designed to keep economic reverses from turning into chronic, vicious-circle poverty. If a personal, family, or social *calamity* temporarily cuts off one's income or imposes emergency expenses, the result can easily be permanent poverty unless something is done before much time elapses.

Some typical calamities include illness, injury, death, or desertion of the main earner in the family; unemployment, a loss of crops, or some other business reverse; floods, fires, storms, or other "acts of God"; theft of one's possessions; war; incarceration; and victimization by the unscrupulous. Some calamities are sudden; some, like the exhaustion of coal or other mineral reserves or the effects of old age upon productivity, come upon an area or a person more gradually.

There are *private* safeguards, such as life insurance and accumulated personal wealth, to keep these calamities from having excessively harmful effects. But *socially*, it is the function of the *welfare system* to keep these calamities from bringing on chronic poverty. Hence, the welfare system is the most important social tool of preventative antipoverty policy.

THE WELFARE SYSTEM

The welfare system consists of *all* social devices and techniques for income maintenance and protection. In the United States in the 1970s, the expression *welfare system* has come to be used by many people to refer to only a portion of the true welfare system, the public assistance program. The true meaning of the term is much broader, and derives from the concept of the *welfare state*.

The most important institutions of the American welfare system—the Old-Age, Survivors', Disability, and Hospitalization Insurance (OAS-DHI) program (Social Security and Medicare), together with federally aided public assistance in the form of Aid to Families with Dependent Children (AFDC) and Supplementary Security Income (SSI) for the aged, blind, and disabled—were all created by the Social Security Act of 1935 or by amendments to that Act. The United States was the last major nation in the world to create such institutions. Many people are under the impression that there was *no* welfare system before the New Deal and that other countries did not have welfare systems before they created government social security systems.

Actually, all societies face the problem of how to deal with the needs of widows and orphans; how to provide for the victims of illness or accidents and their dependents; how to distribute necessities in cases of unemployment; and how to deal with the whole range of calamities mentioned earlier. All societies have some form of welfare system, institutional or traditional, implicit or explicit.

Perhaps the most important welfare system in man's history has been the extended kinship system—the multigenerational family, clan, or tribe that is still encountered in agricultural societies, and even in remote rural areas of the United States. The family unit is often extended not only vertically—to include several generations—but horizontally, with brothers, uncles, cousins, nephews, and other relations living together. If there are more persons in the family than are needed for the tasks at hand (the agrarian equivalent of unemployment), all will do some work and all will be cared for. When men are incapacitated, they and their wives and children will continue to be cared for. The same is true when children are orphaned, when wives are widowed, or when other calamities strike.

A similar unit is the stable village or community where the members are not necessarily related. A home burns down and the community rebuilds it. A man is injured, and the community feeds him until he can get back to work. Sometimes the church has been the institution through which such community "welfare systems" have operated.

A somewhat different "welfare system" was operated by the nineteenth-century American urban political machine. Successful machines kept close tabs on the residents of each block, made sure they were employed, and tried to help out in economic crises, in exchange for loyalty to the organization.

The passage of time and economic development have undermined these more traditional social insurance techniques. Industrialization, urbanization, and related events have made the extended family unnecessary and cumbersome and led to primacy of the nuclear, or two-generation, family (consisting of parents and their minor children). The same events, given the mobility of people and the large populations of urban areas, have undermined the stable community as a welfare device. The Americanization of the foreign-born, together with the concerted efforts of reform groups, has reduced the power of political machines. In fact, local welfare departments were begun or strengthened early in this century partly as a political reform measure, for the very purpose of weakening the political machine as a welfare institution.

In short, the traditional welfare techniques collapsed as a consequence of the direction of history and economic change. In the United States, there was a gap between the collapse of the old techniques around or before the turn of the century and the erection of the new, institutional structure begun in the mid-1930s. The Great Depression of the 1930s was so severe in part because, by then, the United States was a predominantly urban and industrial society without either the old or the new welfare systems. Between 1931 and 1933, the American farm population increased by 2 million persons in the face of long-standing and powerful trends in the opposite direction. This obviously represented a desperate effort to revert to family and community welfare devices and reflected America's failure to provide modern, institutional equivalents.

It was the administration of Franklin Roosevelt which began the process we choose to call the *institutionalization of the welfare system*. The New Deal did not invent the idea of social devices to protect people from the results of calamities; it simply modernized and transformed those devices.

To say our modern institutions had antecedents in more traditional societies may give the false impression that the sick and indigent have always been cared for, at least in more recent eras, and are so today throughout the world. Of course, this is not the case. The traditional methods did not always function well. Sometimes people were left out or ill-treated. The numbers of people in each family, community, or other basic population unit were too small, and their members' risks too interdependent, to provide for the equivalent of a dependable insurance system. Hence their modern, institutionalized equivalents are generally not mere substitutes, but are, in spite of their greater impersonality and bureaucracy, more efficient and at times more humane.

WELFARE PROGRAMS

Just as it would be a mistake to think that welfare began in the 1930s, so also it would be a mistake to think that the modern welfare system consists only of programs like Social Security. As we have noted, the welfare system includes *all* the social means of income protection and maintenance. Welfare programs can be classified as *direct* or *indirect*. Direct welfare programs may be *explicit* or *implicit*. They involve the power of government to tax and spend and to otherwise provide a redistribution of income. Explicit transfer programs are openly and obviously redistributive, taxing some people and making payments to others. They appear, then, on both the tax and expenditure sides of public budgets. Examples are public assistance, Social Security, unemployment compensation, workmen's compensation, Medicare, food stamps, farm price supports, and subsidies for public housing. To most people, the welfare state consists of these explicit transfer devices. They ignore the other types of welfare programs.

Implicit transfer programs redistribute income in less obvious ways. For example, federal tax laws provide an extra dependency exemption for those over 65, in effect increasing their after-tax income. Deductions for medical care in effect give the federal government a share in such costs, as do Medicare and other explicit programs. A tax credit is also given for self-employed persons who wish to set up their own retirement fund. This retirement income credit is comparable to Social Security and other explicit age-related protections.

The name *tax expenditures* has been given to implicit transfer programs in the federal income tax laws. Estimates of selected tax expenditures made by the Tax Analysis Staff of the U.S. Treasury for fiscal 1971 are shown in Table 2-2. (Not every tax expenditure is shown in Table 2-2. Some large items, such as depletion allowances and capital gains, are not included because, although they may create loopholes or tax preferences, they are not forms of "welfare.") The deductibility of medical expenses alone cost the federal government $1,900 million in lost tax revenues in 1971; the added exemption and other tax preferences for those over 65 cost the government $3,250 million.

Tax expenditures reduce taxes for some people and raise taxes for others. Thus they transfer income just as surely—though not as openly—as explicit transfers.

TABLE 2 – 2

Selected Items of Federal Tax Expenditures, 1971
(in millions)

Deductibility of interest on home mortgages for owner-occupied homes [a]	$2,400
Deductibility of property taxes for owner-occupied homes [a]	2,700
Additional exemption, retirement income credit, and exclusion of OASDHI income for the aged	3,250
Additional exemption for the blind	10
Exclusion for "sick pay"	120
Exclusion of unemployment insurance benefits	800
Exclusion of workmen's compensation benefits	320
Exclusion of public assistance benefits	65
Exclusion for employee pensions	3,650
Deduction for self-employed retirement	250
Exclusion of other employee benefits:	
Premiums on group life insurance	500
Accident and death benefits	30
Medical insurance premiums and medical care	2,000
Other	175
Exclusion of interest on life insurance savings	1,100
Deductibility by individuals of charitable contributions	3,200
Deductibility of medical expenses	1,900
Deductibility of casualty losses	165
Deductibility of child- and dependent-care expenses	30
Exclusion of certain veterans' benefits	700

SOURCE: Statement by Edwin S. Cohen, Undersecretary of the Treasury, before the Joint Economic Committee, July 21, 1972. The original list of items was selected by the Joint Economic Committee for estimation by the Treasury Department. The present list of expenditures was selected from that list.

[a] See the appendix to this chapter for a discussion of the effect of this deduction.

Another type of implicit transfer takes place when social policy affects the outcome of market exchanges. For instance, the farm price-support program, radically changed in 1973 when farm surpluses gave way to shortages, not only involved an explicit tax-and-transfer element that appeared in public budgets; it also resulted in higher farm prices, thus bringing about a further transfer of income from consumers to farm owners.

The pre-1973 price-support program and its successor are an interesting example of a shift from one system of transfer payments to another. Under the former, a price was chosen that was deemed to provide sufficient income to farm owners. All of the affected product which could be sold at that price was sold; the remainder, the so-called farm surplus, was acquired and stored by the government. During the administration of President Harry S Truman, his Secretary of Agriculture, Charles Brannan, proposed a major revision in the farm program. The *Brannan Plan*, as it was called, gave the farmers the same income as they had under price supports; but farm products were to be sold for whatever they would bring, and the farmers' incomes were to be supplemented by a check from the government. Thus the Brannan Plan consisted entirely of explicit transfers, whereas the price-support plan consisted partly of explicit transfers (mainly the cost to the government of buying the surplus) and partly of implicit transfers (the cost to consumers of higher farm prices as the result of price supports). Farmers strongly opposed the Brannan Plan when it was originally introduced, partly because the transfers were more explicit; but some twenty years later, in 1973, a version of it was adopted and widely hailed as a major reform.

Minimum wage laws are the other major example (there are a number of minor ones) of techniques for affecting incomes through social intervention in a market exchange.

Even though price supports and minimum wages involve implicit transfers, they are direct welfare programs. Their purpose is to affect income and income security. Powerful welfare benefits may also be achieved indirectly by regulatory programs and laws whose central purpose, at least ostensibly, is not income protection and maintenance. For example, U.S. labor laws guarantee workers the right to elect representatives, the right to bargain collectively, and, in most cases, the right to strike. By strengthening the employee's position vis-à-vis his employer, they protect his job and his income. Laws that regulate insurance companies (who are the purveyors of private income-maintenance programs) are also part of the indirect welfare system.

Those who resist including regulatory agencies and laws as part of the "welfare system" should consider that indirect welfare programs could be substituted for direct programs. Employers, for example, could be *required* to provide private health insurance for all employees, and these private programs could be publicly regulated.

The welfare system, then, seen in full, consists of all explicit and implicit transfers for the purpose of income protection and maintenance *and all indirect, regulatory programs that substitute for such transfers*. A further examination of the U.S. welfare system appears in Chapters 4 and 5.

SUMMARY

Poverty, no matter how it begins, if it is permitted to persist for a significant period, has effects on poor people that, in turn, tend to keep them poor. Thus once people are poor, it takes sustained outside intervention on many fronts to return them to the ranks of the nonpoor. To keep people from falling victim to the vicious circles by which poverty is perpetuated, society must have an adequate and certain welfare system. The term *welfare system*, in this sense, means not merely programs to transfer money to the poor or to other groups within society. It includes all social devices for income protection and maintenance, traditional or modern, direct or indirect, and explicit or implicit.

This is not to say, however, that it does not make any difference what form the welfare system takes. As we shall see shortly, it makes an enormous difference.

APPENDIX

The deduction of mortgage-loan interest and of property taxes on *owner-occupied* housing is considered an item of "tax expenditure," whereas the same deductions apply to *landlord-owned, tenant-occupied* housing, where they are *not* considered a subsidy. It seems prudent to explain why owner-occupied and rental housing are treated differently.

First, let us consider rental housing. The landlord pays income taxes (or corporate profits taxes, if the landlord is a corporation) on his net rental income—that is, on his rent receipts, less deductions for costs incurred. These costs include maintenance and upkeep, depreciation, and the like *and* mortgage-loan interest and property taxes. Like any other businessman, the landlord is permitted to deduct his costs from his receipts, and he pays income taxes only on the difference.

Now consider the owner of owner-occupied housing. Like the landlord, he receives income from his home ownership; but since this income is "in kind" (it takes the form of use of housing, rather than money), he does not have to pay taxes on it. Since he pays no tax, he is permitted no deductions. He is, however, allowed to deduct interest and property taxes.

There are two approaches to estimating the implied subsidy to homeowners. One is to estimate the taxes that would have been paid if home-mortgage interest and property taxes were not deductible by homeowners. This is the approach taken by the U.S. Treasury Department and the Joint Economic Committee and reflected in Table 2-2, which shows estimates of $2.4 billion and $2.7 billion, respectively, for the two items, and a total of $5.1 billion for both together. In 1969, these figures were $1.9 billion and $1.8 billion, respectively, or a total of $3.7 billion.

The other approach is to estimate how much homeowners would have had to pay if the net in-kind rental value of their homes (the rental value of housing used in the year, less the costs incurred) had been subject to tax. This figure was estimated at $4.0 billion for 1969 by Professor Henry Aaron, in "Income Taxes and Housing," *American Economic Review* (December 1970). The two approaches, then, yield very similar results.

REFERENCES

The concept of vicious circles was introduced by Gunnar Myrdal in *An American Dilemma: The Negro Problem and Modern Democracy* (New York: Harper & Row, rev. ed., 1962; orig. publ., 1942) and applied to underdevelopment in *Economic Theory and Underdeveloped Regions* (New York: Harper & Row, rev. ed., 1971; orig. publ., 1958) and other works. The quotation is from *An American Dilemma*. The Lloyd Reynolds quotation is from his *Wages and Labor Mobility Theory* (New York: Harper & Row, 1951). A more recent study with similar results is Reo M. Christenson's *Challenge and Decision*, 3rd ed. (New York: Harper & Row, 1970). Laurence DeWitt's study is his unpublished Ph.D. dissertation in economics for Syracuse University, *Inflation and the Distribution of Unemployment by Income Class* (1969).

The "dual labor market" theory has been developed by a number of economists, including Barry F. Bluestone, Peter B. Doeringer, Michael J. Piore, David M. Gordon, and Howard Wachtel, as well as Bennett Harrison. We have quoted from Professor Harrison's *Education, Training and the Urban Ghetto* (Baltimore: Johns Hopkins Press, 1972). See also David M. Gordon, *Theories of Poverty and Unemployment* (Lexington, Mass.: Lexington Books, 1971) for a thorough survey. Lester Thurow's article on the job competition model is "Education and Economic Equality," *Public Interest* (Summer 1972).

The data on the link between years in school and poverty are from the Bureau of the Census's *Current Population Reports: Consumer Income*, Series P-60 (December 16, 1970). Patricia Cayo Sexton's *Education and Income: Inequalities of*

Opportunity in Our Public Schools (New York: Viking Press, 1964), from which our data on poverty in the urban midwest and the bias against poor and nonwhite children entering college-preparatory programs are taken, is an important work in this area and includes a great deal of narrative, nonquantitative evidence of prejudicial treatment.

The relationship between cultural deprivation, poor health, malnutrition, and lead poisoning on the one hand and low intelligence (including that due to mental retardation and organic brain damage) on the other is discussed most thoroughly in Rodger Hurley's *Poverty and Mental Retardation, A Causal Relationship* (New York: Random House, 1969). This is an important book for everyone concerned with the causes and pathology of American poverty. See also Frank Riessman's *The Culturally Deprived Child* (New York: Harper & Row, 1962); Herbert C. Birch and Joan Dye Gussow's *Disadvantaged Children, Health, Nutrition, and School Failure* (New York: Harcourt Brace Jovanovich, 1972); and A. Dale Tussing's *The Education Strategy: Can Education Solve the Problem of Poverty and Unemployment?* (Syracuse, N.Y.: Educational Policy Research Center, 1972). The last of these includes references to the research literature, especially on the relationship between malnutrition and brain damage. Kenneth Clark's *Dark Ghetto* (New York: Harper & Row, 1965), from which the quotation on p. 38 is taken, is cited by Hurley, *op. cit.*

Moynihan's memo, never officially released to the public, surfaced in a number of places. Our source is *The Wall Street Journal* (March 3, 1970).

The data on workdays missed due to illness and accident are taken from U.S. Public Health Service, National Center for Health Statistics, *Family Income in Relation to Selected Health Characteristics* (July 1963); the data on mental health are from Frank Riessman, Jerome Cohen, and Arthur Pearl, eds., *Mental Health of the Poor* (New York: Macmillan, 1964), especially Benjamin Pasamanick, Dean W. Roberts, Paul W. Lemkau, and Dean B. Kreuger, "A Survey of Mental Disease in an Urban Population: Prevalence by Race and Income"; the data on chronic and acute conditions are from *Medical Care, Health Status, and Family Income* (Washington, D.C.: Public Health Service, National Center for Health Statistics, 1964).

The point on parental rights under slavery is found in Kenneth Stampp, *The Peculiar Institution* (New York: Knopf, 1956). For a discussion of the effects of public assistance on the family, see "Cash Premium to Break Up the Family," *The Wall Street Journal* (November 30, 1967). President Nixon's reference to the same effect appeared in his message to Congress of August 11, 1969 on welfare legislation. The Moynihan report, *The Negro Family*, was published by the U.S. Department of Labor in 1965.

Ramsey Clark's comments appear in *Crime in America* (New York: Simon & Schuster, 1970).

For an analysis of the consumer problems of the poor, see David Caplowitz, *The Poor Pay More: Consumer Practices of Low Income Families* (New York:

Macmillan, 1963); and Anthony Downs, *Who Are the Urban Poor?* rev. ed. (New York: Committee for Economic Development, 1970). Florence Bernstein's comments are from an address to the American Council on Consumer Interests given in Columbia, Mo., on April 9, 1972.

For the arguments in favor of a culture of poverty, see Oscar Lewis, *The Children of Sanchez: An Autobiography of a Mexican Family* (New York: Random House, 1961), from which the quotation on pp. 51-52 is taken; Lewis, "The Culture of Poverty," *Scientific American*, 215 (1966); and Edward C. Banfield, *The Unheavenly City* (Boston: Little, Brown, 1968). For an opposing viewpoint, see Elizabeth Herzog, "Facts and Fictions About the Poor," *Monthly Labor Review* (1969), reprinted in James G. Scoville, *Perspectives on Poverty and Income Distribution* (Lexington, Mass.: Heath, 1971); David Elesh, *Poverty Theories and Income Maintenance: Validity and Policy Relevance*, a mimeographed discussion paper (Madison, Wis.: Institute for Research on Poverty, University of Wisconsin, 1970); Louis Kriesberg, *Mothers in Poverty: A Study of Fatherless Families* (Chicago: Aldine, 1970); and the major study cited in the text, Leonard Goodwin's *Do the Poor Want to Work?* (Washington, D.C.: Brookings Institution, 1972).

3

The Causes
of Poverty

Most of this chapter will be taken up with setting forth and putting to use a "theory of poverty." Our main purpose will be to develop a simple, nonmathematical model of society in which a small number of fundamental elements can be varied and to use this model to explain the presence and persistence of poverty in some regions and among some groups. Like most models, ours will be somewhat abstract and highly simplified. Nonetheless, we will be able to use it to make interpretations and even predictions of a qualitative sort.

Before we turn to the construction of our model, a number of preliminary points must be made.

First, as we mentioned in Chapter 1, it would be a serious mistake to assume automatically that the characteristics of the poor—their age or race, the sex of the head of the family, their type of residence, their level of education, and so on—are necessarily the cause of their poverty. Rural families are more likely to be poor than urban families, but this does not mean that living in the country is necessarily a *cause* of poverty. Blacks are more likely to be poor than whites, but this does not make blackness, per se, a *cause* of poverty. In order to argue that any particular characteristic or combination of characteristics of the poor is a *cause* of poverty, one must be able to explain the process of causation that makes this so. In other words, one must be able to provide a *theory* of poverty.

Second, we must distinguish between the events or phenomena that first make a person, a family, or a group poor and the events or phenomena that keep them poor. It is the latter, as we saw in Chapter 2, that make a vicious circle of poverty. People in every society face all kinds of hazards that, at least potentially, can make them poor: the death or disappearance of a husband or father; illness or accident; unemployment or other business reverses; floods, earthquakes, and other calamities; and wars, riots, or other events that disrupt normal patterns of life. In a country where there is no adequate welfare system or the welfare system itself has been disrupted, these common and universal hazards may create poverty that, for various reasons, becomes chronic.

Third, a society's welfare system is of enormous significance in determining whether there will be chronic poverty. In a developing and growing economy, if growth is fairly uniform among all groups and regions and the welfare system is able to prevent the vicious circles described in Chapter 2 from evolving, there is no necessary reason for chronic poverty to develop. Thus the theory of poverty we shall develop in this chapter will be very much concerned with the development of the welfare state.

Fourth, we must distinguish between the factors which cause poverty in an aggregate sense (that is, those which explain whether and to what extent poverty will exist in a society) and the factors which determine only the distribution of poverty and hence "cause" poverty only in an individual sense. Let us suppose, for example, that a society faces generic, economywide problems which limit the number of employment opportunities and that, because of this, a given number of people will always be poor. Suppose also that there is racial discrimination and that minority groups are last in line for jobs. What is the "cause" of poverty in this case? The poverty of the minority-group members is a direct result of employment discrimination. But at the macro level, racial discrimination is not the cause of poverty. Ending discrimination would not end or even reduce poverty, although it would redistribute it. This fourth point is one of the most important we shall make. It is an example of the *fallacy of composition*—of reasoning from the part to the whole—to assume that what causes individual poverty causes aggregate poverty as well. It may, but often it does not. Whether it does will depend on which theory of poverty is true.

Theories of poverty can be grouped under two headings: *case theories* and *generic theories*. Before turning to our model, we will review briefly these two concepts.

CASE AND GENERIC THEORIES OF POVERTY

The *case approach* to a theory of poverty holds that poverty arises out of the characteristics of the poor themselves: their intelligence, education, skill, handicaps, health, age, marital status, sex, region of residence, family size, and so on. These enter into particular theories in different ways. As we saw in Chapter 2, some writers would include attitudinal characteristics, including a "culture of poverty," in the list of poverty-causing characteristics. Sometimes the characteristics cited as causes of poverty reflect some kind of presumed defect in the poor such as low intelligence or an unwillingness to work. Sometimes, as in the case of race or region of residence, the characteristics cited have nothing to do with personal defects.

Even in societies where the characteristics generally associated with poverty exist, poverty need not be present if the welfare system provides high enough incomes to those affected. Even in case theories, then, *poverty results from a combination of individual characteristics and social policy.*

Generic theories of poverty hold that it results from general, economywide problems rather than from individual characteristics. The most clearcut examples of the applicability of generic theories are in poor, underdeveloped countries, where poverty can hardly be said to derive from individual defects. In advanced economies, the main generic problem is inadequate employment opportunities. Since there is an insufficient number of jobs, some people can find no work at all, while others are able to get only part-time or intermittent employment, or regular, full-time work at wages that are too low. In other words, for reasons unrelated to individual characteristics, there are only so many non-poverty-level jobs in the economy, and those who do not get them will be poor.

This last statement will be true only as long as the economic system and social policy do not work to spread the consequences of generic problems more or less evenly over the entire population. The same decline in aggregate economic activity could, in one economy, yield a general drop in income of around 15 percent and in another no drop in income for most people but unemployment and poverty for about 15 percent. Even in an economy with a chronic unemployment rate of 15 percent, the welfare system could (by means of unemployment compensation payments and the like) ensure that the unemployed and underemployed would not suffer relative to those with good jobs as a result of the economy's inability to provide nonpoverty employment for all. Thus, *poverty arises not only out of generic economic problems such as inadequate employment opportunities, but out of the characteristics of the economic system and social policy.*

If there are generic, economywide problems, and if the structure of the nation's economy together with its social policy translates these problems into poverty for some, *who* are liable to be poor? The *incidence* of poverty is determined in generic theories by the same characteristics that in case theories are said to *cause* poverty: education, race, location, and so on. Which theory holds in practice? As yet, no one knows. Determining which of these theories is true is one of the most difficult problems facing students of the economics of poverty. One reason for the difficulty is the following. Suppose we distinguish between "aggregate causes" of poverty such as inadequate employment opportunities and "individual causes" such as a lack of education. Individual factors *explain* poverty in case theories, but they explain only its *distribution* in generic theories. But no matter which theory one holds, one or more individual factors will be the immediate, proximate cause of the poverty of each poor person. If we examine the poverty of any individual or family, or even of any regional or racial group, there will always be individual factors present. There is no way to tell, when we are looking at the poverty of individuals or groups, whether aggregate factors are also operating.

Similarly (as we will see in Chapter 6), antipoverty policies that *appear* successful may or may not be so. For instance, manpower training programs whose graduates go on to better jobs and lower unemployment rates may reduce poverty (if case theories hold), or they may merely redistribute it (if generic theories hold). If there are only a certain number of nonpoverty jobs in the economy, manpower training programs will not increase that number, but they may help their graduates to get them. Thus these programs may seem highly successful, even when they actually do nothing to reduce either poverty or unemployment.

Although nothing has as yet been settled, there is a good deal of *indirect* evidence favoring generic theories. First, as we saw in Chapter 1, the amount of measured poverty is very sensitive to the ups and downs of the business cycle. Second, the "job competition" model of Professor Lester Thurow, discussed in Chapter 2, supports the generic theory.

According to this model, there are only so many high-, medium-, and low-wage jobs in the economy and educational differences help determine who gets these jobs. Wage levels depend on characteristics of the jobs, not those of the workers. Thus differences in education determine the distribution of a given amount of poverty. Thurow presents some strong, but not conclusive, statistical evidence for his theory. Third, where employers screen applicants by using criteria unrelated to the job—such as a high school diploma for jobs not requiring high school skills—those who lose out do so for reasons other than an inability to perform the duties required. This practice, often called *credentialism* (since an educational credential is required for employment), seems fairly common. And fourth, as we will see in Chapter 6, there is some evidence that compensatory education and manpower training programs *do* merely redistribute given job opportunities, rather than increasing their number.

In spite of this indirect evidence pointing to generic theories, most people—including the poor—probably favor the case theories. Most people are unaccustomed to thinking in terms of aggregates, and what appear to be the causes of poverty for individuals are ordinarily accepted as ultimate causes as well. There is undoubtedly *some* amount of case poverty. But the bulk of the evidence presently available seems to point to generic factors as the predominant cause of poverty.

The theoretical model developed below is not concerned with aggregate causes. Instead, the emphasis is on the individual factors that explain poverty in some theories, and its distribution in others. In addition, the model casts some light on the growth and structure of the welfare system, which is important in determining whether poverty will exist in both case and generic theories.

THE ASSUMPTIONS OF THE MODEL

Three assumptions are necessary to our model, and the failure of any society to satisfy these assumptions will, to some extent, make the model inapplicable to that society. They have, however, been satisfied in most societies in the past century.

1. *A growing real income per person and economic development.* It is assumed that the economy is growing—not necessarily rapidly—

through saving and capital formation, through technological change, through education, and through the other usual sources of economic growth. Note, however, at this stage, that no assumption is made about the *distribution* of the gains from economic growth. All that is assumed is that real incomes (incomes adjusted for price-level changes) are growing on the average, so that there is *enough* growth in aggregate income to provide significant increases in real income for each person if the aggregate increase is sufficiently dispersed among the population.

It is also assumed that, although the long-term trend of the economy is upward, periodic recessions or depressions associated with temporary reductions in per capita income are possible. They do not invalidate the model.

And third, it is assumed that economic growth is accompanied by economic development. These two processes are not the same, though they usually occur together. *Economic growth* refers to increases in output and income. *Economic development* refers to changes in the underlying economic structure, or mix. For the purposes of the model, it means that the economy becomes more unified and integrated, that the market for any single product or producer becomes wider; and that each individual, firm, and region tends to become more specialized and less self-sufficient.

2. *Growing control of the government and the major social institutions by a popular majority*. This assumption does not necessarily imply the existence of an electoral democracy, far less a bill of rights. It requires only that the attitudes of the *majority* of the population find increasing expression in social policy as time goes by. This majority can influence the government in many ways. In some societies, where the government is truly elected, voting power and influence over political parties may gradually expand. In others, even where there are no traditional democratic institutions, the government may nonetheless become increasingly responsive to the will, passive or active, of the majority.

Growing majority control of nongovernment institutions—businesses, religious bodies, trade unions, political parties, and the like—can come either through control of the government or in other ways.

It is not the *extent* of popular control that is crucial here, but the *increasing trend* toward such control.

3. *Growing institutionalization of the welfare system, transforming the society into a welfare state.* Nongovernmental techniques for income protection and maintenance are in the process of becoming institutionalized, in part privately, but largely socially, as discussed in Chapter 2. We do not assume, in our model, that the institutionalization and development of the welfare system is complete. On the contrary, the model applies during the time when most of this transformation and evolution is occurring. Every society goes through such a transformation; but there are marked differences in the way in which it is achieved, and these differences are of the utmost importance.

Let us now consider a hypothetical society in which these three assumptions hold, and into which we shall introduce some or all of the following elements: (1) a traditional and rigid class structure; (2) geographic and regional isolation; (3) an ideology of individualism; and (4) perceived racial and ethnic differences, accompanied by prejudice.

THE ELEMENTS OF THE MODEL

A society in which the three assumptions discussed apply but all four elements mentioned above—a rigid class system, isolation, individualism, and perceived racial and ethnic differences and prejudice—are absent is a special case of our model, which we shall call the *open case*.

THE OPEN CASE

In this open case, there is no reason for the persistence of poverty. The economy is becoming increasingly unified and integrated as development progresses. Agriculture, commerce, manufacturing, and services are all affected by the expansion of real income, even though capital formation or technological change may be concentrated in only one or two of these sectors. For instance, manufacturing may be growing quite rapidly and the gains in income may be shared by the agricultural, fishing, mining, and other sectors. The growth industries may be located in only one area (e.g., in the Northeast), but the growth in income may be shared by the whole nation. Income may be distributed equally or unequally among persons and regions but there are no regional "pockets" or racial or other groups that remain chronically poor in spite of general economic progress.

Even though economic growth and development pervade the whole society, leaving no one behind, the death of a family's chief earners, illness, accident, unemployment, business failure, and similar calamities will still occur. Whether they will create vicious circles of poverty will depend largely on the welfare system, direct or indirect, implicit or explicit. Persistent poverty will be avoided in the open case only if there is no prolonged hiatus between the decline of traditional, nongovernmental welfare techniques and the construction of an institutionalized welfare state, and then only if the institutionalized welfare techniques are sufficiently *certain*, sufficiently *comprehensive* and *uniform*, and sufficiently *financed*. In many ways, the probability of persistent poverty depends upon *how* the welfare state evolves. For instance, if techniques are developed piecemeal for individual groups, so that, for example, unemployment compensation is provided only for factory workers, or life insurance is provided only privately and voluntarily, or if there are programs for the blind but not for the crippled, there is always a possibility that poverty will develop among the members of the unprotected groups and their descendants.

If such poverty develops, will it be a consequence of a particular calamity in each case? Or will it be a consequence of the defects in the welfare system? It will surely *appear* to be the former; but since these calamities occur in all societies, real or hypothetical, and they do not create permanent poverty in all of them, the cause of such poverty is more accurately stated to be the defects in the welfare system.

Fortunately for any members of the "open case" society, there is every reason to expect that comprehensive institutionalized welfare techniques will be constructed promptly. We have not, after all, assumed the existence of an ideology contrary to the establishment of such an order, of insidious racial or other distinctions that would lead to the categorization of some of the population as "deserving" or "undeserving," or of a rigid class structure that would tend to make a low economic station (as opposed to poverty) the result of mere inheritance.

This open case we will call *Case A*. We will alter it by adding, one by one, the four elements mentioned above; we will then examine the effect of introducing these elements in tandem and in different combinations. We shall treat all four factors as if they were either present or absent, although in the real world they are all matters of degree.

A RIGID CLASS SOCIETY

In virtually every society, *some* advantage will adhere to the children of the most educated and best-paid and *some* disadvantage will accrue to the children of those employed in the most menial jobs at the lowest wages, even if we assume that native intelligence and ability are not inherited at all but are distributed randomly among all children. Since it is virtually impossible to do away with all advantages and disadvantages of birth, perhaps a totally classless society is impossible. However, societies may range from nearly classless states to the other extreme, in which caste alone determines a person's occupation, income, type and place of residence, education, diet, and clothing, as well as the group from which his or her spouse and friends are drawn, for generation after generation.

By a "rigid class society" we mean a system intermediate between these two. Although we could of course examine the effect, in the model, of each of a number of types of class or caste systems, a simple, three-class system is sufficient. We shall assume, then (1) a privileged class, clearly demarcated from the rest of society, perpetuated largely through inheritance and intermarriage, possibly landed, possibly with titles of nobility, and certainly cultured and wealthy; (2) a *bourgeoisie* or middle class, of merchants, professional people, and owners of moderate amounts of property; and (3) an unpropertied working class and a largely unpropertied peasantry, the latter probably declining in numbers in favor of the former as development proceeds. (For most of our purposes, however, the first two classes could be merged.)

The system described is, then, on the European pattern, though most features can be found, with some variations, in many other places. Although there can be a small amount of vertical movement (from one class to another), most movement is horizontal. People go from job to job or region to region, but they remain members of the class into which they were born and choose spouses and friends from this class. Most persons regard themselves as permanently members of a particular class, just as most American blacks and whites regard themselves as permanently members of black and white society respectively, in spite of the occasional blacks who move into white society or vice versa, and in spite of a small amount of intermarriage.

Given our three initial assumptions, the rigid class society works as follows.

1. Persons inherit their station in life, though not necessarily chronic and persistent poverty. The lowest classes may have begun the development period in abject poverty, but even they are likely to benefit to some extent from economic and political progress.
2. We have assumed growing control over governmental and other institutions by a popular majority. Assuming that the proletarian-peasant class is a numerical majority, as their control over social policy increases, their points of view will come to be reflected in economic developments, particularly those concerned with income distribution. Their own objectives will tend to be *class* objectives. Their attitudes or, in some cases, their ideologies, will predispose them toward economic policies designed to benefit the group. Their trade unions and political parties will be class institutions, which, compared to their American counterparts, will seem somewhat mixed up. Unions will appear to have political objectives (attempting to influence class gains through political mechanisms), and political parties will have economic objectives.

   We are assuming that the lowest classes are *class-conscious*. The similar economic status of the urban workers and the rural peasantry may create a feeling that they belong to the same group; or, the peasants may be quite separate. We shall construe these two some-times antagonistic groups as a single class in our model, since peasants may leave rural areas and agricultural activity and join the urban work force without difficulty. It is also socially (though perhaps not econom-ically) possible for urban workers to turn to farming, whereas neither group can enter the middle or upper class with similar ease.
3. Economic development, unification, and integration tend to spread the benefits of economic growth, to a greater or lesser extent, through-out the population. If social policy, increasingly influenced by the proletariat, discriminates against the agrarian sector, enough benefits will nonetheless spread, through rural-to-urban population shifts, to keep rural areas from becoming chronically poor. There will be no isolated pockets of poverty untouched by the general progress of the society.
4. Working-class ideology and attitudes will be quite influential in the construction of the welfare state. This fact has two implications: First,

income-security programs, and even programs that put a floor under the level of living, will be designed primarily to suit the needs of urban workers (although casual observation suggests that nearly every country has some kind of program to protect farm income as well). Second, and more important, these programs are liable to be quite comprehensive, both in terms of the hazards insured against (protection "from the cradle to the grave") and in terms of the types of persons covered. Designers and advocates of social insurance programs are liable to believe in them as a matter of principle and to respond in more or less straightforward ways to problems as they arise, although the programs may have an urban-worker bias.

Once the growth in income and the country's political development have reached a certain point, the society just described, which we shall call *Case B*, is unlikely to have or perceive a "poverty problem." All persons may participate in the economy, though clearly not on the same basis. Although everyone's role may be determined by birth, everyone does have a role. Social programs put a floor under the level of living below which no one is expected to fall. Programs and foresight being imperfect, some people may fall through anyway; but such accidents will merely be considered an occasion for repairing the floor. (This metaphor is borrowed from Nathan Glazer.) In this respect, the economy bears a resemblance to the economies of both Western and Eastern Europe; it differs from that of the United States, however, where a certain agony always accompanies the design of welfare programs (because the principles of social welfare and of a floor to the level of living have not been generally accepted), where the design of such programs must always make some concession to contrary ideologies, and where, as a result, self-consciousness is often more important than class-consciousness.

What we have said about the rigid class society does not mean that chronic poverty is not possible, but only that other elements will have to be added for it to develop. And even without such elements and without chronic poverty, such a society may not be a good one in which to live.

ECONOMIC AND GEOGRAPHIC ISOLATION

Early in the process of development, most societies consist of more or less isolated areas and regions whose urban capitals are connected financially and commercially but whose rural and "backwoods" areas are less integrated with one another and the world. The process of development is one not only of growth in output and changes in the input and output mix but also of unification and integration of the economy.

Some areas might, however, remain economically and geographically isolated, becoming enclaves excluded from, but not unaffected by, the progress around them. In fact, as we shall see, some areas may actually become more rather than less isolated as time goes by.

One obvious reason for isolation is natural barriers to transportation. Since what constitutes a barrier depends upon the mode of transport, technological changes in transportation may make an area that was at least as easy to reach as anywhere else (say, by oxcart) more difficult than other areas to get to (say, by truck).

An area may also become isolated if natural resources upon which its economy depends are used up or become obsolete or if the technology best adapted to that area becomes obsolete compared to techniques better adapted to other areas.

Inadequate transportation and communication tend to interact with the obsolescence of resources to produce isolation. Commerce and transportation between an area and the outside world may languish partly because of steep, winding, muddy, or broken-up roads. Conversely, because there is so little commerce, there is no reason to repair or reconstruct the roads. The result may be a vicious circle of isolation.

As long as the change in the outside world is slow, there will be sufficient time for its influence to seep in and for isolated peoples to migrate out, keeping the apparent economic and technological lag small. But there is probably a critical threshold in the size of the lag that will generate a vicious circle: At this point, the faster the pace of change in the outside world, the more isolated the separated area will become.

Though we do not assume that people in an isolated area are perceived as being of a different race, and hence are victims of racism and prejudice, isolation breeds differences in culture and dialect which in turn reinforce isolation.

The consequences of isolation depend, in part, upon its degree. If it is *total*, then there will actually be not one but two or more separate economies and societies, each with its own development pattern. In spite of being "left behind," an isolated area may remain *internally* viable in an economic and social sense, and may in fact become more so. As a consequence, the inhabitants may not feel demoralized or alienated; and the area may not, in its own estimation, be poverty-stricken, in spite of its backwardness.

But this relatively happy outcome is unlikely. More probably, the isolated region in a larger society will exhibit some of the characteristics of a dual economy, as discussed in Chapter 1. Technological and educational standards and prices will be set by the larger society, putting the region at a disadvantage.

If the area maintains some limited trade with the rest of society, its terms of trade are liable to worsen. *Terms of trade* are defined as the ratio of import prices to export prices or, roughly, as the cost of imports in terms of exports. They worsen when the price of imports rises relative to that of exports, so that the community is able to buy fewer goods from "outside" for a given volume of its own goods. Consequently, a worsening of the terms of trade means a lowering of the level of living in an absolute sense. Let us reexamine what happens when a country undergoes an agricultural revolution.

An isolated rural area is unlikely to participate in a revolution in agricultural technology. This is especially true if the area is poor and the revolution involves substituting huge amounts of capital for labor. As overall productivity rises, farm prices will fall and the isolated small farmers, whose methods and costs have remained the same, will suffer. Residents of the isolated areas will gradually become conscious of their worsening relative (and perhaps absolute) position. At worst, large numbers of people will become idle. The most promising young people may migrate to other areas, but their previous isolation in a region with its own cultural forms, forms probably ill-adapted to urban residence and employment, will make adjustment difficult. If significant migration does take place, the emigrés may even form unassimilated colonies in the towns. A similar fate may befall isolated areas dependent on any other industry experiencing a technological change.

This description of what can happen in an isolated area brings to mind the situation in both Appalachia and parts of the American South. There are also isolated backwater areas elsewhere in the United States where one finds the inhabitants living in shacks, poorly fed and educated, and without adequate medical care.

Isolation by itself is sufficient to account for chronic and persistent poverty, unless its effects can somehow be mitigated by the welfare system. For instance, the welfare system may be so comprehensive that it protects and maintains the incomes of those who would otherwise be poor not only because of sickness or unemployment or natural disaster but because their communities and industries have been "left behind." The likelihood that the isolated community will not be well provided for in the welfare system arises from three factors. First, the nation as a whole may be hostile to the isolated community. Such hostility may be caused or aggravated by the cost of redistributive income transfers, as well as by linguistic and cultural differences due to isolation. Second, the isolated area may simply be *forgotten* by policy-makers and by the rest of society. Policy-makers, like others, are always more attuned to the problems of friends, neighbors, and acquaintances than of strangers. Isolated persons may be excluded from adequate welfare coverage not because of a bias against them so much as by an unconscious bias in its own favor on the part of the rest of society. And third, the isolated, rural poor may not take advantage of welfare programs that exist and for which they are eligible because they are unaware of the programs or do not understand them.

If isolated communities are excluded or, through ignorance, exclude themselves from the institutionalized welfare system, the older, traditional forms of social welfare—extended families, neighborhood, church, and community responsibility, etc.—will persist. They are unlikely to have been undermined by urbanization, industrialization, and reform; and moreover, to the extent that nationwide, institutionalized programs are unavailable, the older forms of welfare will be severely needed. They will not work well, however, since they imply carving an already small pie into even more pieces to support the elderly, orphans, and other "nonproductive" members of the community.

Consequently, there are two reasons why poverty is likely to develop in isolated areas in this kind of society, which we shall call *Case C*. Such areas will not share fully the economic growth experienced by the rest of the society. And they are unlikely to share fully in the growth of modern, adequate welfare programs.

John Kenneth Galbraith, who, with a handful of others (including Michael Harrington and Dwight MacDonald), must be given credit for the rediscovery of American poverty in the early 1960s, has drawn a picture of a major source of poverty similar to that discussed here. The two types of poverty persisting in America, Galbraith argues, are "case poverty," resulting from intrinsic deficiencies in the individual (mental retardation, alcoholism, insufficient education, "excessive procreation," etc.), and "insular poverty" in regional pockets that is a product, in part, of the "desire of a comparatively large number of people to spend their lives at or near the place of their birth"—a desire which Galbraith calls the *homing instinct*.

To avoid confusion, we should note that Galbraith uses the term "case" somewhat differently from the way it was used earlier in this chapter to distinguish between theories of poverty. In fact, both of Galbraith's categories, case and insular poverty, are forms of what we have called case poverty. Galbraith's two categories do not cover all, or even most, sources of poverty. Where, for instance, do race and prejudice fall? Moreover, the term "intrinsic deficiencies" seems inadequate to cover the undigested collection of causes grouped together under the heading of case poverty. Why, for instance, is insufficient education regarded as an intrinsic deficiency? And to attribute insular poverty primarily or, through default, entirely to a homing instinct seems a gross oversimplification.

Nevertheless, Galbraith's work contains some valuable insights which have largely been ignored. The significance of insular poverty is too readily dismissed. Consciously or otherwise, we have come to treat poverty as mainly or exclusively an urban problem, maybe because urban poverty causes America so much more difficulty in terms of crime, social pathology, and all-too-visible slums. By concentrating on urban poverty, we ignore not merely the fact that over 40 percent of the poor lived outside metropolitan areas in 1972 (see Table 1-2 in Chapter 1), but also the fact that rural isolation was the original source of a large percentage of urban poverty.

The importance of isolation is underlined by the experiences of Irish and Southeastern European immigrants of the late 19th and early 20th centuries and their descendants, and of the Pennsylvania Germans. The poor from Ireland and Southeastern Europe arrived in the millions, propertyless, often illiterate *and* non-English-speaking, and were, moreover, objects of prejudice and discrimination. Why did they progress politically and economically so much more rapidly than black Americans? One answer often given is that they were white (and hence not easily distinguished on sight) and were never slaves. But another is that they immigrated to large cities, in the very mainstream of and during the peak of industrial expansion, while the majority of blacks were still living in small Southern towns and rural areas. (What would economic and social history have been like had the immigration of such large numbers of people been prohibited, or had the Europeans preferred to stay home?)

The Pennsylvania Germans provide another kind of illustration. These rural people, even the Amish and other culturally and linguistically separatist groups, although purposely committed to obsolete technology (they do not use automobiles, telephones, or motorized appliances), are nonetheless quite affluent. One reason is that the resource which first drew them to Southeastern Pennsylvania—the fertile soil—has not yet been played out, and they are in no sense geographically or economically isolated. In contrast, the descendants of other "Pennsylvania Dutch" who migrated down the Shenandoah Valley into the hills of Virginia and West Virginia, where they were truly isolated, on poor land, live in poverty and backwardness. (Among the latter are the true "Yokums"—or Jochums—from whom Al Capp took the names of his cartoon characters.)

AN IDEOLOGY OF INDIVIDUALISM

Not every American espouses the ideology of individualism, but it is the dominant point of view. It is reflected in most legislation concerning the social order and the distribution of wealth, income, and political power. It has been affirmed by our chief executives and by Congress down the years.

Like most ideologies, individualism has various empirical tenets. That is, it consists not only of subjective judgments about what goals are worth attaining and the best way to reach those goals, but of empirical observations that may or may not be accurate. It is easy to find cases in which people continue to voice the disproven empirical propositions of various ideologies (e.g., that public assistance recipients are primarily unemployed men). Most of the mythology of social systems consists of such disproven empirical propositions.

The American people, despite their adherence to individualism, do not consider themselves ideologists. They think of themselves as pragmatic—as doing what is functional and practical without reference to ideology. But American pragmatism, at least as it affects issues relating to poverty and wealth, is *not* nonideological, and it is conservative. Although it means that we are not wedded to one way of doing things, it also means that change is likely to be accepted only when it is incremental and piecemeal. Moreover, American individualism is really not wholly pragmatic, as we will see.

Individualism is, in part, an ostensible rejection of class structuring and class-consciousness, as well as of sweeping or radical approaches to economic and social questions. It is an ideology that helps explain, for instance, the unique pattern of development of American trade unions and the in many ways similar development of the National Association for the Advancement of Colored People (NAACP). Both of these, after brief experiments with fundamental-change and essentially radical ideologies, chose instead to accept the prevailing economic and social system and to deal with issues one by one, using methods that rapidly became socially legitimate. The American labor movement adopted what has been called "business unionism" or "bread-and-butter unionism"; the policies adopted by the NAACP have not been given such a name, but they could easily have been.

The American ideology of individualism has several components, each of which is discussed briefly below.

The Virtue of Self-Reliance. In America, people are expected to provide for themselves. Society does not owe anyone a living; people make their own living. It is not always clear what "providing for oneself" comprises: It includes, of course, supporting oneself by working, owning a business, inventing things, and the like. It usually includes, for a woman, marrying a man with legitimate income and raising a family. It may or may not include obtaining income from dividends and bonds, by inheritance, or from relatives, although such sources of funds are usually acceptable. It almost surely includes living on pensions to which one has contributed or which one has otherwise "earned," insurance, and the like. It most assuredly does not include the acceptance of charity, welfare checks, and other transfers of income not associated with one's own prior earnings or effort.

This insistence on self-reliance and on individual effort and productivity is frequently ascribed to the influence of the frontier and the Protestant ethic on American thought and behavior. Certainly venturing into frontier areas required self-reliance and self-sufficiency; but so, we might add, would migration in the post-frontier days to urban industrial areas without the protection of an institutionalized and securely established welfare system.

Economic Success as a Reflection of Merit. In the United States, one's income, wealth, and status, the rate at which one is promoted, and the like are considered to reflect one's ability and effort. Poor people are generally assumed to have low incomes not by virtue of their membership in a particular economic class or capricious circumstance, but because they are less useful to society than others and possibly less hard-working, frugal, and responsible.

Hostility Toward Government as a Safeguard Against Tyranny.   The traditional American hostility toward and suspicion of government, deepening as government becomes more remote and centralized, is, like our belief in the virtue of self-reliance, understandable in the light of American history. Moreover, the two are interconnected. A person who is self-reliant does not depend on the government. And in order to preserve one's independence, one does not entrust too much power over social matters to government. Dependent populations and active governments are separately illegitimate; since the one implies the other, they are doubly damned. (Or *triply*. To many, dependence implies leisure, leisure implies idleness, and idleness implies temptation and sin. Many vocal critics of public assistance are preoccupied, if not obsessed, with the recipients' sex lives, their ownership of color television sets, their purchase of alcoholic beverages, and so forth.)

There is, among many American adherents to the ideology of individualism, something of a double standard in this area, which approves of government support and encouragement of business in spite of general hostility toward government "interference" in the social sphere.

The Relevance of Morality.   There is a strong tendency in this country to attach moral weight to all sorts of things, including the preceding three beliefs. Thus self-reliance, personal success, and hostility to government intervention are invested with moral value. The effect is to magnify, without changing, the ideology.

There are two corollaries to this attitude.

1. *A failure to be self-reliant is treated as a moral weakness.* Although poverty may be interpreted as a sort of failure in a success-oriented environment, it is not by itself a sign of *moral* failure. Indeed, until recently there has been a kind of nobility associated with poverty—at least with struggling, self-reliant poverty. Even today, someone who can say "we're poor, but we've never been on welfare" is a kind of heroic figure. It is dependency, more than poverty, that reflects *morally* against one.

This is not to say that poverty is no reflection on a person at all.

Failure of any kind is treated as a reflection on the individual. Poor people are blamed for their poverty, perhaps largely because, in a system in which the legitimacy of income is so important, there is a strong need for the nonpoor to justify the entire system by which income is distributed.

2. *The principles of welfare and social insurance are not accepted.* The ideology of individualism argues strongly against institutional, governmental provisions for income security and maintenance. Social insurance, it claims, encourages dependence, dulls initiative, and encourages idleness. (Of course, people can and indeed should provide, through savings, private insurance, or the equivalent, for their own protection and that of their dependents, and for their own retirement.)

Let us return now to our model. The individualist society that rejects welfare in principle will, paradoxically, develop *more* welfare programs than other societies; and in some, but by no means all, cases these programs will be more generous than those of other societies. This will happen for two reasons.

First, social insurance problems (the need to care for the elderly, to feed and shelter the unemployed, to educate orphans, and so on) will be dealt with one by one, with programs tailormade to the case at hand; indeed, there will be a tendency to subdivide these problems even further, dealing separately with housing for the elderly, health care for the elderly, income for retired railroad employees, income for retired manufacturing employees, and so on. The reason for such a piecemeal approach is simple: Since welfare is not accepted in principle, society will not construct comprehensive programs, but will act only where need is overpowering, and then in a manner responsive only to that particular need. Moreover, we could posit that, because of the need to justify each new program, there will almost inevitably be a lag between the appearance of a need and the response to it.

Second, the *form* of welfare programs will accord with the social ideology. This implies two types of programs: camouflaged and illegitimate.

Camouflaged Welfare Programs. When the dominant elements in a society based on individualism construct welfare programs for themselves, they will be designed in such a manner as to appear to be something other than what they are. They will be called "insurance programs" and given appropriate trappings (account numbers, the appearance of a contributory basis, etc.); they will be called "parity plans" to ensure "fair market prices" or "soil banks" to "conserve resources"; or they will be concealed in tax-law provisions. Even the seemingly neutral expression "social insurance," although it is an entirely valid concept, has the ring of a quasi-private, self-reliant program in harmony with individualism.

Most of the population covered by camouflaged welfare programs will accept them as *part of*, rather than violations of, the ideology of individualism.

Illegitimate Welfare Programs. When the dominant elements in such a society construct welfare programs for weaker groups, the programs will be designed in such a way as to make clear the social illegitimacy of the recipient population. Sometimes application procedures and eligibility standards will be degrading; sometimes recipients' names will be published; sometimes other ways will be found, as in the case of well-identified public housing projects, to mark recipients as dependent on public charity. But in all cases, it will be the explicit definition of the programs as welfare programs and the attendant publicity, rather than other details, that will underline the social illegitimacy of the recipients.

Within the category of illegitimate welfare recipients, a further distinction may be drawn between "deserving" and "undeserving" indigents. "Deserving" recipients will include primarily those *unable* to be self-reliant, such as the elderly, the disabled, orphans, and certain others. "Undeserving" recipients will include able-bodied employables and selected disabled types such as narcotics addicts and alcoholics. However, both groups, as dependents, will be regarded as essentially illegitimate. Elderly persons perhaps cannot work, but they surely should have provided health and payroll insurance for themselves. It may seem irrational to blame orphans or the children of the undeserving poor for their poverty and dependency, but even that is not uncommon. The whole category of "deserving poor" are seen as moral failures because of their dependency, in spite of their moral superiority over the "undeserving poor," who are the least liable of all to have any programs constructed for them and the most likely to find degrading those few programs that do serve them.

The "illegitimate" welfare programs will be primarily, then, for the

poor. They too will be a composite of a large array of individual welfare programs tailormade to solve individual problems—rural assistance programs, urban assistance programs, child-care programs, programs for the elderly, health-care programs, housing programs, and so on. As we have noted, this reflects an unwillingness to accept income maintenance in principle and a consequent tendency to provide it only if and as the need becomes compelling. Moreover, there will be a strong urge to provide only for the clearly demonstrated *needs* of the "illegitimate" indigent population, and hence to provide *goods* rather than income. That is, there will be no social judgment that each family deserves a given minimum level of living; but there may be a judgment that it needs housing or health care or food, and these may be provided.

What is important for the purposes of our model is whether the complex of tailormade income-security and protection programs will be adequate to prevent the initiation of vicious circles of poverty.

In the case of the camouflaged welfare programs—generally meaning the programs for the nonpoor, together with whatever poor people may be included in the categories constructed—the answer is almost certainly yes. Levels of support will probably be adequate, since the protective coloration provided the programs will make society less anxious about the recipients living comfortably and occasionally even well.

It is less likely that the welfare programs considered illegitimate will be either generous enough or dependable enough to prevent vicious circles. Levels of support will be low, both because the popular philosophy provides no justification of comfortable levels and because society believes that the poor deserve to be poor. Moreover, it is unlikely that programs will be dependable or automatic enough to provide security, since such certainty may seem to imply a "right" to welfare, and an individualist society is unlikely to concede such a right.

Thus the individualist society is liable to construct a *dual welfare system* as the welfare system is institutionalized. The American dual welfare system is examined in some detail in the next chapter.

If we now assume an ideology of individualism without a rigid class structure, economic and geographic isolation, or prejudice, we have a type of society we shall call *Case D*. The economy is developing and unifying, average real income is rising, popular control is mounting, and traditional forms of welfare are becoming obsolete and being replaced by governmental programs. As control of the government and of the major institutions of society spreads downward, group after group gains enough power to establish the legitimacy of their instruments of action and leverage (such as political machines, pressure groups, and lobbies) or have already legitimate instruments of power (such as the vote) extended to them. They are thus able to push through legitimate welfare programs designed to apply to themselves.

Will this process continue until every segment of society has the political leverage to protect itself by camouflaged welfare programs? There is a strong danger that it will not—that once a comfortable majority of the population is covered, the motive for continued political and social progress in the area of welfare will be gone.

This point is a most important one for the progress of the welfare state. It suggests a mechanism for the continued development and institutionalization of the welfare system until a large majority are protected and then a more-or-less automatic halt to that progress, possibly perpetuating the poverty of the remaining minority. Moreover, when this point is reached, the dominant majority will be able to believe that, with the exception of illegitimate welfare programs for the poor, *there are no social welfare programs*.

Although satisfaction of the needs of a comfortable majority of the population is sufficient to stop the progress of the welfare state and to bar the construction of new programs for those remaining unprotected, that outcome becomes even more likely if the last group to gain political and economic power feels threatened by the group below them. When that moment comes, when the society changes from one in which a privileged minority oppresses a poor majority into one in which a privileged majority oppresses a poor minority, the need and opportunity to justify the distribution of income and political power will have reached a maximum.

Thus it would appear that the ideology of individualism is, by itself, sufficient for the persistence of poverty in an expanding society, even an increasingly democratic one. Our model does not at this stage predict who it is that will be poor, or for whom society will provide only inadequate and degrading social insurance institutions. These people, whoever they are, will be the last ones to gain economic and political power; consequently, their identity will depend on the process through which popular control spreads and on the structural changes (e.g., the decline of particular industries) that occur in the economy.

PREJUDICE

The last element to be considered in our model is perceived racial or other intergroup differences among members of the society, combined with discrimination against one or more racial, ethnic, or nationality group because of those differences. We shall use the word "prejudice" to describe this discrimination, even though in the United States "racism" is a more apt term, because in some societies religious, tribal, or other differences are the principal source of prejudice.

It is conceivable, but not necessary, that all members of a minority group will belong to the same socioeconomic class. If they do not, and people feel solidarity with other members of their class regardless of race or other group characteristics, we have a class society. Class solidarity and prejudice can exist together, of course; but if they do, this will reduce the number of people with whom each person can align himself and associate. Poor whites (for instance) will feel kinship neither with non-poor whites nor with poor nonwhites. The question of solidarity is important, since it affects the design of economic policy, including the design of welfare systems.

Groups discriminated against are isolated in a sense, but not by historic accident or the depletion of resources, and neither the pace of social change nor outward migration is liable to influence this kind of isolation. Prejudice may also lead to actual separation or segregation of the minority groups. With respect to economic and social development, the two extremes of complete separation and complete integration are probably the most satisfactory. With complete separation, the minority group is nurtured within its own protective culture, maintains its own more or less self-sufficient economy, develops or maintains its own traditional welfare system, and controls its own institutions. Although group and average incomes may be low, patterns of chronic poverty and dependency need not develop. Achievement within the group is possible, and children need not grow up without success models drawn from their own racial or ethnic group. At the other extreme, with complete integration, there are no separate institutions; but there is no discrimination either and, once again, no reason for persistent poverty, or dependency, and no reason for demoralization. There is a spectrum of possible race relationships in between, all probably worse. The situation is worst when the minority and majority groups use the same institutions, but the majority controls them, and when the minority group is prevented from achieving success within the context of those institutions and according to shared values.

Prejudice differs from individualism, but not so sharply as one might think. Individualism is sometimes defined as an emphasis on the worth of each individual and roughly equated with humanism. Seemingly, then, individualism should be incompatible with prejudice. This is not the pattern of behavior one perceives, however, in societies with individualist economic philosophies. On the contrary, one tends to find denial of social responsibility for individual well-being. While prejudice and individualism are different, and a society could have one without the other, prejudice may sometimes appear in the *guise* of individualism, through the process of *rationalization*, which will be discussed momentarily.

The world has known several types of prejudice, and each type can affect the persistence of poverty and the progress of the welfare state in a different manner. We shall attempt to deal here only with a few fundamental problems.

Rationalization is a common psychological phenomenon: when the real reasons for a persons' behavior are unacceptable, his mind may construct acceptable reasons. Prejudice itself, for instance, may be a rationalization of behavior that actually results from hidden phobias or sexual feelings, but we will not explore that question. In a society whose nominal ideology emphasizes individual worth and democracy, and in which prejudice itself has become morally unacceptable, it is necessary to rationalize racist behavior in other terms. But when a person—or a society—develops a rationalization, the entire rationalization must be acted out. That is, the person or group must do all the things implied by the rationalization.

For example, the United States, which has had one of the most libertarian and democratic nominal ideologies, nonetheless entertained one of the most virulent forms of slavery. The rationalization of this institution, based on the "inferiority" of the enslaved and sponsored even by organized religion, had to be really powerful in order to overcome the libertarian passion that had prompted the world's first successful colonial revolution and formation of the first modern republic. The rationalization for black slavery was essentially that Africans were not quite human and hence did not have human rights. Acting out this rationalization produced not just economic exploitation, but brutality and inhumanity. The same argument is used today by some to justify discrimination and segregation, though it is gradually giving way to other rationalizations. (The controversial findings of psychologist Arthur R. Jensen and others, who claim to show that racial differences in intelligence are genetic rather that environmentally caused, may revive the issue of black "inferiority"; but thus far they have shown little sign of doing so. Perhaps they have not because inferiority is no longer viewed as ample justification of inequality before the law, so that modern rationalizations must be more sophisticated and devious. Jensen's research is discussed in Chapter 6.)

Throughout history, various rationalizations have been used to justify racism, as well as sectarian, tribal, and other prejudices. Those discriminated against have been accused of immorally holding divergent religious views (of being "pagans," "infidels," or "Christ-killers"); of natural indolence or stupidity; and of many other faults. Some have even comforted themselves with the attitude that various minority groups *prefer* discrimination, segregation, and even slavery to the insecurity of independence. The rationalization which seems at the same time the most common and the most pernicious, at least in modern societies, is that a minority group represents a *danger* to the rest of the society. This rationalization, like many, may be self-fulfilling: Minority groups that are the objects of continued oppressive discrimination may well be pushed into pathological behavior patterns that represent a danger to others or into resistance by force.

For the purposes of this chapter, we shall call a society in which prejudice is present *Case E*. Although prejudice and the rationalizations for it may take a number of forms, these will tend to affect our model in similar ways, except for details. Because of economic discrimination —with respect to systems of land tenure, employment, education, and so on—the minority group may not share in the growth of average real income; and even if it does, its share may lag far enough behind to create an easily perceived gap. For similar reasons, its members may not share in the popularization of control of the government and other institutions of society. The techniques they use to attempt to gain and use power may not be legitimized, as those of others have been. Prejudice and its rationalizations will almost certainly be sufficient reason for the development of welfare devices that deal with minorities in a way different from the way the majority group is treated. The following points might be considered:

1. If prejudice is open or deeply rationalized, so that whatever inferiority or danger ascribed to members of the group is coextensive with the group, then welfare differences will also be coextensive with the group. Such is the case, for instance, under Apartheid. On the other hand, if the society professes to make no legitimate racial or ethnic distinctions, but to make distinctions only among individuals on the basis of their "true" performance and behavior, some minority-group

members will escape discriminatory treatment, while some majority-group members will suffer it. Indeed, these exceptions are of great importance if the society is to convince itself that its rationalizations are true and it is not prejudiced.

2. There is sufficient reason in either case for chronic and persistent poverty, a product of both economic discrimination and categorical welfare programs. In the case of highly rationalized prejudice, other persons caught in the net created for the minority group may also be persistently poor. If these nonminority poor are, as is common, those most threatened by the putative dangers presented by the minority, they may, oddly, be the most prejudiced members of the society. Here the differences between a class-oriented and a prejudiced society become most patent.

3. Since poor people in a prejudiced society will tend to be equated with the undesirable, the inferior, or the dangerous, we can describe some of the possible characteristics of the welfare system that might be constructed for them. At one extreme, they may simply be excluded from all protection on some grounds (e.g., they haven't "earned" it). If they are not excluded, the system may be designed in such a manner as to blame recipients for their poverty, that is, to confirm and prove the rationalizations for discrimination. Then too, welfare programs may be designed in such a manner that they can be used to manipulate minority-group members, moving them into or away from a region and into or out of the labor force.

Thoroughgoing prejudice provides one final and powerful reason for the persistence of poverty. Its rationalization is liable to be subtle enough, consistent enough with a higher moral code, and possessed of a sufficient germ of truth to be convincing not only to the majority who practice discrimination but to much of the minority who suffer it. To the extent that the minority group itself accepts and acts out majority rationalizations, engulfing itself in what has been called group self-hate, the progress of the group through "bootstrap" methods becomes difficult if not impossible. That this is true when the group accepts itself as inferior or rejects its own heritage as savage and barbarian is fairly obvious. It is less obvious, but probably no less true, that this is the case when the group accepts society's definition of it as dangerous. One suspects that the violent character of American inner-city, predominantly black schools, for instance, represents in part the acting out by black youth of the picture white society draws of them.

THE ELEMENTS OF THE MODEL COMBINED

Figure 3-1 shows all the various combinations which our model can accommodate, on the extreme assumption that the four elements are always either present or absent. If we allowed *degrees* of presence or absence (reflecting, for instance, the fact that all prejudiced societies are not equally prejudiced), there would be no end of possible combinations. Readers will have to construct the in-between cases, however, for themselves.

SIXTEEN CASES

Figure 3-1 sets out 16 "cases," A through P. Of these, the first five have already been discussed. Case A, where the three assumptions of economic growth and development, growing majority control, and institutionalization of the welfare system all apply but where none of the four elements is present has been identified as the open case, where there is no reason for poverty to develop. Cases B through E are those in which each element, in turn, appears by itself. In B, where there is a rigid class structure, there is sharp inequality, but not necessarily chronic, vicious-circle, pathological poverty. In C, D, and E, poverty is possible.

We shall now examine cases in which two or more of the elements are combined. It is important to know, in each situation, whether the groups of people that make up the lowest economic class in a class-structured society, the racial minority in a racist society, and the isolated segments where there is isolation are the same, overlapping, or wholly different. In general, if each is a different group, then the descriptions already given of Cases B through E will apply. Suppose, for example, that a society has a rigid class structure and also that a significant group of people is isolated geographically and economically. If that isolated group and the lowest economic class are wholly different, then instead of Case F, we really have Cases B and C side by side in the same society. For F to occur, some overlap is necessary. For that reason, our discussion of F, and of cases G through P, assumes just such an overlap.

Case F: Class Structure and Isolation.   We have assumed, for the reasons just mentioned, that the lowest economic class and the isolated group in Case F are not wholly different. It remains an important question whether they are identical or merely overlapping groups. The greatest danger of chronic poverty occurs when the isolated group constitutes a

FIGURE 3 - 1

All Possible Combinations of the Elements in the Model

Case	Class Structure	Isolation	Individualism	Prejudice	Characteristics
A					The open case: There is even development, an adequate welfare system, and no reason for poverty.
B	■				Chronic inequality may be followed by worker control, but there is no chronic poverty.
C		■			Uneven economic, social, and political development produces poverty and gaps in the welfare system.
D			■		A dual welfare system makes the poor, who are seen as illegitimate failures, vulnerable.
E				■	Discrimination produces minority-group poverty. Development is uneven, and there are gaps in the welfare system.
F	■	■			Isolation may turn chronic inequality into chronic, vicious-circle poverty.
G	■		■		If the nominal ideology is a myth and the class structure is hidden, the poor may be blamed for their poverty, which is actually due to their membership in the lowest class.
H	■			■	If the lowest class and the racial minority overlap or are the same, poverty will be harder to eliminate.

FIGURE 3 - 1 (Continued)

Case	Class Structure	Isolation	Individualism	Prejudice	Characteristics
I		▓	▓		Development is uneven, and members of the isolated group are victimized by a dual welfare system.
J		▓		▓	Isolation reinforces prejudice and group stereotypes and accentuates real group differences.
K			▓	▓	Prejudice is rationalized and the resulting poverty attributed to personal defects.
L	▓	▓	▓		As in F, the class structure may reinforce isolation; as in G, poverty is attributed to the failings of the poor.
M	▓	▓		▓	Massive alienation based on distance, class, and racial or ethnic group guarantees poverty.
N	▓		▓	▓	The factors operative in G and K are combined. Poverty caused by prejudice and class is blamed on the poor.
O		▓	▓	▓	Poverty caused by prejudice is aggravated by isolation, rationalized as case poverty.
P	▓	▓	▓	▓	All four elements combine to bring massive alienation, self-deception, and poverty.

NOTE: Shading indicates the presence of an element in the society.

powerless minority in society, when it thinks of itself as constituting a separate (low) socioeconomic class, and when there is great interclass hostility. On the other hand, if the two groups are only overlapping, the class structure may mitigate some of the effects of isolation. If, for instance, the isolated group is thought of by others across the land as containing fellow members of a large, nationwide class, the other members of this class may, out of solidarity, insist upon development schemes and welfare programs which include them.

Case G: Class Structure and Individualism. This is an important case, and one that requires some discussion. It involves a combination that may at first seem odd: How can a belief in a rigid class structure coexist with individualism, a competing philosophy? In most circumstances, it cannot. The individualist ideology makes people responsible for their own economic success or failure. It imposes no constraints, so that in principle anyone can be poor or rich. Where there is a rigid class structure, on the other hand, one's economic role is broadly determined by the class into which one is born. The two seem mutually inconsistent as a basis for the social order.

There is one circumstance, however, in which the two may be combined. That is where the ideology of individualism is a myth (or contains large elements of myth) and where the class structure on which the society is really structured is largely *hidden*. It is entirely possible for a society to be based on one social and economic arrangement and yet articulate a widely shared point of view, passed down from one generation to the next, that it is based on quite another. Indeed, all societies do this to some extent. There is always some difference between the day-to-day realities of a necessarily imperfect world and the idealized self-portrait most societies develop and nurture. They see themselves as democratic, as holy, or as communistic. This view is reinforced in schoolbooks and in patriotic speeches and pervades popular discussion of politics or the country. In Case G, this rather natural disparity between the real and the ideal is magnified to an unhealthy extreme.

Case G is unhealthy both because of the social psychopathology implied by a radical difference between the national ideology and reality and because of the economic consequences. By combining individualism and a rigid class structure, a society gets the worst of both. In Case B, there is a rigid class structure, but chronic poverty is unlikely because class-consciousness ensures that social legislation put into effect by a working-class majority will not exclude large groups of people. But in Case G, there is a class structure without class-consciousness. This fact has four very important consequences.

First, although the class into which a person is born will largely determine his economic performance and status, people will *think* that his achievements reflect his ability and effort. Low-income people will tend to blame themselves for their poor economic position, and society as a whole will agree with them. One consequence may be low morale, a feeling of defeat, and perhaps other aspects of a "culture of poverty."

Second, the institutionalization of the welfare system may proceed in a patchwork and categorical manner, with invidious distinctions being made between legitimate ("social insurance") and illegitimate ("charity") programs. Such a dual welfare system, as we shall see in Chapter 4, may help keep people poor.

Third, if the society develops antipoverty programs—which it may or may not do—it will probably develop techniques for dealing with the putative defects and shortcomings of poor people, not of the class structure. (For instance, manpower training programs may be established, thereby seemingly validating the theory that poverty arises out of a lack of skills; or welfare payments to the poor may be conditioned on work requirements, thus seemingly validating the theory that poverty arises out of an unwillingness to work.)

And fourth, where poverty does derive from the class structure but antipoverty policies are based on individual-deficiency theories, these policies are almost certain to fail. Paradoxically, the failure of these programs will *reinforce* the individual-deficiency theories. People will conclude that even when society ("the taxpayers") makes an effort to help the poor they are too unintelligent, too lazy, or too dishonest to succeed.

Case H: Class Structure and Prejudice. Our concern here is with instances in which the lowest class or classes overlap substantially with the subordinate racial or ethnic minority. There are three major possibilities (as well as cases in between). The first is where all racial or ethnic groups are represented in all classes, and vice versa. Prejudice cannot be too potent in such a society, since it does not seem to confine the minority group to the lowest class. Such a society would resemble Case B more than Case E.

The second possibility is a society in which all or virtually all members of the subordinate group are in the lowest economic classes, but so are a significant number of members of the dominant group. What happens then depends on whether class or prejudice is stronger. In the first case, working-class or lower-class solidarity may transcend racial or ethnic lines, mitigating somewhat the effects of prejudice. In the second case, however, lower-class members of the subordinate and dominant groups may view each other with anxiety, hatred, or fear; their mutual antagonism may undermine what joint strength they might command, particularly that which they might otherwise acquire as a numerical majority. And if the society will not admit that it is prejudiced (and so must rationalize its prejudice), it may find ways to persecute *all* lower-class people in an unconscious attempt to get at the minority group.

Poverty will be hardest to eliminate when the racial minority and the lowest class are identical. Instead of the usual three social classes, this society may in fact have four: a landed upper class with inherited wealth, a middle class of business and professional people, a lower class of workers and farmers belonging to the dominant racial group, and an even lower class of workers and largely landless farm laborers from the subordinate racial group.

Case 1: Isolation and Individualism. We have seen that, where individualism appears by itself, both the growth in popular control over the country's institutions and the institutionalization of the welfare system may come to a halt when a majority of people are satisfied with their socioeconomic position. Thus individualism can leave a persistently poor and powerless group in society. Ordinarily, there is no way of knowing in advance exactly who will be left out when the motor for democratic and social progress stalls. But if individualism is combined with the isolation of certain groups, it is obviously likely that the isolated population will be prominent among those on the lowest economic rung.

The isolated group, poor and powerless, will tend to be blamed (and will probably blame themselves) for their own poverty. To the extent that they stay isolated, the uneven development of the economy will keep them poor; and they will be dependent on welfare payments by the majority. Since the individualist ideology implies a dual welfare system, these payments will be "illegitimate" (rather than camouflaged).

Even if the isolated groups migrate to more prosperous areas, they may remain handicapped, possibly for generations, not only by their past separation but by their acceptance of the label and role of "dependents" and "failures."

Case J: Isolation and Prejudice. If, as we assume, the isolated group and the racial or ethnic minority are substantially the same (as has historically been the case with black Americans), isolation and racism will reinforce each other. Prejudice against the isolated poor will make it less likely that transportation and communication networks will be developed and maintained. They will make the movement of industry into the region more unlikely, they will encourage barriers to migration, and they may even lead to the development of a welfare system that reinforces isolation (e.g., through residence requirements). At the same time, distance and the unfamiliarity created by isolation make it easier to treat the minority poor as a group rather than as human beings and individuals. This in turn facilitates the retention of stereotyped pictures of minority-group members. Isolation enhances whatever cultural, religious, and linguistic differences already exist and creates new ones. Even if isolation diminishes over time, its effects on both the majority and the minority may take generations to overcome.

Case K: Individualism and Prejudice.   Like Case G above, Case K is important. And like Case G, it involves an apparent paradox. How can a society be individualist and prejudiced at the same time? Anyone familiar with history will realize that such societies have existed—and indeed do exist. The explanation resembles that of Case G: Prejudice is either thoroughly rationalized or concealed. It may even be rationalized in terms of individualism itself. A society such as K has an enormous capacity for self-deception. It probably has a dual welfare system; but the programs for the nonpoor are camouflaged, largely unconsciously.

The poverty of the minority group will be largely a result of unconscious prejudice, but most members of society—poor and nonpoor—will accept the proposition that poverty results from personal deficiencies such as those that produce Galbraith's version of case poverty. As in Case G, antipoverty programs may be based on this assumption. As in Case G, they will probably fail. And, as in Case G, that failure will only reinforce people's belief in the fallacious assumptions that caused the failure.

Case L: Class Structure, Isolation, and Individualism.   This, our first case to include as many as three elements, is based on the important Case G, discussed above. In G, where individualism is mythical and the class structure is hidden, the resulting poverty is attributed to personal failings. In L, the aggravating handicap of geographic and economic isolation is added, as in Case F. To the extent that, as we have assumed, the lower-class people and the isolated groups are the same, the resulting poverty will be all the more difficult to eradicate. There is little basis for thinking that it will go away by itself.

Case M: Class Structure, Isolation, and Prejudice. This case contains a very great potential for social and economic disunity and alienation. Some people are isolated, economically and geographically, from the mainstream of society. Some people, perhaps the same ones, are objects of racial or ethnic discrimination. And some people, perhaps the same ones, find their economic opportunities determined by the class into which they are born. To the extent that these three groups are the same, they will form a sharply segregated, truly subordinate, and oppressed subgroup for whom poverty is almost inevitable.

Of course, in the real world a society could contain some persons who fell into all three groups, some who fell into any two of them, and some who fell into only one. Such a society would have elements of Cases M, J, H, F, E, C, and B, and hence contain several different poor groups whose poverty arose from different causes. It would thus be more intractable in some cases than in others.

Case N: Class Structure, Individualism, and Prejudice. We have already discussed two cases—G and K—that involved apparent paradoxes, cases where individualism was combined, respectively, with an apparently conflicting belief in a rigid class structure and with prejudice. In Case N, all the factors operative in G and K are operative. Individualism, although it may be the official ideology, is not the true basis of the social order. Income and status are the result of class and minority-group membership.

Because of the individualist ideology, and to keep up the people's faith in it, whatever poverty results from the class structure and from racism is blamed on individual shortcomings. As we have seen, this means that antipoverty policies will be directed at overcoming these deficiencies and hence are liable to fail.

Case O: Isolation, Individualism, and Prejudice. Case O is built on Case K. To the problems imposed by K's unhappy combination of prejudice disguised as, rationalized by, and combined with individualism, we add the problems and alienation wrought by isolation. Where the isolated group and the minority group are the same, we have, as in Case J, a powerful reinforcement effect. Oddly, where the two groups are different, society may nonetheless think of them as basically the same since it will tend to explain and deal with poverty on an individual, case-by-case basis, as the result of personal failure.

Case P: Class Structure, Isolation, Individualism, and Prejudice. All four elements are present in this last case, where chronic poverty seems all but inevitable. There is a rigid class structure, which (depending on how rigid it is) tends to condemn a fraction of the population to limited economic opportunities. But since this class structure is combined with an ideology of individualism, its existence is unrecognized, either officially (as a basis for policy) or informally (as a basis for attitudes about poverty). There is group prejudice which, too, may remain below the surface. Society may also explain the poverty that results from prejudice as reflecting individual shortcomings, an approach which seems to require that token members of the dominant group be found among the poor and token members of the subordinate group be found among the nonpoor. Finally, whatever consequences arise from this combination are aggravated by the economic and geographic isolation of parts of the population. Depending on the extent to which the affected groups overlap, there may be a great many poor groups in society whose poverty arises out of circumstances resembling those in virtually *all* the preceding cases except, of course, the open case, A.

We can be sure that there will be uneven economic, social, and political development and that some groups will be left behind. We can be sure that the society will develop a dual welfare system, with camouflaged (and hence socially legitimate) welfare programs available primarily to the nonpoor and obvious, ideologically illegitimate, and generally inadequate programs for the poor. We can be reasonably sure, also, that poverty will be explained in personal terms and that, because of this, antipoverty programs will be constructed to correct personal defects and will, by and large, fail.

EXOGENOUS SHOCKS TO THE SYSTEM

In the cases discussed above, we talked about *processes* rather than *conditions*. Differences among the cases were due to differences in the direction in which the societies were tending during the course of economic and political development rather than differences in where they were at a given moment. In any given case, these processes will follow the paths described only if we assume that exogenous events (events not caused or determined by forces within the model) will not alter the course of history. The two exogenous events most likely to do this are major depression and war.

A depression is more likely to occur in a developed economy than an underdeveloped one, since it entails ruptures in patterns of trade, exchange, and economic integration. (Of course, less developed economies have other problems, such as periodic famines.) In developed economies, a depression is more likely to occur, and more likely to have a powerful effect when it does occur, if little progress has been made in institutionalizing the welfare system and if traditional, nongovernmental welfare systems have been made obsolete by industrialization and urbanization. A depression in such circumstances is liable to cause widespread poverty and initiate vicious circles that will continue even after the depression. Some of the elderly poor in the United States today are probably poor because they lost their assets in the depression of the 1930s. A major depression in a society where popular political control has reached a certain point is liable to speed up the institutionalization of the welfare system tremendously; where popular power has not reached this point, the result may be a revolution. Revolution is also more likely when there is a rigid class structure.

The exogenous shocks produced by wars may be economic or political and military. On the economic side, all-out war, with the attendant need for capacity production, is likely to reduce poverty significantly. The number of people isolated and the degree of isolation will decline rapidly as the society seeks added manpower for urban factory jobs and the armed services. For many, the added income from these sources, even if it lasts only for a relatively short period, will be sufficient to break permanently the vicious circle of poverty. (Whether the poverty-reducing effects of war can be simulated during peacetime through a tight full-employment policy is one of the questions we shall consider in Chapter 6.)

Not every country finds war an economic boon, however. The discussion above ignores the political and military consequences of war. The destruction of wealth during wartime can be random and capricious and constitutes a calamity it is virtually impossible to insure against with any kind of welfare system. The nation that loses a war, of course, is more likely to be impoverished than the victor.

THE USA: WHICH CASE ARE WE?

In Cases A through P we have seen 16 different types of economies, representing all conceivable combinations of the basic four elements in our model. Which of the 16 cases represents the United States? The cases in the model are, of course, ideal types. Real societies will diverge from these types for one or more of three reasons. First, there may be divergences between our *assumptions* of growth and development, the popularization of control, and the institutionalization of welfare and the actual experience of the country. Second, the four variables in our model have been treated as discrete (either present or absent), whereas in fact they are continuous (present or absent in various degrees). Countries are not just prejudiced or nonprejudiced, for instance; they vary with respect to the *degree* and *type* of prejudice that is reflected in their institutions and behavior. Thus there are a virtually infinite number of cases in the real world, not merely 16. And finally, no list of causal variables can ever be exhaustive, unless they are tautological (true by definition). The four included in our model were chosen because they are the most significant recurring and fundamental causes of poverty. But unique historical forces and events (such as slavery in the United States) can have an impact apart from the model.

Nonetheless, the model fares well in explaining the American case. Let us review, briefly, the four main elements in attempting to place the American experience.

CLASS

The United States does not have the rigid class structure found in most other countries. This is not to say that it is a classless society; far from it. The children of the rich are very likely to be rich, the children of the middle class are very likely to remain in the middle class, and the children of the poor are very likely to be poor. The main reason class is generally inherited is a cycle of cumulative causation, of which vicious-circle poverty is a special case. There is some upward and even a little downward mobility, however—more than in most other countries, but probably less than most Americans believe.

INDIVIDUALISM

Our discussion of the ideology of individualism was based on the dominant American point of view on the social order, the distribution of income, and economic morality. Even so, before we turn around and confirm the presence of this ideology in the American case, we must make one qualification. It is one thing to say that individualism is the dominant American ideology, which it clearly is; but it is quite another to say how dominant it is. There is a significant and perhaps growing minority of Americans, primarily young, who, although they have not settled on a substitute, are uncomfortable with or reject outright the traditional ideology.

The attitudes of this minority have yet to be manifested in *any* significant piece of social legislation, which is overwhelmingly based on individualism as described in these chapters; but it is increasingly represented in significant public debates over social policy.

In Cases G, L, N, and P, above, individualism is widely held to be the prevailing belief and class structure is a powerful but hidden determinant of behavior and events. The American situation diverges somewhat from these cases. The class structure is much weaker and individualism is less mythical. The class structure that does exist, though it is not trivial, is largely hidden. In many ways the situation in the United States resembles the situation in Case G, where "the class into which a person is born will largely determine his economic performance and status, [but] people will *think* that his achievements reflect his ability and effort. Low-income people will tend to blame themselves for their poor economic position, and society as a whole will agree with them."

In all societies in which the ideology of individualism is a factor, the development of a dual welfare system is a possibility. The dual welfare system of the United States will be examined in Chapter 4.

ECONOMIC AND GEOGRAPHIC ISOLATION

The applicability of the isolation argument to the United States has already been discussed and needs only to be reviewed here. Most American groups among whom poverty is high are isolated or have been isolated for significant periods from the economic progress of the mainstream. This is true of blacks, of American Indians, of Appalachian and other rural whites, and of smaller groups such as Franco-Americans and other poor whites in New England. The converse is also true: Poor people, even where they have been objects of racist types of discrimination, have progressed much faster in areas of economic expansion. In the past, these areas have generally been urban centers. One might assume, then, that the migration of blacks and other isolated poor people to cities means that their chronic poverty may end within a generation or so. Unhappily, this is not necessarily true. The centers of major cities are no longer at the heart of economic expansion. Almost all economic expansion, industrial or not, is now occurring in suburban areas. And blacks, who suffered in the past in part because they were in the rural South when robust growth was occurring in the central cities, may suffer again because they are in the central cities when robust growth is proceeding in the suburbs.

PREJUDICE

Clearly, racial discrimination exists in the United States and is an important cause of poverty among blacks, American Indians, Mexican-Americans, Puerto Ricans, and others. It is not clear how much vicious-circle poverty among blacks is attributable to racism and how much is due to isolation, their membership in the lowest economic class, and the powerful historical effects of slavery. Enslavement, the special extremes of American slavery, and the American manner of emancipation (which had an effect similar to the abrupt firing of massive numbers of property-less workers wholly unprotected by any welfare system) amounted to a calamity as the term is used in Chapter 2, a calamity more extreme and destructive than that experienced by any other group of significant size in America, with the exception of the Indians. The effects of slavery *by itself*, with no subsequent prejudice, class stratification, or isolation, would have been sufficient to generate a powerful vicious circle of poverty whose effects could easily persist until the present.

Racist attitudes and behavior have been rapidly becoming illegitimate in the American ideology. This process has had two important effects. It has meant a decline in racist behavior, permitting accelerated economic and social progress among blacks. It has also pushed much of the very substantial remaining racism "underground," so that it is camouflaged or rationalized in other terms.

In sum, then, the United States' economy comes closest to Case P, although the class structure is weaker. And in Case P, the model predicts poverty, primarily among minority races, people born in the lower classes, and people who have been isolated from the mainstream of the economy or who have inherited the effects of such isolation. All these forms of poverty are present and important in the United States.

OTHER CAUSES OF POVERTY

It would be surprising indeed if there were not a great many explanations of poverty that are independent of and in addition to the four discussed in this chapter. Let us review briefly some of these other explanations.

PERSONAL INADEQUACIES

Some persons are permanently handicapped by low intelligence, chronic physical ailments, crippling deformities, or mental illness. Since they are consequently less productive (or totally unproductive), their earned incomes are less and they are chronically poor. Concerning this cause of poverty, three comments are in order.

First, a substantial percentage of such cases are a *consequence* of poverty, as well as its cause. Health and nutrition, as we have noted, are crucial in influencing intelligence. In a great many cases, therefore, personal inadequacies are not the ultimate cause of poverty.

Second, when people are poor because of such chronic problems, their poverty is the result of an implicit social decision. It is not inherent or automatic. There is no necessary reason (unless the whole society is poor) why handicapped persons must live on what they are able to earn or on poverty-level transfers. Hence when such people are poor, their poverty is a consequence of *two* factors—their handicap and society's reaction to it.

Third, it would be interesting to know whether poverty arising out of such handicaps will be inherited by the next generation, even when the handicap itself is not. Are the children of cripples, themselves not crippled, more likely than others to be poor? If so, their poverty can be considered, in many instances, a consequence of inadequacies in the welfare system, one of whose main functions should be to prevent the inability of parents to be productive from permanently impoverishing their children.

LACK OF EDUCATION AND TRAINING

Among the working poor, there is a very high concentration of persons without either skills or an adequate education. Since no nonpoor society has achieved or seems on the verge of achieving equality in the distribution of education and since there is a strong link between education and earnings (some of that linkage presumably being causal), it seems appropriate to attribute some poverty to a lack of education or other training.

It is very hard to ascertain how much difference years of education make in determining income. Education is correlated with other variables that are important in influencing the income of parents: social class and position, health, race, and intelligence. Moreover, employers tend to use educational attainment—as represented by degrees, diplomas, or years in school—as a *proxy* for desirable traits, such as ability, knowledge, and ambition, traits often possessed in ample quantities by those with less formal education. And where the number of job applicants exceeds the number of positions (in depressions, recessions, or prolonged periods of economic slack), employers are even more likely to use education as a job-rationing device, to weed out applicants and simplify the hiring process. In such circumstances, it is the distribution of education that influences the allocation of jobs. More education for some people will not necessarily mean more jobs; it will only mean a different distribution of jobs. More education for *all* will not alter the situation if it does not alter the distribution.

The influence of education upon income may be exaggerated. But this is not to say that it is not vitally important. It may be.

As we saw in Chapter 2, the association between education and poverty creates a vicious circle of poverty. Lack of education may not be the *ultimate* cause of poverty in every case in which it is the apparent or proximate cause.

In every society, education is in some sense and to some extent a social rather than a private good. Hence its amount and distribution is influenced by public policy. If public policy provides an uneven distribution of educational benefits, and if that uneven distribution leads to unequal incomes or even to poverty, we can attribute inequality of income in part to public policy. Once again, lack of education may not always be the *ultimate* cause of poverty.

It may be true that poor children lack the *motivation* to learn that others have, and their parents may fail to encourage a desire for learning. In such a case, even if society provides what *appears* to be equal educational opportunity for all, the performance of poor children in school will be inferior. Economist Thomas Carroll has shown that educational preferences, desires, and motivations can be endogenous, *caused by* poverty and characteristics associated with poverty.

The role of educational policy in fighting poverty will be discussed in Chapter 6. The fact that education is not an ultimate, independent variable—a fundamental cause of chronic poverty—but a reflection of the distribution of income does not mean that there is no role for an educational strategy in the fight against poverty.

ECONOMIC SYSTEMS

Is poverty caused by capitalism? Or, for that matter, by socialism or some other form of economic organization? Although it is certainly not possible to review all the arguments here, we should note that there are widely held theories which ascribe poverty and other social evils —unemployment, militarism, imperialism—to one or another economic system.

The notion of an economic system is a massive abstraction, including not only the means of production and distribution, but many other things as well. So if the question is asked, "Does a nation's economic system influence the likelihood of chronic poverty?" the answer is obviously yes. It is hard to see how it could be otherwise. In fact, much of the discussion so far has concerned economic systems, though the expression itself has not been used.

Whether poverty is necessarily strongly associated with socialism or capitalism is another question, and one to which a flat yes-or-no answer would probably be carrying oversimplification a step too far. Having said this, we shall go on to make the following observations about capitalism.

1. Capitalism is based on the fundamental argument that *by maximizing his own self-interest, each man also maximizes the social interest*. Consequently, self-interested and competitive behavior is seen as not only defensible and legitimate, but laudable.
2. Capitalism arrives at the conclusion that *insecurity is useful and functional*. In theory, at least, each firm faces competition from other firms, each employee faces competition from other employees, and

each capitalist faces competition from other capitalists. The ultimate economic sanctions for poor performance are business failure, the loss of one's job, the collapse of stock values, and the like. Lesser sanctions include decreasing profits, low wages or frequent layoffs, and market losses. The capitalist system depends upon these sanctions for the effective functioning of the system. Although many American critics of public assistance and income-maintenance proposals may not use these words, they are essentially arguing that guaranteed incomes are inconsistent with the insecurity necessary under capitalism. (Of course, there is some competition under socialism as well, and to an extent insecurity is functional in that system too.)

3. Although capitalism is not *necessarily* based on the economic philosophy of individualism set forth in this chapter, the beliefs described above lead most proponents of capitalism to espouse that philosophy.

4. Occasional recessions and depressions are much more common under capitalism. The ever present threat of unemployment arising out of them and out of functional insecurity makes workers under capitalism more unemployment-conscious than workers under other systems. As a result, they react with vigor against policies that threaten competition for jobs—minority apprenticeship programs, manpower training programs in certain fields, government employment programs, and the like. Fear of unemployment also has other harmful consequences, which will be discussed in Chapter 6.

5. The preceding points imply that poverty is probable under capitalism. However, the relationship is not a necessary one. There is much more job security under Japanese capitalism, for instance, than under the American variety, and unemployment consciousness is much less of a problem. Other varieties of capitalism are also possible. Presumably, the U.S. Congress could pass a set of bills and appropriations that would virtually abolish poverty (see Chapters 5 and 6) without changing the economic system from a "capitalist" one to a "socialist" one. Alternatively, it could conceivably pass quite a different set of bills nationalizing basic American industries and creating a "socialist" system without materially affecting the incidence of poverty.

Upon consideration, then, it does not seem warranted to include the economic system as a separate variable in our model, even though many aspects of economic systems are important in determining the likelihood and character of chronic poverty.

CAUSES AND CURES OF POVERTY

Quite obviously, most of the elements in our model cannot easily be manipulated by government as a matter of antipoverty policy. Instead, governments must take action with respect to such things as jobs, education, and the welfare system. One might well ask, then, what is the relationship of the model to national policy?

Since our concern in this book is with poverty in a dual economy where only a minority is poor, our paramount interest is in questions of *distribution* rather than aggregate output. It is for this reason that our inquiry into the causes of poverty has concentrated on social factors, particularly ideological and attitudinal ones. It is a very different thing to deal with explanations and effects of the poverty of whole societies and nations.

Because the social factors we have discussed are influential in shaping policy, an understanding of them will help us to understand why a society produces or tolerates chronic poverty. But that does not mean that antipoverty policy will logically consist of efforts to change the class structure, the national ideology, or racial and intergroup attitudes. (The problem of isolation is somewhat different and may be influenced by policy.) Moreover, since governments tend to reflect, rather than determine, ideological and attitudinal variables, they are not the most apt vehicles for antipoverty policy.

As we shall see in Chapters 5 and 6, promising antipoverty strategies lie in another direction. Whether these will be earnestly undertaken, or efficacious if truly tried, is likely to depend on what happens to society in the meantime and in particular to the elements of the model discussed in this chapter.

REFERENCES

A more extended discussion of case vs. generic theories of poverty appears in A. Dale Tussing, "Poverty Research and Policy Analysis in the United States: Implications for Ireland," *Economic and Social Review* (Dublin: October 1973). The remainder of Chapter 3 is based on and adapted from Tussing, *A Social Model of Poverty and the Progress of the Welfare State*, mimeographed working draft (Syracuse, N.Y.: Educational Policy Research Center, 1969).

Nathan Glazer's "floor" metaphor appears in "A Sociologist's View of Poverty," in Margaret S. Gordon, ed., *Poverty in America* (San Francisco:

Chandler, 1965). John Kenneth Galbraith's discussion of case and insular poverty appears in *The Affluent Society* (Boston: Houghton Mifflin, 1958). Arthur R. Jensen's study of genetic aspects of intelligence appears in "How Much Can We Boost IQ and Scholastic Achievement?" *Harvard Educational Review* (Winter 1969). Other sources of information on this issue are cited at the end of Chapter 6.

Thomas Carroll's analysis appears in his "Education and Income: An Analysis by Fable," *American Economist* (Fall 1972).

4

The Dual

Welfare System

The expression "welfare system," as it is used in this book, has a very broad definition. It includes all *social* (as opposed to private) techniques of income protection and maintenance, no matter what form they take.

We said in Chapter 2 that welfare programs can be grouped into two categories—*direct* and *indirect*; that direct programs consist of *explicit* or *implicit* transfer payments from some people to others; and that indirect programs consist of techniques for influencing and controlling private behavior to produce the same results. Unemployment compensation, old-age benefits under Social Security, and public assistance are examples of explicit programs. Certain tax deductions and the higher prices caused by farm price supports are examples of implicit programs. Collective bargaining and minimum wage laws are examples of indirect programs.

TWO WELFARE SYSTEMS

An examination of the programs that make up the American welfare system shows that they fall more or less neatly into two main groups —those for most Americans, whether they are working class, middle class, or even well-to-do (in short, those for the nonpoor) and those for the poor. In spite of the greater publicity and attention given the latter group, the former is far bigger and much more comprehensive. As Professor Gordon Tullock (who is by no means considered a liberal) has observed:

114

Almost all standard discussions of redistribution imply that it is normally from the rich to the poor. Some such redistribution does indeed go on, but it is a trivial phenomenon compared to the redistribution within the middle class. I find the concentration of [the] discussion of redistribution upon the very minor phenomenon of redistribution from the wealthy to the poor and the general ignoring of the major phenomenon—redistribution back and forth within the middle income groups . . . most remarkable.

The major components of the two systems are listed in Table 4-1. (Veterans' relief, a poor people's program with characteristics of programs for the nonpoor, is omitted from Table 4-1 and from this chapter. A discussion of it appears in Chapter 5.) The separation between the two systems is not perfect, but the overlaps are strikingly few. The separation arises out of the *categorical* nature and *productivity* basis of the programs for the nonpoor.

PROGRAMS FOR THE NONPOOR

The categorical basis of the programs for the nonpoor derives from the less-than-universal eligibility for them. For instance, under Old-Age, Survivors', Disability, and Hospitalization Insurance (OASDHI) —usually referred to as Social Security—the old-age, survivors', and disability provisions cover only 90 percent of those regularly employed, and beneficiaries of the old-age provisions include only 84 percent of those over 65. Between 10 and 16 percent, then, are not covered at all; and some of those who are covered get only partial support. This is one main reason why some 2 million elderly persons require public assistance under the Supplemental Security Income (SSI) program. Medicare or hospitalization insurance (the "H" in OASDHI) covers almost exactly the same group as OASDI.

Unemployment compensation covers about 80 percent of wage and salary workers who are regularly employed (excluding, then, both those who are not regularly employed and 20 percent of those who are). At any given time, about half of the unemployed are not covered by unemployment compensation! It is very odd, when one thinks about it, that U.S. social policy should protect workers against unemployment but exclude certain workers from coverage. Those excluded are excluded both on the

TABLE 4 – 1

The Major Components of the Dual Welfare System, by Type of Assistance Required

RESPONSE OF WELFARE SYSTEM

Type of Assistance Required	Regular System	Poor People's System
Unemployment benefits, supplementary income	Unemployment compensation	Aid to Families with Dependent Children; General Assistance
Survivors' benefits	Social Security (survivors)	Aid to Families with Dependent Children
		Public assistance: Supplementary Security Income [c]
Old-age benefits	Social Security (old-age benefits); additional income tax exemption for elderly and related tax provisions;[a] exclusions of pensions and related income tax provisions[b]	
Medical benefits	Medicare under Social Security income; income tax deductions[d]	Medicaid; clinic and emergency room care
Food benefits	Farm subsidies[e]	Surplus food distribution; food stamps
Housing benefits	Income tax deductions for home-owners;[f] FHA and related programs	Public housing; other housing programs for the poor[g]
Disability benefits	Social Security (disability benefits); workmen's compensation; "sick pay" income tax adjustment[h]	Public assistance: Supplementary Security Income[c]

Footnotes on next page.

basis of the irregularity of their employment (part-time and irregular employees are not covered) and on the basis of the industry in which they are employed. Similarly, minimum wage laws are not universal but exclude workers in some industries. The same is true of the right to vote on whether to be represented by unions, and to bargain collectively. Even child labor laws exclude some industries, notably agriculture, but not because there are no health or safety hazards, and not because there is no danger that children may be exploited in agricultural work.

Although the list of eligibles and ineligibles varies from program to program, those most commonly excluded are employees in the service industries (such as workers in hospitals, hotels, restaurants, and laundries) and agriculture—precisely the industries in which most poor employees are concentrated. These are the jobs that make up much of the unstable, low-wage "secondary labor market" discussed in Chapter 2.

Poor people are also excluded from coverage by the *productivity basis* of the mainstream programs. That is, programs for the nonpoor require, without exception, that benefits be based on *earnings*—either those of the beneficiary or those of the person (father, husband, etc.) upon whom the beneficiary would normally be dependent. OASDI and Medicare are financed through payroll taxes paid by both employers and employees. One has to have been employed and had earnings to be covered by Social Security. Unemployment compensation is financed by a payroll tax paid only by the employer. Once again, only the regularly employed are

Footnotes for Table 4 - 1

a Additional exemption, retirement income credit, and exclusion of OASDHI income for aged.
b Exclusion for employee pensions and retirement fund deduction for self-employed; exclusion of group life insurance premiums.
c The Supplementary Security Income Program, which became effective in 1974, combines three previous programs: Old-Age Assistance; Aid to the Blind; and Aid to the Permanently Disabled. (See Chapter 5.)
d The excess over 3 percent of adjusted gross income of the sum of one-half of medical insurance premiums; the excess over 1 percent of adjusted gross income of the cost of medicine and drugs; and other medical deductions — this excess to be added to the other half of medical insurance premiums.
e Until 1973, price supports; after 1973, the Brannan Plan. See text.
f Deduction of interest on mortgage loans and property tax payments. (See Appendix to Chapter 2.)
g Rent supplements; leased housing programs.
h Payroll income becomes tax exempt after 7 days if the employee is absent for health reasons.

eligible. Since poor people are often not in the labor force at all or work irregularly, any program that is based on regular employment tends to exclude a great many of them. It might be said that the American system of social insurance constitutes a system of "poverty insurance" which makes it less likely you will *become* poor if you or your family is not poor but which does little for those *already* poor. Like medical and hospitalization insurance, it covers new conditions but not pre-existing ones.

Other programs for the nonpoor also depend upon productivity. Farm price-support systems, for instance, pay a subsidy only to farms that sell their output, excluding the many small, noncommercial, subsistence farms; and they pay subsidies in proportion to output. Minimum wages help only the employed. Even welfare-type provisions in the income tax laws are effective only for those with a taxable, earned income. An extra exemption means nothing, for example, to persons over 65 with no taxable income.

PROGRAMS FOR THE POOR

Since the large mainstream (or nonpoor) welfare programs are categorical, excluding many or most poor persons, and since, in any case, they are productivity-based, again excluding most of the poor, it has been necessary to provide a system of welfare programs specifically for poor people. This system consists of public assistance, Medicaid, public housing, food-stamp and surplus-foods programs; clinics; fresh-air programs; and a number of smaller programs. (Some of the largest of these programs will be examined in detail in Chapter 5.)

Like the programs for the nonpoor, programs for the poor are categorical rather than universal. But the categories are of a different sort. Whereas the nonpoor, generally, are categorized according to the industry in which they work or the source of their earnings, the poor are categorized according to their age, their physical condition, or some other indicator of "deservingness." For instance, public assistance recipients consist in most states of four groups of people: the aged, blind, and disabled, covered by the Supplementary Security Income program (SSI), and dependent children, covered by Aid to Families with Dependent Children (AFDC). These four groups comprise what seem, in the United States, to be considered the "deserving poor." The fact that public assistance is *not* available to everyone who needs it (although some states have additional General Assistance, or "GA," programs that are not federally funded) illustrates an important point. The welfare system for poor people is *not* a residual system, protecting those left uncovered by the categorical, productivity-based regular programs. Instead, it too is categorical, leaving some people wholly unprotected.

There is no productivity basis for poor people's welfare. Instead, there is a *means test*—almost the complete opposite of a productivity basis. The poor must show that they do *not* have an income, or that their income is insufficient for their needs.

PRODUCTIVITY AND LEGITIMACY

The productivity basis of the mainstream, or nonpoor, welfare programs not only excludes most poor people, but it makes mainstream programs appear more socially legitimate than programs for the poor. This is because it appears as though the beneficiaries of these programs have provided for their own protection, whereas the beneficiaries of poor persons' programs appear to be *dependent upon* the nonpoor.

The legitimacy of one's income, and especially one's position in the overall distribution of income curve, is a central preoccupation in America. *No* welfare programs are inherently legitimate in the United States, because the dominant ideology of individualism still appears to reject the principle of the welfare state. (The fact that it applies this principle in practice produces a conflict of some significance for what follows.) In the view of many people, jobholders are members of and contributors to society; the unemployed are not. Holding a job also legitimates one's political role; local, state, and national politicians seem to talk more about "taxpayers" than about "citizens."

Other socially legitimate sources of income exist, but their legitimacy can be traced directly or indirectly to someone's job. For instance, a person can *save* some of his earnings to provide income for his own retirement, either through a bank or through a formal pension scheme. Similarly, one can provide through savings or insurance for an income while sick or for one's family when one is "no longer there." Virtually all private provisions of this sort are automatically legitimate.

When a recently urbanized and industrialized America found that it could no longer rely on the old, nongovernmental forms of income protection and maintenance—the extended family, the community, and informal systems of obligation—and had to create a governmental welfare apparatus, a way had to be found to bypass the problem caused by the fact that the American ideology opposed welfare devices. If both the need for welfare programs *and* the ideology were to be satisfied, either the ideology would have to change or the welfare programs would have to be carefully designed to make them seem to fit the ideology. In particular, they would have to have (or seem to have) a productivity basis.

Two systems were created. Professor Clair Wilcox has labeled the explicit transfer parts of these systems "social insurance" and "public charity," a distinction which, though invidious, cannot be blamed on Wilcox, since it merely reflects the forms created by society.

"Social insurance," the heart of the welfare system for the nonpoor, has been constructed in such a way as to be accepted as legitimate, to protect the integrity and dignity of the people involved. To a large extent, this legitimacy is provided by some form of camouflage—by protective nomenclature such as "parity," "compensation," and even the term "social insurance" itself; by the paraphernalia of private programs, such as Social Security account numbers; and by burying welfare benefits in tax laws.

"Public charity," or the welfare system for the poor, has been constructed in a way that reflects its "illegitimacy." Thus it too leaves the ideology intact. The illegitimacy of poor people's welfare is multifold. There is, first, the inherent illegitimacy of government spending financed by taxation. Most welfare programs for the nonpoor either do not entail government spending (tax relief, for example, is not considered an expenditure item) or are financed through earmarked payroll taxes and segregated trust funds. Spending financed in this way is thought of, and officially treated as, generically different from spending out of the general revenues of the government.

The three examples below illustrate the importance of the *form* of a program and the association of form (rather than content) with legitimacy.

In 1968, Wilbur Cohen, then Secretary of Health, Education and Welfare, advocated a program of "income insurance" to be financed through a form of payroll tax on all employed persons, an approach he considered preferable to guaranteed income plans, negative income taxes, and similar schemes, to cover both the unemployed and victims of chronic poverty. Cohen pointed to the greater acceptance of Social Security and other programs financed by payroll taxes and with separate trust funds, and he argued that the poverty gap could be closed in America—that there were no economic reasons why we could not afford

to redistribute income to eliminate poverty altogether, and that the only barriers to such a redistribution were psychological.

In New York State, union members on strike have been eligible for public assistance checks. In one upstate city, a prominent labor leader, an outspoken critic of public assistance recipients, was asked to justify the acceptance of these checks by members of his union, both in light of his general antipathy for public assistance and in light of the argument that public assistance was created to help the poor, not to underwrite strikes. His response was that the union members drawing relief checks had been taxpaying members of the community for years and were now drawing on only a fraction of what they had paid in. In fact, he argued, regular welfare recipients were *less* entitled to public assistance, since they had not (he said) been taxpayers. He was, in effect, converting the program into a contributory one for which his own followers, but not the poor, were eligible.

In both cases, viewing the welfare program as contributory made it "legitimate."

The importance of form is also illustrated by the history of the Brannan Plan, discussed in Chapter 2, which was proposed in the late 1940s to replace price supports with a direct government check to the farmer. For over two decades, farmers as a group opposed this plan, in spite of its general superiority to the price-support programs (it would eliminate storage costs and would lower food prices) because a market subsidy was less explicit and therefore more socially legitimate than a direct cash transfer. Opponents used words like "socialism" to describe the Brannan Plan. More revealing still, some said they "didn't need charity." But in 1973, when farm surpluses gave way to shortages, much of the price-support program was replaced by a version of the Brannan Plan with surprisingly little fanfare.

SOCIAL SECURITY—A CLOSER LOOK

We have already stated that the legitimacy of welfare programs for the nonpoor is provided by some form of camouflage and that the acceptability of welfare programs depends on their *form*, not their *content*. The paradigmatic legitimate welfare program is the OASDI (more recently OASDHI) provided under Social Security. Social Security has been in existence for more than 35 years and has covered millions of beneficiaries, yet it is almost uniformly misunderstood. Its protective camouflage consists in part of a widespread mythology.

As of mid-1973, the Old-Age, Survivors', and Disability Insurance programs were financed by an employee tax of 5.85 percent on the first $12,000 of payroll income and an identical tax paid by employers. Economists believe that the employers' share is passed on to employees in the form of lower wages. Thus it is fair to say that OASDI was financed as of 1973 by an effective tax of 11.70 percent on the first $12,000 of payroll income. There is a relationship between the amount a worker pays in and the amount to which he is entitled, but only a rough one. Each person is given an account number, and a record is kept of his tax contributions. Each year's benefits (approximately $40 billion annually in the early 1970s) are paid from that year's tax contributions. Since there is typically a small surplus, over the years a balance has built up in the OASDI trust funds of about $45 billion. (This was the figure as of 1972.)

MYTH No. 1

Many people conclude from the way that OASDI is financed that it is not a welfare program at all, but merely a compulsory pension or compulsory saving scheme. Note, for instance, the language used in a Gallup Poll question asked in September 1936, just before the system became operative: "Do you favor the *Compulsory Old-Age Insurance Plan*, starting January first, which requires employers and employees to make equal monthly contributions?" A question asked by a National Opinion Research Center poll in April 1943 reflected even greater confusion about the nature of the program. It ran as follows: "As you may know, under the present Social Security Law, workers in certain occupations *have to save money* so that when they are too old to work they will receive money from the Government, like insurance. Do you think this is a good idea or a bad idea?" In both these cases, the wording of the question is more significant for our purposes than the answers. As recently as June 1971, NBC newsman David Brinkley, commenting on a news item to the effect that Social Security was the largest program of government payments to persons, made this remark: "Social Security is not a government payment to individuals. It is just the government giving the *people's own savings* back to them." (As in the two preceding quotes, the emphasis is added.)

MYTH NO. 2

Before attempting to deal with Myth No. 1, let us review a second, somewhat more subtle myth that often appears in the conservative press. This is the myth that Social Security is inefficient and that individuals could do better by saving on their own and putting their money into banks, private pension plans, and the like. The reasoning is as follows: If a man were to "tax" himself at current Social Security payroll tax rates (putting aside an amount equal to the employer and employee payments combined) and deposit the proceeds in a savings account, and if at age 65 he were to stop paying and start drawing a "pension," he would be better off (on the average) than he would be under the present Social Security program.

Unfortunately, this argument contains a serious conceptual error: It misunderstands the nature of Social Security. Myth No. 2 compares *present* benefit levels and *present* tax rates. Yet no one will spend a lifetime paying *present* tax rates, nor will future retirees receive *present* benefits. Tax rates have continued to rise since the inception of Social Security, and benefit levels have risen even faster. Tax rates are scheduled by Congress to rise automatically over the next few years. Social Security payments have amounted to, on the average, well over *four times* the amount paid in by each taxpayer (counting employer and employee shares and interest) and not slightly less than he or she could have earned by banking the same payments.

How is it possible for a trust-funded program to have paid over four times as much to each beneficiary as he or she paid in during his or her working life? Three things have made this possible: a growing population and work force, which has meant that more people have always been paying current taxes than were receiving benefits; a rising level of aggregate income; and rising tax rates. Could a private pension program have done the same—relying on having a growing number of clients and paying out more to each retired person than he has paid in, even taking into account earned interest? Obviously not. Only a government unit could be sure enough of its ability to continue growing, just as only a government has the power to tax.

Social Security is not, then, essentially a scheme by which individuals pay into a fund from which they later withdraw. Instead, it is a scheme by which those who are now working are taxed to pay benefits to those who are now not working. It is a transfer *at this time* rather than *across time*. It is a welfare program, as we have defined such programs, and not a savings program.

The resemblance between Social Security and private, funded pension programs becomes even more illusory when we consider (1) the weak link between taxes and benefits and (2) the nature of the Social Security trust fund assets. In a funded pension program, the more you pay in, other things being equal, the more you get. The later in life you enter the program, other things being equal, the less you get. And finally, your eligibility is typically not affected by your eligibility for other pension benefits. None of this is necessarily true of Social Security. As Professor Milton Friedman has written,

> the relationship between individual contributions (that is, payroll taxes) and benefits is extremely tenuous. Millions of people who pay taxes will never receive any benefits attributable to those taxes because they will not have paid for enough quarters to qualify, or because they receive payments in their capacity as spouse. Persons who pay vastly different sums over their working lives may receive identically the same benefits. Two men or two women who pay precisely the same taxes at the same time may end up receiving different benefits because one is married and the other is single.

Then, too, because private pension programs are a form of individual savings plans, under which beneficiaries receive what they have paid in, plus interest but less administration costs, these programs *do* save for their members. In the process they acquire massive amounts of stocks and bonds. Because, over the years, OASDHI members have paid in more in payroll taxes than has been paid out to beneficiaries, the Social Security trust funds have also acquired massive assets. However, these assets are in the form of U.S. government securities. Thus one agency of the federal government, the U.S. Treasury, owes money (some $45 billion in 1972) to another federal agency, Social Security. (The other dozen federal trust funds—most of which, like the Railroad Retirement, Medicare, and unemployment compensation funds, are linked to welfare programs similar to Social Security—owned an additional $40 billion or so in U.S. government securities.) Since receipts exceed payments almost every year, the assets of these trust funds continue to grow, though they are far below the level necessary to place the system on the same actuarial footing as a private insurance company.

To the extent that Social Security taxes exceed benefit payments and the excess is "lent" to the U.S. Treasury, Social Security taxes are actually being used to finance expenditures for defense, education, environmental projects, and other budgetary items. The "lending" is merely a bookkeeping entry. The taxes that finance these trust funds are nominally "earmarked" for use only in their respective programs. But to the extent of about $2 billion per year, they are not really earmarked after all. The point is not that Social Security taxpayers are being bilked or that their money is being siphoned off into the Treasury. After all, they receive, on the average, over four times what they have paid in and so can hardly claim to have been defrauded. Instead, the point is that the Social Security system is not a segregated, quasi-private, compulsory insurance scheme, but rather a government welfare program, fully integrated in fact if not in form with other government functions.

This makes it all the more important that OASDHI payroll taxes are America's most regressive major tax—interest, profit, rent, capital gains, and all payroll income over $12,000 are exempted from the tax base, and no allowance is made for the number of dependents a person has. Moreover, the higher one's income, the larger is the ratio of benefits to taxes. Friedman, a noted conservative, has called Social Security "the poor man's welfare payment to the middle class."

FIVE DIFFERENCES BETWEEN THE TWO SYSTEMS

We do not argue that the dual welfare system is the result of either a conscious design or a conspiracy. No one sat down and decided to establish one set of programs for most people and another set for poor people. The system merely grew somewhat haphazardly out of our needs and our ideologies. This being the case, the regularities that exist are all the more striking.

There are five major differences between the welfare programs for the nonpoor and those for the poor. They are (1) the amounts of money involved; (2) the camouflage that makes programs for the nonpoor appear to be something else; (3) the level of government—federal, state, or local—administering the programs; (4) the varying incentive and distributional side effects of the programs; and (5) the degree to which the programs intervene in personal and family life.

LEVELS OF SUPPORT

Both in the aggregate and on a per-person basis, the welfare system for the nonpoor is more liberal than that for the poor. Side-by-side comparisons are hazardous because coverage varies from program to program according to circumstances (e.g., the age or number of children of those covered), because the specifications of welfare for the poor and nonpoor are different, because there are state-to-state differences in a number of programs, and because some recipients are covered by more than one program. Nonetheless, something can be learned from the following figures. In March 1973, the average unemployment compensation recipient received $256.76 per month; the average family receiving General Assistance (including, among others, the families of unemployed persons ineligible for unemployment compensation) received $114.15. The average retired worker covered by OASDHI received $164.30, while the average recipient of Old-Age Assistance under public assistance received $78.65. On the whole, programs for the nonpoor seem to provide 20 to 30 percent more than comparable programs for the poor, though in some cases the difference is 100 percent or more.

There are interesting differences even among various segments of the public assistance program. Payments per person averaged as follows for various programs in March 1973: Aid to the Blind, $110.10; Aid to the Permanently and Totally Disabled, $106.55; Old-Age Assistance, $78.65; General Assistance, $68.81; and Aid to Families with Dependent Children, $54.20. (See Table 5-1, in the next chapter, for more information on benefits.) As of 1974, benefits for the aged, blind, and disabled became the same.

Far more dramatic differences than these exist. In Mississippi the average monthly AFDC payment per recipient was only $14.39 in March 1973. In that same state, a corporate farm called Eastland, owned by the family of a U.S. Senator, received over $250,000 in farm subsidies annually.

And, as we shall see later, programs for the nonpoor have this in common with each other: They provide more for those who need less and less for those who need more.

Neither of our welfare systems distribute benefits on the basis of need.

Rather, they seem to distribute them on the basis of *legitimacy*. Poor people are viewed as less legitimate than the nonpoor; and among the poor, those who are disabled, blind, and old are seen as more legitimate than those who are receiving General Assistance or AFDC. There is a social judgment implied here that—rhetoric to the contrary notwithstanding—America's poor are poor because they *should* be poor. This judgment is also implicit in the other differences between the two welfare systems discussed below. Most nonpoor Americans would probably be willing to agree that poor people are poor because of circumstances rather than lack of merit, except that to do so would be to imply that they themselves were comfortable, affluent, or rich because of circumstances rather than because of merit. It is not that poor people are thought to be inferior. It is rather that nonpoor people are thought to be superior. The distinctions we make between successes and failures, the deserving and the undeserving, lead us to create categories of assistance that on the surface appear to be functional, but which on deeper examination prove to be moral and ideological rationalizations. Deep down, we feel that poverty reflects inadequate performance and that high levels of welfare for the poor are tantamount to rewarding sin.

THE NOMINAL NATURE OF THE PROGRAMS

By and large, welfare programs for the poor are obvious, open, and clearly labeled, whereas welfare benefits for the nonpoor are either concealed (in tax laws, for instance) and ill-understood or clothed in protective language and surrounded by procedures that disguise their true purpose.

Indeed, one rule of thumb for determining whether a person is poor may be to look at the names of the programs he is eligible for. If he is receiving "relief," "welfare," "assistance," or "charity," he is surely poor; if he is receiving "insurance" or "compensation," is protected by a "parity" program, or is part of a "compulsory savings" plan, he is very likely a member of the large majority of the nonpoor, who do not even think of themselves as receiving welfare payments.

The degree of concealment in a program in turn influences the level of support in a number of ways. First, welfare programs for the poor are, for the most part, more noticeable, more often in the public eye, and more likely to attract the wrath of taxpayers' groups. A dramatic example of the "low profile" of transfer payments for the nonpoor, on the other hand, is provided by two "tax expenditure" items from Table 2-2 in Chapter 2. As we noted in Chapter 2, the deductibility of interest on home mortgages and of property taxes cost the federal government $2.4 billion and $2.7 billion, respectively, in 1971. Individually, these tax deductions, which serve as a massive "rent supplement" for homeowners, constitute the largest two federally funded housing programs in existence. Together, they cost more than quadruple the budget of all the federal programs for housing the poor combined, yet they receive little publicity. According to U.S. Treasury figures, 85 percent of the benefits from these provisions goes to taxpayers with over $10,000 of adjusted gross income, whereas less than one-hundredth of 1 percent goes to those with adjusted gross incomes of $3,000 or less.

Second, the openness of poor people's welfare reinforces the illegitimacy of the poor in the eyes of many Americans. One reason poor people are condemned is that they are viewed as idle and dependent. The considerable publicity given to public assistance and public assistance recipients is likely to (and often calculated to) create the impression that poor people as a group tend to be idle and dependent.

Third, the difference in visibility between the two systems permits taxpayers to demand and legislators to provide different levels of support without conscious discrimination. Those who have convinced themselves that they are wholly independent and self-reliant, in spite of vast camouflaged welfare programs, do not feel that they have provided less generously for poor people. In their opinion, they have provided *only* for poor people.

Fourth, the degradation and humiliation involved in some poor people's programs and the sense of having failed in life that is instilled in those who accept poor people's welfare make poor people strive mightily to "stay off welfare." This is undoubtedly a major reason why a numerical majority of those legally eligible for public assistance do not receive it. The number who decline to claim special tax deductions and other tax preferences in order to preserve their dignity is, by contrast, surely quite small.

And fifth, the techniques used to camouflage welfare programs for the nonpoor often tend, as a byproduct, to provide for automatic increases in the amounts disbursed as the years go by. This is especially true of tax expenditures, which require no annual appropriations, but only that the tax structure remain the same as income rises.

THE LEVELS OF GOVERNMENT INVOLVED

The third difference between welfare for the poor and welfare for the nonpoor is in the levels of government involved. Welfare programs for the nonpoor tend to be federal programs, federally financed and federally administered, with decisions on eligibility and on levels of support made nationally. There are two exceptions (unemployment compensation and workmen's compensation), and those exceptions involve federal-state partnerships. Programs for the poor, on the other hand, although they may be partially or almost totally supported by federal funds, are characteristically administered as *local* programs, primarily by county welfare departments (or as state programs in states where welfare departments are state-operated). In fact, not only is almost every program listed in column two of Table 4-1 a local program in this sense; even the "War on Poverty" efforts of the Office of Economic Opportunity and such related programs as "Model Cities" have been tied to local government and local politics.

There is one important exception to this statement, and it is an exceedingly revealing one. In 1969, President Nixon proposed a major revamping of the public assistance system, including federal administration and a federally determined minimum payment level for all four federally aided groups—families with dependent children, the aged, the blind, and the disabled. For nearly four years, Congress labored over the proposal, and in 1972 it produced a mouse. Major changes were rejected and a bill was passed that contained few departures from the existing welfare system. The most significant of these was the establishment, effective in 1974, of a federal Supplementary Security Income program (SSI), replacing three federally aided state and local programs: Old-Age Assistance (OAA), Aid to the Blind (AB), and Aid to the Permanently and Totally Disabled (APTD). (SSI was mentioned briefly earlier.) Benefit levels in the SSI program are, however, lower than those of a number of states in the antecedent OAA, AB, and APTD programs. Since states are permitted to supplement the federal payments (making the federal benefit the floor, or minimum payment), and since a number of states are expected to do so in order not to reduce payments, even the 1972 legislation does not fully federalize assistance to these groups. Benefit levels still depend on state decisions, and state taxes are still involved.

Thus the public assistance system is left with three levels of federalization. There is the new, semifederal SSI program for the most "deserving" poor—the aged, blind, and disabled. There is the federally aided Aid to Families with Dependent Children, in which eligibility and support-level decisions are made by the states, which is administered at the state and local level, and which is viewed by many people as a "ghetto mother" program. And finally, there are General Assistance (GA) programs, which receive no federal funds at all and cover the least socially legitimate of all the dependent poor—unemployed single and childless married persons and unemployed fathers. (See Chapter 5.) It is clear that the degree of federalization of a program depends on its legitimacy or the "deservingness" of those it helps.

All three of these degrees of federalization are in contrast to the complete federal control, administration, and financing of such regular, mainstream welfare programs as OASDHI under Social Security.

Except for the programs described above, which are partial exceptions, the rule mentioned earlier consistently applies: Programs for the nonpoor are federal programs; programs for the poor are state or local programs. This difference between the two welfare systems interacts with the two other differences we have discussed, aggravating them both. It increases the exposure of poor people's welfare, not only because these programs are subject to local decisions, closer to home and easier to see, but because poor people's welfare legislation will be debated and acted upon at at least two, and probably¹ three, levels of government. This difference also aggravates the differences in levels of support, primarily because poor people's welfare is tied more often to inelastic local and state revenue sources, such as the property tax, whereas the regular welfare system is tied to the overproductive federal tax system.

But the locus of control over welfare programs also has a far more important implication. Just as many cities, counties, and states compete with one another to attract and keep industry and a high-income population, so also do they (with less fanfare, of course) compete to discourage or drive away low-income people. Before Department of Agriculture reforms prompted by the Poor People's March and Resurrection City, hundreds of counties, primarily in the South, refused to participate in surplus food distribution, and a few openly stated the motive: to drive away once-needed farm workers, tenant farmers, and sharecroppers made obsolete by technological changes in agriculture. The competition to get rid of poor people is not limited to the South, however. A city councilman in a Northern metropolis, commenting on the council's negative vote on a public housing issue, once noted that the majority would be delighted to build more public housing for the city's poor, except that construction of public housing would merely attract more poor people to the community. The logic is clear: Don't build public housing and you keep down the poor population. Suburbs have steadfastly refused (with Supreme Court approval since 1971) to provide public housing. And despite the fact that residence requirements for public assistance were declared unconstitutional in 1969, states continue to adopt and try to enforce them. (New York State adopted such a law in 1971, which was promptly declared unconstitutional.)

There is no point in trying to deny the logic of such behavior on the part of states and localities. In most cases, poor people's welfare programs will cost state or local tax money; and even when they do not, the taxes paid by poor people will not cover the added costs of public education, police, fire, and other services for them. Even those who feel no qualms about the morality of trying to drive people away for purely economic reasons must realize, however, that no amount of *local* competition to get rid of poor people will reduce the *national* total of poor people; it will just affect their geographic distribution. In fact, there is good reason to believe that such policies increase poverty, in two ways. First, they reduce the mobility of poor people and discourage them from moving. Consequently, they are less likely to leave unpromising regions for growing and prosperous ones, and less likely to escape poverty. And second, when competition holds down levels of services and support to the poor, it reinforces the vicious circles that keep them poor.

In short, states and localities are led by the system of poor people's welfare to adopt policies that are intended to reduce the number of poor people in their jurisdictions, but which in fact, by raising the total number of poor people, raise the average number in each jurisdiction as well.

INCENTIVE AND DISTRIBUTIONAL SIDE EFFECTS

Poor people's welfare programs are so constructed as to discourage the poor from becoming self-supporting, from being thrifty, and from leading a regular family life. The regular welfare system is frequently so constructed as to provide nothing to those in the greatest need and to provide increasing benefits as need declines. These two side effects, disincentives to the poor and inverseness to need, will be discussed separately.

Disincentives to the Poor. The best-known disincentives are those of the public assistance programs, particularly Aid to Families with Dependent Children. The manner in which recipients (other than under WIN —see below) are covered provides that every dollar they *earn* reduces their assistance check by a dollar. If it has been determined that a family is entitled to $150 per month, and if the family earns nothing, it will get a check for $150; if it earns $50, it will get a check for $100; and so forth. In effect, then, there is a "tax" of 100 percent on earned income. Since businessmen with far lower marginal tax rates complain of the disincentive effects of taxation, it should hardly be surprising that the motivation of someone with a tax rate of 100 percent is likely to be affected adversely.

In some poor people's welfare programs, the effective marginal tax rate may even exceed 100 percent. This is true wherever a food stamp, public housing, medical care, or other program has a fixed eligibility threshold—an income level above which families or individuals become ineligible to participate in the program. A family may find that any further increase in its income will force it to leave public housing and pay a rent increase that exceeds the pay increase; force it off food stamps, increasing its grocery budget by more than the pay increase; and force it out of other programs as well.

Such a family is in a position illustrated by Figure 4-1. Even when earned income is zero, the family still has a certain amount of income in the form of assistance payments and subsidized goods and services (medical care, food, etc.). As earned income (shown on the horizontal axis) increases, the family's total income remains unchanged or actually *falls*. The range over which total income (including goods and services) is constant or falls is called the *welfare trap*. This trap discourages the poor from earning more; if they can get past it, however, the relationship between earned income and total income becomes positive.

The Work Incentive (WIN) program for certain AFDC parents, discussed in Chapter 5, reduces the effective tax rate from 100 to 66 2/3 percent. President Nixon's proposed welfare reforms, also discussed in Chapter 5, would have reduced the rate to 50 percent. These lower rates would not constitute a welfare trap in the sense described above, but they are still high enough to discourage effort.

Although recent research indicates that this kind of disincentive is less potent than was once thought, it nonetheless constitutes an added burden on the poor, a sandbagging of those who need no such handicap.

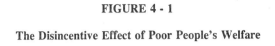

FIGURE 4 - 1

The Disincentive Effect of Poor People's Welfare

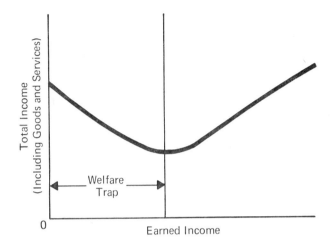

There are other kinds of disincentives in poor people's welfare too. The best known is the incentive to break up the family. In a majority of states, AFDC, the largest public assistance program, is available only if there are no employable unemployed adults in the household. In practice, this means that virtually all AFDC families are headed by husbandless mothers. As we pointed out in Chapter 2, chronically unemployed husbands often must desert their families in order for the families to become eligible for assistance.

Benefits Inverse to Need. Mainly as a byproduct of their camouflage, many mainstream welfare programs provide benefits inverse to need. The most glaring examples are found in welfare programs buried in the tax laws. Generally, the dollar value to the taxpayer of any item that reduces his taxable income, whether it is a deductible expense, a dependents' exemption, or an exclusion (a nontaxable income item), is equal to the size of that item multiplied by the highest marginal tax rate he pays. Thus a $100 deduction for someone in the 25-percent marginal tax bracket is "worth" $25. With a progressive income tax, the dollar value of any given deduction, exemption, or exclusion rises as income rises.

Since this is a very important point, let us examine a number of examples. The simplest is the extra dependents' exemption allowed those over 65. The extra $750 exemption is worth nothing to the person whose taxable income is so low that he or she pays no taxes; it is worth $105 (14 percent of $750) to a person in the 14-percent bracket, a person with up to $1,000 in taxable income; and it is worth $525 to a person in the highest (70-percent) bracket, for families with over $200,000 in taxable income. So the added exemption is worth the least to those whose need is greatest and the most to those whose need is the least.

Even though the *amount* of this extra dependents' exemption is the same for all people, its *value* to the taxpayer rises as his income rises. This effect is aggravated whenever the amount of the deduction or exclusion also rises with income. This is true, for instance, in the case of mortgage-loan interest, whose deductibility was mentioned earlier as part of the federal government's most costly housing program. Poor people are less likely to be buying a house and less likely in any case to itemize deductions on their income tax returns. Moreover, as income rises, so does the price paid for a house, as a rule, and so does the amount of interest paid on mortgages.

The "income-splitting" provision (which allows husband and wife to file joint returns) also provides benefits that increase with income. Although it was not mentioned in Table 4-1, this provision is an interesting contrast to poor people's welfare. The effect of the joint-return provision is to double the size of each tax bracket. Thus the 14-percent rate applies to the first $500 for single persons, and the first $1,000 for married couples filing jointly. The 15-percent bracket is $501-$1,000 for single persons and $1,001-$2,000 on a joint return, and so on. The greatest benefit comes at the highest end of the income scale, because the brackets are much wider (e.g., $100,000-$200,000). People with high incomes are, in effect, paid thousands of dollars to be married (which helps explain why many rich persons are well known for having wife after wife, or husband after husband—they are encouraged to formalize their affairs, for tax reasons). As incomes decline, so do the tax advantages of being married. When the family is so poor that it qualifies for public assistance, it is even paid to break up!

There are ways of designing income tax provisions, using credits instead of exemptions and such devices as disappearing deductions, so as to avoid making their benefits inverse to need. Such regressive effects as are found in the U.S. law are not inherent in progressive taxes. They are a byproduct of concealed welfare programs. Can anyone believe that the American people would permit Congress to establish an *explicit* old-age pension that paid nothing to those with no income, or only Social Security or public assistance income; paid $105 to a person with $1,000 in income; and paid $525 to someone with over $200,000 a year? The same question might fairly be asked of farm programs that pay the largest benefits to the largest farmers.

INTERVENTION IN PERSONAL AND FAMILY LIFE

A final distinction between the regular, or nonpoor, welfare system and that for poor people concerns the degree to which they intervene in personal and family life. Programs for the nonpoor rarely intrude on sensitive family decisions; programs for the poor exact, as part of the price of assistance, a degree of control over the family, a surrender of some of its autonomy. They do this in three principal ways.

First, by controlling the family's *budget*, they control important family decisions. Whenever someone tells you what to *buy*, he is really telling you how to live. The poor people's welfare system does so in two ways: by providing goods instead of money (public housing, medical care, uplifting symphony concerts for ghetto children, etc.) and by controlling the use of money transfers (through vouchers, such as food stamps, or through close administrative supervision, as in the case of AFDC).

Second, they affect the composition of the family. Can anyone doubt that one reason there are so many husbandless mothers heading poor families is that the government has for years *paid* husbandless mothers? Can anyone doubt that some poor people have children because most states do not provide assistance for childless people, no matter how impoverished? President Nixon's family assistance reform proposals would have corrected the first, but not the second, of these problems. And they would have denied part of their assistance to mothers who did not work, unless they had children of preschool age. Who can doubt that *some* mothers, faced with a choice between having to work outside the home and having another baby in order to continue to have preschool children, will choose the latter in order not to lose benefits? This is not to say that such choices are coldly calculated. But by influencing the environment in which decisions are made and the way in which they are rewarded, the government subtly influences those decisions, in precisely the manner described by former Selective Service Director Lewis Hershey in his famous "Channeling" memorandum. Just as college students were led to think that becoming engineers or clergymen was their own decision, so poor people are led to think that having children or breaking up the home is their decision.

Third, poor people's welfare programs monitor the behavior of their "clients." Public assistance caseworkers, public housing tenant-relations officers, and social workers for a variety of agencies may view their role as anything from advisor and family friend to parent-or-husband-surrogate to warden. Mothers have had assistance checks held up because they were seen in bars. Families have been evicted from public housing because of delinquent children. People have been denied surplus food for having a television set.

The use to which a Social Security or unemployment compensation check is put, on the other hand, is never monitored. Families get an income tax exemption for each minor child, but no one checks to make sure that the family spends at least as much as the exemption on the child. Home-buyers who hold orgies do not have their FHA loan insurance revoked. Farmers may spend their farm-surplus money on wine, women, and song. In fact, an upstate New York farmer achieved some notoriety by using subsidy money to buy a Cadillac; using the name "Cadillac Smith," he then began a political career that led him to the State Senate.

What is the significance of this double standard? It makes the stronger poor people liars and cheats and the weaker ones psychologically dependent. Neither outcome is particularly conducive to personal development. As we have so often pointed out, moneylessness is only one aspect of chronic poverty; it is aggravated by a concomitant sense of powerlessness. Although some poor people's programs attack this feeling of powerlessness, a great many of them increase it. By stunting independence and reinforcing dependence, they help to keep poor people poor.

The differences between poor people's and regular welfare programs are systematic and significant. They mean minimal living conditions for poor people and reasonable comfort for the nonpoor; they mean degradation for poor people and dignity for the nonpoor; and, most important, they imply continued poverty and dependence for many of the poor and continued security and apparent self-reliance for the nonpoor.

In the next chapter, we will examine the major poor people's programs in more detail and review the major features of various reform proposals, from family assistance to a guaranteed income.

REFERENCES

The most thorough account ever assembled of the American welfare system—both for the nonpoor and for the poor—appears in the President's Commission on Income Maintenance Programs, *Background Papers* (Washington, D.C.: Government Printing Office, c. 1969). Although the data in that volume are growing rapidly out of date, it remains the outstanding reference work in the area.

Cited in the text is Clair Wilcox, *Toward Social Welfare* (Homewood, Ill.: Irwin, 1969).

The 1936 and 1943 public-opinion-poll questions are referred to in Michael E. Schiltz, *Public Attitudes Toward Social Security, 1935-1965*, Social Security Administration Office of Research and Statistics, Research Report No. 33 (Washington, D.C.: Government Printing Office, 1970).

Data on average and total payments under OASDHI, unemployment compensation, workmen's compensation, and public assistance programs can be found in two monthly periodicals published by the federal government, *Social Security Bulletin* and *Welfare in Review*.

The single best source of information on the U.S. federal tax system is Joseph Pechman's *Federal Tax Policy*, rev. ed. (New York: W. W. Norton, 1971). This volume also discusses the taxes, trust funds, and benefits under the Social Security system. On Social Security, see also Milton Friedman, "The Poor Man's Welfare Payment to the Middle Class," *The Washington Monthly* (May 1972), from which we have quoted on p. 124. See also Carolyn Shaw Bell, "Social Security: Unfair to Those Who Pay It; Unfair to Those Who Receive It," *Challenge* (July-August 1973).

Other articles that explore some of the characteristics of the dual welfare system include Gordon Tullock's "The Charity of the Uncharitable," *Western Economic Journal*, 9 (1971), quoted at the beginning of the chapter; Phillip M. Stern's "Uncle Sam's Welfare Program for the Rich," *New York Times Magazine* (April 16, 1972); and A. Dale Tussing's "Our Two Welfare Systems," *Social Service Outlook* (June 1968).

Gilbert Y. Steiner, in his book *The State of Welfare* (Washington, D.C.: Brookings Institution, 1971), distinguishes between "crude" and "subtle" relief systems, which correspond very roughly to systems for the poor and the nonpoor. This distinction is drawn at the start of his admirable book, the remainder of which is concerned solely with the "crude" system.

With kind permission of the publisher, St. Martin's Press, this chapter was pre-published, in modified form, in the January/February 1974 issue of *Society*.

5

Welfare and Poverty: A Closer Look

In the final two chapters, we shall turn at last to antipoverty policy. In this chapter we shall discuss ways of dealing with poverty through the welfare system—still using the broad definition of that system we have used throughout. In Chapter 6, we shall discuss a variety of nonwelfare strategies for addressing the problem of poverty.

In this chapter, we will look at the details of a few of the most important poor people's welfare programs: public assistance, public housing, food stamps, Medicaid, and veterans' relief. We will then examine some proposals for reforming the welfare system and evaluate their merits.

In Chapter 2, a distinction was drawn between preventative and curative antipoverty policies. At that time we observed that the welfare system is society's most important institution for preventing poverty. That is not, however, its only function.

In fact, the welfare system may have *three* separable social functions. First, it is, as we have just noted, the principal social device for preventing the calamities that befall the nonpoor from precipitating vicious circles of poverty. It may also, if its benefits are substantial enough and certain enough to create a sense of security, interrupt existing vicious circles, and *cure* existing poverty. (This is the so-called income strategy point of view, upon which we shall comment in the next section.) Finally, the welfare system, even when it does not provide enough money or enough security to cure poverty, may at least sustain large numbers of poor people and ensure their *survival*.

THE INCOME STRATEGY ARGUMENT

The argument in favor of an *income strategy* can be summarized as follows: (1) The principal characteristic of poverty is moneylessness. Even if powerlessness, which we discussed in Chapter 1, is more important, the main reason for powerlessness is moneylessness. The principal difference between poor people and nonpoor people is how much money they have. (2) The most certain way of getting money into the hands of the poor (and hence make them nonpoor) is to give it to them through jobs or guaranteed incomes, or both. Strategies for combating poverty through expenditures on education, health services, social services, and the like (the so-called service strategies, a rival of income strategies) actually put money primarily into the hands of nonpoor teachers, doctors, health-care workers, social workers, and administrators. Their effect on poor people is, at best, uncertain. Thus the main effects of large-scale expenditures on services for the poor is to create a substantial "poverty industry" that supports a large number of people, few of them from the poverty group. Daniel P. Moynihan, a leading advocate of the income strategy, likens the service strategies to "feeding the sparrows by feeding the horse."

Those who oppose the income strategy argue (1) that transfer payments are a "palliative" and deal only with "symptoms" and (2) that any kind of guaranteed income will not only fail to act on the fundamental causes of poverty, but will reinforce them by impairing motives to work.

These criticisms reflect an imperfect understanding of the problem of poverty. Three points can be made in response to them.

1. It is sometimes correct to deal with symptoms. The terms often used in talking about poverty, such as "prevention" and "cure," "symptoms" and "palliatives," are all borrowed from the practice of medicine, where it is quite common to deal with symptoms (for example, by using pain-killers), either together with or in place of therapy. The fact that a policy deals only with symptoms is not necessarily reason to reject it. This is particularly true if a cure for the problem has not been found.

2. Wherever there are vicious (or benign) cycles of cumulative causation, like those discussed in Chapter 2, the distinction between causes and symptoms is not always clearcut. Those who would have us deal

with the fundamental causes of poverty rather than the symptoms usually point to education or attitudes toward work as examples of the former. But the evidence is fairly clear that both of these are causally dependent on poverty as well as causes of it.

This is an important point, and one worth emphasizing. A sustained and certain income strategy that guaranteed nonpoverty incomes for all might eventually break the vicious circle of poverty for most people. In that case income transfers would be not just a palliative but a cure.

3. Research does not support the view that modest income guarantees have a serious negative effect on work motives. Working under a contract from the Office of Economic Opportunity, the University of Wisconsin's Institute for Research on Poverty has been experimenting with income guarantees in New Jersey by varying the terms of these guarantees to determine the effect they have on, among other things, work incentives. The research findings indicate that they have no significant influence. Similar results were found by Leonard Goodwin, whose major study of the work orientations of poor people, *Do the Poor Want to Work?* was cited in Chapter 2. According to Goodwin,

> Excessive concern that a relatively low level of guaranteed income—around the poverty level—would cause people to drop out of the work force reflects a misunderstanding of the life and work orientations of the poor. They are no more likely to settle for this meager income and cease working than are middle-class people.

Parenthetically, we might note how unusual the OEO's New Jersey income-maintenance experiments are. Large-scale social or psychological experiments on people are not at all common, at least in democratic countries. One wonders whether we will ever see them practiced on any but poor people, convicts, and school children.

POOR PEOPLE'S WELFARE

Some of the major characteristics of poor people's welfare programs in America, particularly the generic features that distinguish them from mainstream (nonpoor people's) welfare programs, were discussed in Chapter 4. We have seen that programs for the poor tend to have a means test, as opposed to a productivity basis, and that they categorize people by criteria that tend to reflect their "deservingness" rather than by their occupation or the industry in which they work. We have seen that they tend to provide less money than mainstream welfare programs, they are more open and less camouflaged, they are more often functions of local or state government, they tend to contain more disincentives that create a "welfare trap," and they tend to be associated with greater intervention in personal and family decisions.

In this chapter, we will look more closely at the operation of these programs, particularly those that provide public assistance, public housing, and food.

PUBLIC ASSISTANCE PROGRAMS

By far the largest, most costly, and most discussed programs in the poor people's welfare system are the public assistance programs. In 1972, these programs paid an estimated $11 billion to an average monthly total of 15 million recipients.

Over 60 percent of the expenditures and over 70 percent of the recipients are in the largest program, Aid to Families with Dependent Children, which is also the fastest-growing public assistance program. Public assistance is also provided by the Supplementary Security Income program and General Assistance programs. The SSI program is, as we noted in Chapter 3, a federal program. GA programs rely wholly upon state and local funds. Slightly over half the states administer public assistance directly; the others supervise local (mostly county) administration.

Eligibility and payments are determined as follows for AFDC and, in many cases, for General Assistance. Each state calculates its own minimum standard of income, or *cost standard*. Those whose incomes fall below the standard and who meet the other eligibility requirements are considered "needy" and hence eligible for payments. There is considerable state-to-state variation in minimum standards, reflecting different costs for rent, utilities, food, clothing, and other goods as well as different points of view on what constitutes a minimum standard of living. In 1968, for example, the monthly cost standard for basic needs for a four-person AFDC family ranged from $144 in North Carolina and $172 in South Carolina to $307 in Connecticut and $419 in Alaska. Payments are based on the difference between a family's income and the minimum standard, but not every state makes up 100 percent of the difference. In 1970, only 20 states did so under AFDC. (The others made up from 27 to 95 percent of the difference.) This is a remarkable fact, and one worth emphasizing. Many states—a majority, as far as AFDC is concerned—*provide less than the minimum income necessary*, by their own calculations, to purchase the most basic necessities.

Payment levels are determined somewhat differently in the new SSI program. A flat $130 a month for an individual, or $195 for a couple, paid by the federal government, is the national minimum. This exceeds the amounts paid in most states by the programs SSI replaced. Some states, however, were paying more, and these (as indeed all the states) will have the right to supplement the federal minimum.

A summary of the operating statistics of the five programs in existence in 1973 (the first three of which are now part of SSI) is shown in Table 5-1. The great disparity in average payments per recipient from program to program reflects in part (as we mentioned in Chapter 4) the acceptability, or "legitimacy," of the recipients and how "deserving" they are. The combination of OAA, AB, and APTD into SSI does, of course, reduce the disparity among the first three groups. It will, however, *increase* the disparity between them and the AFDC and GA recipients.

The federal contribution to AFDC is computed on the basis of a complicated, open-ended grant formula. States determine the benefit levels themselves, and there is enormous state-to-state variation. Ignoring Puerto Rico and the Virgin Islands, average monthly payments per recipient in March 1973 ranged from a low of $14.39 in Mississippi to a high of $93.83 in Massachusetts, a ratio of 6.5 to 1. Variations under OAA, AB, and APTD were comparable. Statistics indicate an even greater ratio—26 to 1—for General Assistance payments, to which the federal government does not contribute. GA payments per recipient ranged, again in March 1973, from a low of $5.20 in Arkansas to a high of $135.53 in New Jersey. These figures are less meaningful, however, because of differences in state GA programs.

State benefit levels in turn determine the amount of the federal contribution. With some variations based on circumstances, the AFDC formula (as of 1972) provided that the federal government would pay five-sixths of the first $18 per recipient and 50 to 60 percent of the next $14, or a total of $22 to $23.50 of the first $32 per recipient.

Such a formula encourages low payment levels since the percentage contribution of the federal government is the largest (83.3 percent) in

TABLE 5 – 1

Monthly Money Payments Under Public Assistance, March 1973

(Numbers of recipients, families, and cases in thousands; total money payments in thousands of dollars)

Program	Total Number of Recipients	Number of Families or Cases	Total Money Payments	Average Payment per Recipient	Average Payment per Family or Case
Old-Age Assistance [a]	1,880		$147,902	$ 78.65	
Aid to the Blind [a]	78		8,639	110.10	
Aid to the Permanently & Totally Disabled [a]	1,190		126,846	106.55	
Aid to Families with Dependent Children	11,155 [b]	3,173	604,356	54.20	$190.50
General Assistance [c]	811	529	60,364	74.40	114.15
Totals and Overall Averages [d]	15,114		948,107	62.73	

SOURCE: Social Security Administration, *Social Security Bulletin*, August 1973.

[a] Merged into Supplementary Security Income, effective 1974.
[b] Includes 8,037,000 children.
[c] Data incomplete.
[d] Details may not add to totals because of rounding.

states with the lowest benefit levels ($18 or less). Above these minimum levels, as benefits rise, the federal share drops. Beyond the maximum of $32, the states (together with localities) are on their own. States are also given grants to help cover administrative costs and for other purposes.

Let us look briefly at each of the three categorical programs for the poor.

Supplementary Security Income. As we have noted, this program combines three older programs, Old-Age Assistance, Aid to the Blind, and Aid to the Permanently and Totally Disabled. Since there is, as yet, no data available on SSI itself, we can only review the three antecedent programs.

Of the approximately 2 million OAA recipients in 1972, more than 1 million also received some benefits under OASDHI (Social Security), but these benefits were so low that they had to be supplemented. This left just under a million persons who received only OAA.

According to a 1965 study, the percentage of OAA recipients who were black (about 20 percent) was larger than the percentage of blacks in the population, but smaller than the percentage of poor people who are black (about 30 percent in 1965 and 1972). Moreover, every other public assistance program has a higher percentage of blacks. This situation is presumably explained primarily by the shorter life expectancy of blacks.

In terms of social legislation, the blind have traditionally been the elite of the handicapped, a fact that reflects their superior organization as well as the character of their handicap. Blind persons are given an extra personal exemption when they file their income tax returns, and until 1974 they had their own public assistance program, Aid to the Blind. Although it was a very small program (it had only about 78,000 recipients), its average benefits have consistently been higher than those of any other public assistance program. As of 1962, 28 percent of AB recipients were black.

As of 1971, about one in seven recipients of Aid to the Permanently and Totally Disabled also received disability benefits under OASDHI. As of 1962, approximately 30 percent of APTD recipients were black, about the same as the proportion of poor people who were black.

People are disabled in a vast range of ways. Some are mentally deficient, some are permanently bedridden, and some are confined to their homes. Others need help to get around. Many need more than income allowances. They need special rent for an apartment with an elevator, the services of a practical nurse or other professionals, special diets, and so on. Very few APTD recipients ever received this kind of supplemental aid.

Aid to Families with Dependent Children. AFDC is the largest, most costly, fastest-growing, and most controversial category of public assistance. As of March 1973, there were 11 million AFDC recipients, of whom 8 million were children. The total annual payments to these people (which are not the same as the program cost, because of administrative costs) amounted to just over $7 billion. Average payments to AFDC recipients were the lowest of any federally assisted public assistance program.

AFDC has the highest proportion of black families (40 percent as of 1967) of any public assistance program. Although this figure exceeds the proportion of poor people who are black, it is approximately the same as the black proportion of poor families with female heads, which is the main group from which AFDC recipients are drawn.

Eligibility rules vary considerably. Federal standards require that there be a dependent child whose dependency is occasioned by the death, incapacity, or "continued absence" of at least one parent. States may, under the AFDC-UP (unemployed parent) program, define a child as dependent if the parents are unemployed; however, somewhat more than half the states have elected *not* to have an AFDC-UP program. There are also state-to-state differences in the definition of "continued absence."

A 1967 survey estimated the following frequencies for reasons for dependency: father dead, 5 percent; father absent because of divorce, separation, desertion, unmarried parenthood, imprisonment, etc., 71 percent; father incapacitated, 16 percent; father unemployed, 5 percent; and other, 3 percent. Since there were unemployed fathers in only 5 percent of the cases, and since wives were almost always, and children always, included in these families, only about 2 percent of the AFDC recipients, according to the survey, could be unemployed men. (That percentage has presumably risen somewhat since 1967, even discounting increases in the rate of unemployment, as additional states have adopted the AFDC-UP option.) Since no unemployed employable men are covered by SSI (just as none were covered by OAA, AB, or APTD), there are virtually none in any federally supported public assistance program. There are more, however, in GA programs.

In 1967, Congress established a *work incentive program*, dubbed "WIN" for short (the sound of the actual initials having a rather unfortunate connotation). Actually, the program features both the carrot and the stick. Employable AFDC parents (interpreted by the Department of Health, Education and Welfare to include female family heads) can be required to accept either employment or employment training, or lose their assistance payments. Once employed, AFDC parents (mostly mothers) are allowed to keep the first $30 per month, plus one-third of the excess over $30, of earned income (in addition to certain costs of employment, such as carfare). Thus WIN mothers, unlike other AFDC parents, have an effective marginal tax rate on earned income of 66 2/3 percent (instead of 100 percent). As of February 1970, 1.5 million AFDC recipients had been screened for referral to the WIN program; 199,000 had been placed in it; and only 22,000 had been employed. A year later, in February 1971, the job placement rate was still only 20 percent. By June 1972, 30 percent of those in the program were being placed in jobs, while 70 percent were dropping out. Many of the 30 percent held jobs for only a short time, and many of those who held jobs for longer periods presumably would have found jobs even without WIN. Since the education and skills of most welfare mothers are limited and their potential hourly earnings are low, and since WIN enrollees work, in effect, for one-third of their nominal wages (many for one-third of the minimum wage), work disincentives would seem to be almost as strong under WIN as before.

Paradoxically, the WIN program may have had a net *negative* effect on the work attitudes of welfare recipients. Goodwin's study of the work orientations of the poor, which examined the relative acceptability of welfare dependency and work among black women, found that

women who find welfare most acceptable tend to show the lowest work activity. By itself, this finding might suggest that poor women prefer welfare to work. The data also indicate, however, that ratings on this orientation are sensitive to encounters in the work world. Women in the WIN program who were terminated from it without jobs—who experienced another failure in the work world—showed a marked increase in the acceptance of welfare score over their score when they entered WIN, demonstrating that the concrete experience of failure directly and negatively influenced this work orientation. The picture that emerges is one of black welfare women who want to work but who, because of continuing failure in the work world, tend to become more accepting of welfare and less inclined to try again.

The situation is hardly better for the minority of WIN mothers who do get jobs if these pay, as they typically do, very low wages.

Just as failure in the WIN program increases mothers' acceptability of welfare, working in jobs that do not pay them enough to support their families is likely to reinforce just those psychological orientations that characterize the poor and discourage them from further work. . . .

These findings ought to be instructive to advocates of work requirements like those recently added to the food stamp program, which —under the name "workfare"—were included in President Nixon's welfare reform package. A policy of requiring work without providing adequate jobs is not only certain to fail, but creates circumstances that are psychologically intolerable and can only reinforce the sense of failure of many poor persons.

Because of obvious failures in the original WIN program, a revised scheme called WIN II was introduced in 1972. The main features of the revision were a further tightening of the mandatory character of the program, the introduction of federal tax credits for employers willing to hire WIN enrollees and give them on-the-job training, and subsidies for the employment of enrollees in public and private nonprofit agencies.

The other widely criticized incentive side effect of AFDC laws and regulations, the incentive to break up the family, was discussed in Chapters 2 and 4.

We have already seen that most AFDC families are white, that unemployed men constitute a very small fraction of AFDC recipients, and that recipients in general prefer working to assistance, despite popular myths to the contrary. Other myths also surround AFDC. For instance, it is popularly thought that AFDC recipients tend to have larger families. The evidence indicates, however, that non-AFDC families who have low incomes and are in the same age group have the same number of children, or slightly more children, than AFDC families.

The most serious criticisms of AFDC are that its procedures are degrading, that it is inequitable, and that it is inadequate.

The charge of degrading procedures is based on, for example, the fact that applicants for AFDC must appear in person, must (usually) wait several hours for an interview, and must submit to a searching personal inquiry, including a "social study" of their personal history leading up to dependency. They must submit to periodic visits by caseworkers, in part to determine continued eligibility. If the applicant is a woman who claims desertion, she must report the father to the legal authorities and, usually, swear out a criminal warrant for his arrest. Some states and localities have added special touches to the procedure by using policemen as caseworkers or using lie detectors to verify applicants' statements.

The charges of inequity and inadequacy are based on the fact that 45 states and the District of Columbia leave recipient families *below* the official poverty line *after* assistance. Perhaps most shocking is the estimate that 58 percent of the poor children in America are not covered at all, either by AFDC or by OASDHI.

General Assistance. It is somewhat misleading to compare General Assistance to SSI and AFDC as if there were a specific, national General Assistance program. There is not. There are merely various state and local programs grouped together under the name General Assistance.

The federally aided programs provide assistance (based on state eligibility rules) to the elderly, to the blind, to other disabled persons, and to certain families with children. This leaves an unprotected residual group of poor people who are under 65, who are not handicapped, and who are single or childless; of families with children, where the head of the family is unemployed; and of the "working poor," those who are regularly employed but at poverty-level wages. Some states provide, to varying degrees and in specified circumstances, for some of these people. Though these programs have various names (some of which, such as "home relief" and "outdoor relief," are hangovers from the old poor laws, which used the terms "home" and "outdoor" to distinguish those recipients of public charity who did not actually live in the poorhouse from those who did) and though they serve various purposes, they are usually discussed together.

Since there are no federal rules, state-to-state variations are greater here than in other programs. For a variety of reasons, within-state variations are also common. Some states give welfare commissioners complete discretion to accept or reject applications (guided only by such language as "dire emergency"); some require localities to foot the entire bill.

The President's Commission on Income Maintenance Programs, in

Background Papers, cites a 1962 study of the California GA system by Laurin Hyde Associates. According to the study, the California program, which is probably typical—neither better nor worse than that of most states—

cared for persons without means who were being investigated for the categorical programs [those now merged into SSI and AFDC], persons with no residence for the categorical programs, and persons ineligible for the categorical programs. At the time, the program also supported, in those counties which permitted it, children whose parents are unemployed. California has since added an AFDC-UP program, but the observations which are appropriate in the absence of that program are pertinent to States which today have no such program.

Payments are always less than those of the corresponding categorical program. For example, a woman with three children was getting $215 [a month] from AFDC while her husband was in jail. When he got out, he was unable to find work. The family, now five instead of four, was put on General Assistance at $177. That was in a county which allowed a payment of that size. In some counties, in the winter months, the average payment for the family cases was only slightly above the average for one-person cases and in many counties there was a severe limit on the duration of payments.

County policies varied widely regarding assistance to families with unemployed members. Four counties made no provision other than surplus food commodities. Twelve others gave aid only occasionally in circumstances described variously as "extreme hardship," "dire emergency," "extreme destitution," etc. Twenty-two counties provided aid only during periods of seasonal unemployment, usually between November and May. Only 20 counties granted aid without regard to season. The counties with seasonal limitations tended to be agricultural, but three which were agricultural and became mainly urban and industrial continued to place seasonal limits.

Several counties limited assistance to families to 30 days, others to 90 days, and one county limited assistance to two weeks in any given 30-day period. In some cases elaborate formulas were derived to determine the length of time assistance would be granted. In one county General Assistance was paid for only 15 days if the unemployment rate for the county was below 5.5 percent and up to 60 days when the unemployment rate was 7.5 percent and over.

In some counties General Assistance to unemployed families was regarded as emergency short term assistance. The usual items provided were food, shelter and utilities, but a substantial number of counties gave only food. Others would pay rent and utilities only when eviction was imminent or utilities about to be shut off. Clothing was rarely provided except in such emergencies as a family being burned out. . . . Of the [California] counties studied by Laurin Hyde, those with the most adequate General Assistance standards used the AFDC cost schedules as a base, but generally scaled downward. . . . In contrast to federally aided programs, payment may be in kind or by voucher. In 1962, 13 of 58 California counties had local commissaries in which food and, in some cases, clothing was issued. Approximately 14 counties gave no General Assistance in cash, 16 gave less than one-third in cash, and 4 were paid less than 5 percent in cash.

The state-to-state variations in General Assistance seem to resemble those within California, as described. (The word "seem" is used because reliable data are not available.) All the evidence available suggests that virtually every criticism made of public assistance in general applies, only more so, to General Assistance.

PUBLIC HOUSING PROGRAMS

There is not space, in a book of this scope, to give adequate attention to the subject of housing for the poor in America. Nonetheless, it would be unwise to discuss public housing without providing some background information on the subject, however brief. Before turning to the public housing program per se, then, we shall quickly survey America's dual housing system.

The Dual Housing System. Just as the United States has a dual welfare system with different programs for the poor and nonpoor, so also it has a dual housing system with largely different markets and systems for the poor and nonpoor.

In the 1930s, a series of probably independent but functionally related policy decisions were made that radically changed America's housing system. The Federal Housing Administration (FHA) was established and put home ownership within the reach of millions of middle-class Americans by providing mortgage-loan insurance and by encouraging monthly payments on mortgage loans (rare until then). At the same time, savings and loan associations, which had been hard hit by the depression (and which were to become the major financers of home mortgages), were shored up and strengthened. They became eligible for federal charters and deposit insurance. A system of Federal Home Loan Banks was created to stand behind them. These were the major, but not the only, policies that pushed the American housing system firmly in the direction of single-family, mainly detached, owner-occupied homes and made the suburban explosion of the postwar decades possible.

In the postwar years, other institutions were created that encouraged this trend, among them a system of mortgage-loan guarantees (as opposed to insurance) provided to veterans through the Veterans Administration. And, as we have already seen, the tax revenue foregone by the federal government, which allows homeowners to deduct mortgage-loan interest and property taxes, is enough to make these deductions, in effect, the two largest housing programs in America. In another way, the expanded federal highway system also contributed to the growth of the suburbs.

Not all nonpoor Americans live in owner-occupied, single-family dwellings, of course. The low-cost availability of this kind of housing has helped, through market competition, to keep down the cost of middle-income rental housing, and FHA aid is also available for financing new apartment structures.

Poor people, particularly in urban areas, live primarily in two kinds of housing: old and public. This is so mainly for two reasons. One is cost and the other is discrimination. It seems virtually impossible to build housing that is both new and inexpensive. Therefore, unless housing costs are subsidized (through, for instance, the provision of public housing), poor people are limited to older structures. At the same time, racial discrimination also limits poor (and many nonpoor) blacks and Puerto Ricans, and other minority-group members, to old housing in the centers of cities or to public administered housing.

Of the three "establishment" groups who are most often targets of the anger of the urban, ghetto poor—the police, ghetto merchants, and slum landlords—only the landlords seem to be getting rich. Few policemen have incomes much above the U.S. family median. Ghetto merchants may exploit, mislead, and victimize their customers (though not all do), but rarely do they themselves become really wealthy. On the other hand, some slum landlords, abetted by favorable tax treatment from the federal government and from local governments; by a frequent failure to enforce housing codes; and by their political influence with housing inspectors, judges, sheriffs, and the like, have come to be very rich and powerful indeed.

Besides public housing, there are a number of smaller programs that provide federal subsidies for low-income housing, including rent supplements, which will be discussed in the next section.

Some people confuse urban renewal with public housing. Urban renewal may, on occasion, result in public housing; but they are not the same, nor do they usually go hand in hand. *Urban renewal* consists of programs to acquire, clear (demolish the structures on), and resell land on which slum buildings or blighted structures stand. Since most of the structures demolished thus far have been high-density slum housing, and since most of the new structures have been commercial buildings, middle- or high-income rental apartments, or public or civic buildings, the effect of urban renewal has been to reduce substantially the supply of low-income housing, not to increase it. Moreover, since this has meant an increase in the population density in low-income neighborhoods elsewhere, it has typically meant the exacerbation, rather than the elimination, of slum conditions.

The Public Housing Program. There are a series of interlocking defects in public housing in America which make that program one of the least successful elements of the poor people's welfare system.

The first is the inadequate number of housing units. Approximately 2 1/2 million persons, less than 10 percent of those who are eligible, live in approximately 750,000 public housing units. Long waiting lists testify to the inadequate supply of such units, and at the same time discourage many people who would like to move into public housing from even bothering to apply.

Like urban renewal, the construction of public housing projects probably results in a net reduction in the number of low-income housing units available. This is because the density of the demolished structures often exceeds that of the new housing.

The public housing deficit is attributable both to an unwillingness on the part of Congress to provide funds for the construction of enough units, largely because of opposition from private housing interests, and to an unwillingness on the part of localities to accept and operate enough units. Local control has led to regional disparities in the availability of public housing far more extreme than the disparities in public assistance programs described earlier. New York City has one-fourth of the public housing units in the United States. Thus the New York City Housing Authority supervises housing with a greater total population than either San Diego, California, or Des Moines, Iowa. San Diego and Des Moines, incidentally, have no public housing at all.

Few people want public housing tenants as neighbors. For this reason, there are virtually no public housing projects in suburban areas, in spite of the steady movement of employment opportunities to the suburbs. Even within cities, there are strong objections to low-income housing. In Cleveland, middle-class blacks protested plans by black mayor Carl Stokes and his administration to build public housing in their neighborhood; while in Queens, a borough of New York City, angry whites protested white Mayor John Lindsay's plans to construct public housing in middle-class Forest Hills.

Whatever the cause, the public housing deficit, unfortunate in itself, has had an undesirable secondary effect. Local public housing authorities are able, because of shortages and long waiting lists, to be very selective in accepting applicants. The result is a phenomenon called *creaming*. When programs for the poor are small and selective, they often take only the best of the available applicants (the "cream"), a practice which has the dual effect of improving the program's apparent performance and results while doing little or nothing for the poorest and most disadvantaged. This has often been the case with public housing. Alcoholics, prostitutes, addicts, and the like are barred by most authorities. Some have refused to admit unwed mothers or families with illegitimate children; some have evicted those who were unable to control delinquent children. There have even been cases of eviction of tenants who were active in tenants' rights organizations. Some of this discrimination has been declared illegal by the courts, but it seems to continue on an informal, *de facto* basis.

This kind of tenant selection obviously makes life easier for the local authorities. But barring the most troublesome tenants does not make them disappear, since they have to live somewhere. On the other hand, the best tenants are probably public assistance recipients. They have dependable incomes, and they and their children are probably more docile than most other poor people.

The tenant selectivity arising out of the public housing shortage combines with the method of financing public housing to create still another problem for the poorest of the poor. In brief, the federal government pays the capital costs of public housing, but the local housing authority must pay operating costs out of rental revenues. Rents range from 20 to 25 percent of family income, adjusted for family size, and income limits are determined locally. In 1969, the national median maximum income allowed for a family of four was $4,100. Whatever the income limit for admission, local authorities must permit family income to rise by 20 percent of that amount before evicting tenants.

Since rents are a percentage of a tenant's family income, and since housing authorities are required to cover operating costs out of these same rents, they are forced to limit the number of very poor people they admit. Many authorities have what is, in effect, a quota system, designed to admit a predetermined percentage from each eligible income range. Income quota systems or their equivalent, like creaming, would not work were there not a severe shortage of housing units and long lists of applicants from which to choose.

Studies indicate that tenants tend to dislike public housing far more frequently than they dislike private housing, even in slums, in spite of lower rents and better physical surroundings. Gilbert Steiner, in *The State of Welfare*, cites the most frequent complaints from tenants and applicants. These include invasion of privacy ("Why does the maintenance man have the right to walk into our dwelling any time of day without advance notice?"), injustice ("Why must I pay for a broken window when I didn't break it?"), poor management ("Why is our apartment only painted every six years?"), bureaucratic rigidity ("Why must I lose a half-day's pay to see the Manager—why can't the office stay open one night a week just as the stores do?"), and discourtesy ("Why doesn't your staff address me as *Mister*?"). Presumably, many if not all of these problems would receive more attention if the authorities did not have a backlog—a "reserve army"—of potential applicants.

About 40 percent of public housing tenants' units are reserved for the elderly, and this percentage is growing. There is, apparently, less political and neighborhood resistance to housing for the elderly than to housing for the younger, predominantly black poor families.

Rent supplements and leased housing are available to the poor under newer, smaller programs. Under the rent-supplement program, the federal government contracts with private developers in local communities to provide housing to low-income families subject to rent and profit ceilings. The structure of this program, too, makes it difficult for the lowest-income families to participate; it also discourages developers from offering units with more than two bedrooms, thus limiting its utility to large families. Under leased housing programs, the local housing authority contracts with private landlords to provide housing to low-income families; tenants pay their rent to the authority, who pays the owner. Both programs have rents calculated in ways similar to rents for public housing. Both have the potential advantage of providing "scattered site" public housing (with tenants living among the nonsubsidized population). Thus the stigma and pathology of life in "brick city" projects are avoided, and some racial integration may even be possible.

Urban Land Reform. A possible alternative to public housing is *urban land reform*. In most underdeveloped countries, land ownership is highly concentrated; most of the people who work the land do not own it. Absentee ownership of this type poses a major barrier to economic development, for it makes the peasants reluctant to undertake costly or risky investments to improve the land.

A similar situation exists in America's urban areas. In most poor areas, urban or rural, those who occupy housing do not own it. Absentee ownership of poverty housing means that neither owner nor tenant has much of a motive to maintain and improve the property. Indeed, absentee ownership is part of the cycle of urban decay.

In agrarian land reform programs, the government may confiscate the land and give it to those who work it, or it may purchase the land and then resell it on easy terms. What is needed today in America is a form of urban land reform under which tenants come to own properties in which they live if the property is worth saving.

The place to begin such a program is in areas already inhabited by poor people, where the properties have not yet deteriorated enough to make maintenance impractical. Tenants could use their efforts to maintain and improve buildings in which they live as a form of "sweat equity," to make a down payment on the property.

FOOD STAMPS AND COMMODITIES

The food stamp program, like the public housing program, has serious weaknesses. Just as public housing has, on balance, probably reduced the supply of rental housing available to low-income persons, so too food stamps have probably reduced the number of persons who are assured of a more nutritious diet by a federal food program.

The food stamp program is, in effect, the successor to the surplus commodity distribution program. Both programs are in operation in the United States (though not in the same counties), but the food stamp program is gradually displacing the commodity program. As of 1970, participating counties were fairly evenly divided between the two programs. Some counties have neither, since participation is a local option except in emergencies.

The essence of the two programs is as follows. Both are administered by the U.S. Department of Agriculture (USDA); legislation is written by, and legislative oversight provided by, the Agriculture Committees of the House and Senate. Appropriations are passed upon by the Agriculture Appropriations Subcommittees of the two houses. As a consequence, both the executive and the legislative branch are ambivalent, at best, over whether the programs should be farmer-oriented or poverty-oriented. Public assistance recipients, together with other persons selected locally, are eligible for the programs. But eligibility standards, like those for other poor people's welfare programs, vary widely throughout the United States.

The *commodity distribution program* provides for local distribution, through welfare departments, of surplus food products provided by the USDA. Counties distribute anywhere from 8 to 22 commodities, at their own option. *Food stamps* are sold, at prices varying with income, to eligible poor persons, although the very poorest families (most of which are in the rural South) can be given stamps if their incomes are at a starvation level (such as $600 a year for a family of four).

The food stamp program was developed to correct a number of significant defects in the commodity programs, over which it has a number of built-in advantages; or so it would seem. Commodities are distributed from a central point in each county once a month. In the past, the commodities selected depended primarily on what there was a surplus of at the time rather than on nutritional needs. Improvements have been made in recent years, and counties can supplement federally provided food through purchases of their own, though few do. Because many of the food products (lard, flour, skimmed milk, etc.) are bulky, and because an entire month's supply is distributed at once, picking up food can be difficult, particularly for the elderly and those without automobiles. People queue up, and it may take hours to get an allotment, even in periods of subfreezing temperatures, rain, or other inclement weather conditions. The scene is a familiar one to a great many Americans because, on slow news days, television newsmen in hundreds of

areas habitually film (or used to film) the lines of poor people, many with children's wagons, baby buggies, or shopping carts, others arriving or departing in taxicabs. Besides the obvious indignities it entails, the commodity program has other defects. Poor families cannot select the foods they wish. By dictating a certain diet, the program not only intervenes excessively in personal and family decisions, but it ensures that some food will either be thrown away or sold, since people often will not eat food they find distasteful no matter how low their income is.

It would be hard, one would think, to create a welfare program worse than the commodity distribution setup. But that is what Congress and the USDA succeeded in doing, at least at first, with food stamps. Stamps have, to be sure, a number of important advantages over commodities. Although they are bought monthly, the food itself is bought as it is needed, from regular grocery stores. There is no transportation problem, no standing out in the cold or the rain, and no waste, since families can choose their own food items. The stamp program is less demeaning, although it too can be embarrassing, particularly to people new to the program, who often must learn by experience that nonfood items (light bulbs, cigarets, toilet paper, napkins, toothpaste, etc.) and imported foods (coffee, many brands of tuna fish, bananas, etc.) sold in grocery stores cannot be bought with stamps.

The advantages of food stamps should have made them very attractive to poor people—certainly more attractive than commodities. But in *every* county where food stamps were substituted for commodities, participation went down—sometimes to only 15 percent of the participation rate under commodities. By late 1969, only about one in five of those poor persons eligible for the program were in it. The food stamp program was greatly liberalized and expanded between 1969 and 1972, and the number of participants doubled. And yet, a numerical majority of eligible poor people still do not participate.

There appear to be a number of reasons for nonparticipation. One is that all but the very poorest families must put in some of their own money, and the program dictates how much of their budget must be spent on food. Since one purpose of the program is improved nutrition, the amount of food that must be purchased takes a considerable bite out of poor people's budgets. Participants cannot buy more or less than the number of food stamps for which they are eligible, and they must use every month's food stamps in the month for which they are issued.

Whether they like food stamps will depend on how much they have been spending on food. In general, they will not have been spending as much on food as food stamps will require; consequently, they must either increase their food budget (as those who designed the program intended they should) or not participate at all. A very large majority do not participate. One can either say that most poor people do not feel they can afford to participate, or (as some do say) that poor people are too ignorant of nutrition or too apathetic to participate; whatever their motives are, the result is the same.

Even if food stamps require a family to spend about the same amount as they have been spending on food, they may not want to lock themselves into spending that amount by committing so much money at the start of each month. Doing so reduces their financial options and increases their vulnerability. A forced commitment of a large part of their income contributes to the sense of powerlessness and domination by others that is part of the pathology of their poverty.

Families who want to participate in the program but do not want to spend as much on food as is required cannot simply buy stamps one month and skip buying the next; if they miss more than two months out of six, they are disqualified from participation.

Working poor people find it much harder to participate than public assistance recipients because, if they are paid weekly, they find it almost impossible to raise an entire month's food money at once.

The food stamp and commodities programs share one serious disadvantage with each other and with public housing, Medicaid, and a number of other poor people's welfare programs. Instead of providing poor families with the incomes they need and trusting them to spend it to their families' advantage, they provide commodities or restricted vouchers such as food stamps, thereby determining the makeup of the poor families' budgets. Thus poor families must give up some of their independence in exchange for assistance in survival. The fact that some poor people refuse to make this exchange undoubtedly helps explain the high rate of nonparticipation in food stamp programs.

MEDICAID

Medicaid, a major poor people's welfare program, with more participants and a greater budget than public housing or the two food programs combined, was born almost by accident. It was, reports the staff of the President's Commission on Income Maintenance, almost an afterthought on the part of the designers of Medicare [part of OASDHI]. It was tacked onto the Medicare Bill moments before it went to Congress in order to provide a means by which premiums, required under Part B of Medicare (physicians' and other medical services other than hospitalization, financed by monthly premiums), could be paid for the poor and near-poor elderly on a State-Federal sharing basis. While providing such financing, Congress went a step further by guaranteeing payments for the cost of Medical Assistance [under Medicaid] to all Public Assistance recipients.

Besides public assistance recipients, states were permitted, but not required, to cover "medically indigent" persons—those who were poor but who were not receiving public assistance payments.

Virtually everyone at the federal and state level underestimated the backlog of unmet medical needs among the poor, and consequently expenditures for this purpose exceeded expectations by a considerable margin. Moreover, Congress supplied massive new funds for medical care in the two new programs, but failed to provide for similarly expanded health-care facilities and services. The resulting pressure of demand on supply forced costs up even more rapidly. Most governors and state legislators interpreted the result as a budget problem, rather than as evidence of a health-care problem, and several states cut back sharply on eligibility to balance their budgets, thus leaving large numbers of people without the means to finance adequate health care.

Medicaid closely resembles public assistance in its financing and operation. The federal government pays between 50 and 83 percent of the cost for the richest and poorest states, respectively. The program operates through state and local welfare departments. As in other programs for poor people, eligibility standards vary considerably around the United States.

Payments are made directly to vendors (i.e., hospitals, physicians, druggists, etc.). This procedure seems to make for delays in payment and a great deal of paperwork for the vendors. This fact, together with a maximum fee schedule that many doctors complain is too low, has led a great many to refuse to do business with Medicaid clients. Class or racial biases may also play a part in some of these refusals. Thus one of the theoretical advantages of a program like Medicaid—the fact that poor patients are able to choose their own physicians and other purveyors of medical services, rather than being forced to accept treatment at public emergency rooms or clinics—does not work so well in practice.

Moreover, in some areas the quality of physician's services has been affected adversely, since, quoting again from the analysis of the Commission staff, "preliminary evidence suggests that the pattern of the receipt of care may often be that patients are receiving care from a small percentage of practitioners who are frequently without hospital privileges and reside in low-income neighborhoods and who are involved in large volume practices."

In 1971, medical payments under Medicaid totaled just under $7 billion; payments under Medicare, by way of comparison, totaled just over $7.5 billion.

VETERANS' RELIEF

Veterans' relief, consisting of veterans' pensions and death pensions, constitutes a poor people's welfare program of considerable magnitude, and one that is in many ways in a class by itself. These two pension programs should not be confused with veterans' compensation, which pays those with service-connected disabilities and surviving dependents of veterans who died of service-connected causes. Veterans' relief is paid to wartime (though not necessarily combat) veterans, or to the widows or orphans of wartime veterans, who are incapacitated or who die as a result of causes that have no connection whatever with their service in the armed forces. There are approximately 3 million recipients, of whom 40 percent are veterans and 60 percent are widows and orphans. Total benefits of approximately $2.5 billion were paid in 1971.

Veterans' pensions and death pensions qualify as poor people's welfare programs, as defined in Chapter 4. They have a means test (veterans, widows, and orphans must be "needy," with incomes of $3,500 or less, and without excessive assets) rather than a productivity basis, and eligibility is based on "deservingness" (because of their veteran status). Being 65 or over is considered incapacitating. But these programs have features which separate them from all other poor people's welfare programs. As Steiner puts it,

Persons in a position to make a choice are well advised to opt for a veterans' pension rather than for Old Age Assistance or for Aid to Families with Dependent Children. The veterans' program usually pays better and comes easier. Unlike most public assistance beneficiaries, recipients of veterans' pensions are not conditioned to believe that they are a drag on society, are not subject to investigation

to insure that their claim continues to be valid, are presumed to be telling the truth, are assisted in making a claim by a large network of volunteers and of agents of governmental units other than the unit paying the benefit, are not obliged to account for their spending behavior, may have significant amounts of income from other sources, are able to move freely without jeopardizing their benefits, and are not badgered to get off the rolls. Added to all this is an administrative agency instructed by law to be and naturally disposed to be sympathetic; a finely tuned Congressional committee preoccupied with the problems of the veteran population but also sensitive to the importance of avoiding excesses; a financing system that depends exclusively on appropriations from Federal general revenue without the need for any state participation whatever; and an appeals procedure that keeps disputes within the family, handles them informally, and strives to find an interpretation that will permit a favorable ruling.

Thus these two pension programs, though they are forms of poor people's welfare, have most of the attributes of the nonpoor welfare programs discussed in Chapter 4. The benefit levels are higher; the programs themselves, if not camouflaged, are at least administered in such a way as to protect the dignity of the people involved; they are administered exclusively by the federal government; and they intervene very little if at all in vital personal and family decisions.

Veterans' pensions go back to the early 19th century, long before the passage of the Social Security Act or legislation creating any of the other modern welfare programs. Once these had been created, there was no longer a need for a separate set of veterans' programs, except to compensate for service-connected disabilities and deaths. But the U.S. welfare system, for the reasons explained in Chapter 3, does not generally develop comprehensive social welfare programs to replace existing selective ones; instead, it grows in a capricious and patchwork fashion, reflecting the play of circumstances, political power, ideology, racism, and change. Thus most old programs never die, or even fade away.

WELFARE REFORM AND INCOME-MAINTENANCE PLANS

Many major reforms have been proposed in the area of income maintenance and welfare. Some of these reforms would replace federally supported public assistance with other forms of aid. Some, like

Milton Friedman's negative income tax, would replace the entire welfare system.

Since reform proposals are so numerous, and since the possible variations of these proposals are almost endless, we cannot hope to examine them all here. Instead, we shall examine what seem to be eight desirable characteristics, or "desiderata," of a comprehensive, fair welfare system. We shall then evaluate, briefly, a few of the principal reform proposals.

Eight Desiderata of Income-Maintenance Schemes

The following elements would seem to be desirable in any comprehensive welfare system:

1. an adequate floor to the level of living,
2. a cut-off point for assistance,
3. an incentive to earn income,
4. noncategorical and certain coverage,
5. equal treatment for intact and broken families,
6. uniform, national eligibility standards and benefits,
7. federal financing, and
8. a separation of social services from financial assistance.

We shall postpone our discussion of the first three elements until we have examined the other five.

Noncategorical and Certain Coverage. The welfare system should, if possible, contribute to a solution of the poverty problem, providing more than simple support (the first desideratum) and more than an incentive to earn (the third desideratum). To accomplish this requires an income strategy, though not necessarily in isolation. In the case of the U.S. welfare system, it would mean (1) raising support payments to an adequate level, (2) making the present programs more comprehensive, (3) making them more certain, and (4) reducing intervention in personal and family life. As the Kerner Commission Report stated in 1968,

> The [public assistance] system is deficient in two critical ways:
> First, it excludes large numbers of persons who are in great need, and who, if provided a decent level of support, might be able to become more productive and self-sufficient;

Second, for those who are included, it provides assistance well below the minimum necessary for a humane level of existence, and imposes restrictions that encourage continued dependency on welfare and undermine self-respect.

As we have noted, the vast majority of states leave public assistance recipients' family incomes below the poverty line. It seems obvious that a subpoverty income cannot break vicious circles of poverty. Moreover, less than one-third of the poor receive public assistance. Some of the remainder are ineligible because they do not fit into the available categories; some are put off by demeaning application and administration procedures; some do not know they are eligible, since public assistance agencies (unlike OASDHI, veterans' relief, and other programs) make no effort to find qualifying recipients; and some would not want assistance under any terms. A welfare system that is able to break vicious circles of poverty must be available to most poor people. In spite of continuing gradual reforms, much poor people's welfare, especially General Assistance, is available only at the discretion of administrators and hence is not certain enough to provide economic security. The resultant vulnerability is one of the characteristics that separate the poor from the nonpoor. Moreover, administrative discretion gives public assistance overtones of charity; a comprehensive welfare system should make support as much of a legal right as OASDHI payments. We have already discussed at length the ways in which excessive intervention in poor people's personal and family lives via welfare programs reinforces dependency.

Equal Treatment for Intact and Broken Families. Welfare aid should not contribute to breaking up families. The way in which it does, in the United States, has already been discussed, primarily in Chapter 2. To prevent this problem, a welfare program must provide assistance to needy families in which both parents are present and able-bodied as well as to families in which one parent is absent. A merger of all the major welfare programs (public assistance, OASDHI, unemployment compensation, farm programs, etc.) into a single, comprehensive, income-maintenance system would help greatly to accomplish this. However, either the present public assistance categories based on ''deservingness'' would have to be abolished, or new categories would have to be added to make coverage truly comprehensive.

If, in addition, a family could always keep some of its earned income without having its welfare benefits reduced dollar for dollar, it could never do better disbanded than intact and welfare would not compete with husbands' and fathers' attempts to provide for their wives and children.

Uniform, National Eligibility Standards and Benefits. Standards of eligibility and benefits should be uniform and national. As we have seen, both eligibility standards and benefit levels in poor people's welfare programs vary widely from state to state. Existing arrangements permit the fiction that public assistance, public housing, commodities, food stamps, and Medicaid programs are merely "state" or "local" programs financed in part by federal subsidies. Thus the anomaly of a nonuniform federal program is justified.

This sixth desideratum does not necessarily imply that there should be a uniform national *dollar* standard of either eligibility or benefits, since prices, and hence living costs, may vary from place to place.

National standards are important for two reasons.

First, it is unjust for society—and particularly unjust for the federal government—to treat its citizens (all of whom are supposedly equal in the eyes of the law) differently simply because they live, say, in South Carolina or Indiana rather than Connecticut or Alaska.

Second, varying standards and benefits violate the principle of *neutrality*. This principle, which is found mainly in discussions of taxation, applies also to welfare, which is in a sense the mirror opposite of taxation. It holds that taxes—and welfare payments—should have no capricious or unintended effects on such private economic decisions as where people live, what they buy, or how firms produce their output. It is violated whenever interstate differences in welfare benefits lead people to migrate in quest of higher payments. (It should be noted, however, that existing research provides little convincing evidence that differential public assistance support levels really have much to do with migration of significant numbers of low-income people.)

Federal Financing. Since welfare problems are national problems, the techniques of financing welfare should accord with tax-equity standards applying to the whole nation. All welfare costs should be paid from federal revenues.

Geographic mobility makes state and local participation in the financing of poor people's welfare unfair. If agricultural workers leave South Carolina when job opportunities dry up and go to Philadelphia, does that make any temporary or chronic poverty that results just a Pennsylvania problem? Similarly, if housing and other policies in suburban New York force poor people to stay in the central city, does that make poverty a purely urban problem? The economic forces and policy decisions giving rise to the dependency of some groups are national in scope. Poverty and dependency are *not* local problems, and the cost of eliminating them should not be borne by local taxpayers alone.

Some people, of course, will ask what difference it makes whether welfare costs are paid by the federal government, since all federal taxpayers are also local taxpayers. But it does make a difference. Those who live in states and localities with high concentrations of recipients, or where eligibility or benefit levels are more liberal, pay more than those in other areas.

Moreover, the federal government's tax problems differ markedly from those of state and local governments. The federal tax structure is highly income-elastic; as income rises, federal tax revenues tend to rise even faster. As a result, the federal tax structure automatically tends to depress the economy unless expenditures also increase rapidly. This problem of "fiscal drag" was the major reason for tax cuts in 1962, 1964, and 1965; and by 1965 a consensus had developed that tax reductions would have to be fairly regular thereafter. The Indochina War, of course, altered the situation in the late 1960s. States and localities, by contrast, have far less elastic tax structures. Yet they bear the brunt of the urban, welfare, education, highway, and other costs, which create their well-known fiscal crises.

Separately Administered Social Services and Financial Support Programs. Noncash social services should *always* be separated from financial support programs. Welfare departments provide a range of social services in addition to disbursing money. They do case and social work; provide public nurses, family counseling, and day-care centers; and work closely with other agencies providing retraining or basic adult education, family planning, and the like and with important authority figures such as probation officers, school administrators, and the courts.

It has become increasingly clear, however, that the combination of social services and financial assistance in one program is anomolous in the extreme. It is all the more so in the present public assistance system, in which welfare departments have a measure of discretion over the amount of assistance given to recipients (and seem to recipients to have even more power) and in which caseworkers possess and exercise the right to withhold support checks for a variety of reasons. Advice, counsel, information, and teaching offered by those who control the means of survival, even when the two are not actively linked, will often be interpreted as commands. Paradoxically, such a system is as likely to result in resistance to good advice (owing to the love-hate relationship involved in dependency) as in the unquestioning acceptance of bad advice. It reinforces those attitudes of dependency that are such crucial barriers to personal and economic development. Obviously, local welfare departments should continue to function and to provide a wide range of services; but the distribution of income-maintenance grants, their major and best-known function, should be given to a federal agency.

The First Three Desiderata. It is time now to return to the first three desiderata of a comprehensive, workable, and just welfare system. These are, once again, an adequate floor to the level of living, a cut-off point for assistance, and an incentive to earn.

Any income-maintenance plan should provide at least a basic, adequate level of living. A floor to the level of living should be established, and no one should be permitted to fall below it. We shall refer to this below as the "floor" desideratum.

Establishing such a floor requires a more sophisticated approach than defining a poverty line. The latter is a device for determining how many people are poor; determining, in general, the characteristics of the poor; and getting a geographic fix on poverty so that neighborhood antipoverty programs can be set up when they are needed, the eligibility of school districts for aid can be ascertained, and so on. But determining how many people are poor amounts to determining the level of living below which the people of the United States will not permit their fellow citizens to fall. According to desideratum 4, above, this level must be fairly high—high enough to interrupt vicious circles of poverty. And according to desideratum 6, this level should be the same throughout the nation.

We now come to our second desideratum, a cut-off point. No one whose nonwelfare income is above the floor established should receive assistance. We shall refer to this below as the "no-leakage" desideratum. It is, in effect, a criterion of efficiency: A program that spends a great deal of money on a nontarget population must provide relatively less to the target population dollar of tax revenue. Of the existing programs, those designed for the nonpoor violate this leakage requirement far more often than those for the poor.

Our third desideratum for a welfare system is an incentive to earn. Thus those who earn money should fare better than those who do not. Those who are receiving assistance and who also work should be able to keep some fraction of their earnings. We shall refer to this below as the "incentive" desideratum. As we saw in Chapter 4, work incentives are related to the effective tax rate on earned income, which is presently 100 percent for most public assistance recipients and 66 2/3 percent for those in the WIN program. High effective rates may create a welfare trap. However, there is some doubt as to the importance of effective tax rates in influencing the work orientations of the poor people. The issue is by no means settled. Even if very high effective tax rates do not seriously impair work incentives when adequate jobs are available, this requirement still holds. After all, community standards of equity hold that those who work should, in general, earn more than those who do not. Moreover, no income-maintenance scheme will enjoy much popular support if it is viewed as a program mainly or wholly for the totally dependent, as opposed to the working poor and near poor. When there is an effective tax rate of 100 percent, there is a sharp dividing line between those who are eligible for assistance—people below a given income level, who will tend to be mainly nonworkers—and those who are not. When the effective tax rate is less than 100 percent, instead of a sharp dividing line between eligibles and ineligibles, there is a range over which benefits gradually drop off as earned income increases.

The first three desiderata of a welfare system are being discussed together because they are inconsistent. It is *impossible* to design an income-maintenance scheme that simultaneously achieves all three. The best that can be done is to incorporate two—any two—of these desiderata.

The systematic relationship between welfare, total income, and the cut-off point for welfare can be expressed as follows:

$$(1) \ Y = F + E - t(E\text{-}B)$$

$$(2) \ W = Y - E$$

$$(3) \ C = B + \frac{F}{t}$$

where Y is the recipient's total income from all sources; E is earned income; W is the welfare or income-maintenance payment; F is the income floor (the minimum income that would be received by a family with no earned income); B is the basic amount, if any, which can be earned with no reduction in welfare benefits; C is the cut-off point, or the amount of earned income that makes a recipient ineligible for welfare benefits; and t is the average effective tax rate, that is, the fraction of earned income the recipient is not entitled to retain.

For example, under the proposed Family Assistance Plan, which will be discussed later, B is \$60 per month and t is .50. Suppose a family is entitled to \$133 in monthly benefits (F). Equation 1 tells us that if the family *earned* \$100, its total income would be \$133 plus \$100, minus .5 of \$40 (\$100 − \$60), or \$213. If it had earned income of \$200, Y would be \$263. Equation 2 tells us how much of that total income is welfare benefits—\$113 and \$63 respectively in the two cases just mentioned. (Notice that as earned income rises by \$100, total income rises by exactly one-half that amount, as a t of .50 implies). Equation 3 tells us how high income can go before the family loses all benefits. In this case, C is \$326. If the family earned \$326 per month, it would receive no welfare benefits at all. (If it earned just \$1 less, or \$325, it would be entitled to a total income of \$325.50, or a monthly income from welfare of just 50 cents.)

Presumably, once income rose above C, the family would begin paying regular income taxes.

It should now be clear why our first three desiderata of an ideal welfare system are inconsistent. Number 1 demands an income floor adequate to meet basic needs. Number 2 says that no one whose income is above that floor should receive any assistance. This means, in effect, that the cut-off point, C, must be the same as the floor. This is possible only if B is zero and t is 100 percent. Such a situation, of course, provides no incentive to work, our third desideratum.

It is, however, possible to combine *any two* of the first three desiderata. The following combinations are possible.

A Floor Plus No Leakage. Combining the first two desiderata gives us a program similar to traditional public assistance programs and to a variety of other poor people's programs already discussed. This combination seems best-adapted to programs for the permanently dependent, where incentives are superfluous. One hesitates, however, to label any population "permanently dependent."

No Leakage Plus Incentives. The implication of this combination is that no one whose earned income is above that needed for a basic, adequate level of living can receive benefits, but that someone below that level is not necessarily brought up to it. To take a simple example, suppose it is determined that a four-person family needs $4,800 for a basic, adequate income; and suppose, to satisfy desideratum 3, that an effective tax rate of 50 percent is chosen. Then a program might be developed which provided a floor of $2,400—far less than the adequate level—and which allowed recipients to keep half their earned income. Thus the cut-off point would be $4,800, satisfying the leakage desideratum. Friedman's version of the negative income tax and President Nixon's proposed Family Assistance Plan both resemble this combination.

A Floor Plus Incentives. This would vary the case immediately above by providing for an income floor instead of a cut-off point that equalled the basic, adequate level. In the preceding example, the floor would be $4,800, and the cut-off point would be $9,600.

A cut-off point of $9,600 may seem very high; but welfare benefits become very low—amounting to only a few dollars—as the cut-off point is approached. Some welfare programs for the nonpoor—especially those hidden in the tax laws—have no cut-off point whatever.

We have assumed in our examples that t remains constant, but it could vary. For example, t could be fairly low at low levels of earned income in order to encourage poor people to seek employment and get them accustomed to the nonmonetary rewards of work. The disincentive of higher rates as income rises might well be offset by ambition and work-connected satisfactions. In equations 1 and 3, t need not be constant; in fact, it can be interpreted as the *average* tax rate, over the relevant range of incomes in 1 and over all incomes in 3.

One of the first three desiderata must be sacrificed, and the one with the lowest priority is 2 (no leakage). Both the floor and the incentive desiderata can be used to fight poverty by providing enough money to break the vicious circles that keep people poor and by encouraging them to earn more. Both are also related to equity. The second desideratum relates, by contrast, mainly to economy.

A floor-incentive combination costs the most, however. And it has one important characteristic. It is an income-redistribution scheme which, by transferring money from those with incomes above *C* to those earning less, assists not only the dependent poor, but the working poor, the near poor, and possibly, to some extent, the lower middle class.

Major Income-Maintenance Proposals

We shall now examine four prominent proposals for the reform or replacement of large parts, or all, of the existing welfare system—the universal income supplement, the negative income tax, children's allowances, and the Family Assistance Plan—to see which of the eight desiderata just discussed they provide. The results of this examination are summarized in Table 5-2.

A Universal Income Supplement. A universal income supplement (UIS) was proposed in 1969 by the President's Commission on Income Maintenance, a body appointed by President Johnson in 1968 and one of a series of presidential and congressional commissions—on riots (the Kerner Commission), on crime, on pornography, on marijuana—whose findings have been either disparaged or ignored.

The Commission proposed a national system of federally financed welfare benefits of $750 per adult and $450 per child as a floor, with a reduction in benefits of 50 cents for every dollar of earned income. Thus it would provide a $2,400 income floor for a family of four. A family with no other income would be left below the poverty line. Instead of various categories of assistance, there would be one universal program for all.

A Negative Income Tax. First proposed by Milton Friedman, the negative income tax plan, in effect, extends the concept of an income tax so that, below a certain income, it becomes "negative." (That is, it turns into a transfer payment.) This scheme would pay a family half of the difference between its income and the poverty-line income. In Table 5-2, we have assumed the poverty line to be $4,500 for a family of four. Like the universal income supplement, the negative income tax would leave a great many families below the poverty line. It would, however, separate financial assistance from social services, since it would be administered by the Internal Revenue Service.

Children's Allowances. Though children's allowances are often proposed as an antipoverty measure, they are an extremely inefficient device. They entail payments to the parents of all children, regardless of

TABLE 5 – 2

**A Comparison of the Universal Income Supplement, the Negative
Income Tax, Children's Allowances, and the Family Assistance Plan**

Characteristics	Universal Income Supplement	Negative Income Tax	Children's Allowances	Family Assistance Plan
Income floor (annual benefit with no earned income)	$2,400	$2,250	$1,200	$1,600
Cut-off point for benefits	4,800	4,500	none	3,920
Effective tax rate	.5	.5	0	.5
Amount of earned income disregarded in computing benefits	0	0	all	720
Program is non-categorical and comprehensive	yes	yes	no	no
Coverage is certain	yes	yes	yes	yes
Family is not discouraged from remaining intact	yes	yes	yes	yes
National standards for eligibility and benefits	yes	yes	yes	no
100 percent federal financing	yes	yes	yes	no
Separate administration of transfers and services	yes	yes	yes	probably

NOTE: The description of the characteristics of these programs is based on Theodore R.
Marmor's *Poverty Policy* (Chicago: Aldine, 1971). The figures are those for a four-person
family consisting of two adults and two children. In the case of children's allowances, children are assumed to be of preschool age. In the case of the Family Assistance Plan, the floor
and cut-off point exclude state supplements and food stamps. The figures for the negative
income tax assume a poverty line of $4,500.

family income. Thus in order to get money into the hands of poor families, it is necessary to give it to nonpoor ones as well, thus reducing the funds available for the poor. Some versions, however, couple the proposal for children's allowances with one to abolish the children's personal dependency exemption. The net effect of these two changes would be a transfer from high- to low-income families. The version considered in Table 5-2 is that proposed by Alvin Schorr, which provides for $50 a month per preschool child. (School-age children are not covered.) This version would also achieve something of a transfer to large, young families.

The Family Assistance Plan. The Family Assistance Plan (FAP) was first proposed by the Nixon administration in 1969 and was rejected by Congress in 1972. Unlike the universal income supplement, the negative income tax, and children's allowance, which represent major departures from present welfare programs, the FAP represents a reform of the existing public assistance structure, mainly AFDC. Since incremental change is the typical progress by which the American welfare system has developed, something like the FAP will probably, ultimately, be adopted.

The original FAP proposal provided benefits of $500 each for the first two persons in a family and $300 for each additional person, regardless of age. Thus a four-person family would receive $1,600, an amount that would leave them substantially below the poverty line. The administration, recognizing this, attempted to "sweeten" its proposal with an added $800 subsidy via food stamps. (However, we have already seen that food stamps are not voluntarily used by most poor families.) The first $720 of earned or other income would be disregarded in computing benefits; beyond that, each $1 earned would reduce welfare benefits by 50 cents. Thus the cut-off point for aid would be an income of $3,920.

The FAP has four major advantages over the AFDC program. The first is a set of national standards for eligibility and benefits. However, at the time the proposal was made, thirty states were paying more in benefits than the proposed levels, so some state supplements would be necessary to maintain current benefits. Thus the national standards actually provide national minimums rather than uniform benefit levels. This is an improvement, but it is not ideal. (The same situation obtains under Supplementary Security Income.) The national minimums would be a major improvement only for 20 states. (The FAP proposal also included a federal subsidy toward the state supplements, constructed so as to guarantee that if the states continued their previous levels of support, their costs would be no more than 90 percent of what they were paying before.) The second advantage of the FAP is that families with fathers present are eligible. Thus families would not be encouraged to break up, and some families previously eligible only for General Assistance would become eligible for family assistance. But single persons and married persons without children would remain ineligible, and there would still be a great many persons who would be, as now, left out of all federally supported or aided programs.

The third advantage of the FAP is that it reduces the effective tax rate to 50 percent. Thus it would supplement the incomes of the working poor, as well as aiding totally dependent families.

Finally, eligibility for family assistance would be determined initially by obtaining a declaration of need from the applicant and later by reviews and spot checks. This would eliminate the present demeaning and complex application procedure.

Both the administrative supporters of the plan and its critics have made much of the "work requirement," but its importance is probably exaggerated. Able-bodied adults must accept a job or, if they lack suitable skills, job training, unless they (1) are ill, incapacitated, or aged; (2) are the "caretaker relative" (usually the mother) of a child under six; (3) are a mother in a family where the father is present; (4) are the caretaker of an ill household member; or (5) are already a full-time worker. This requirement represents a change in policy in that it requires all mothers in fatherless homes to work unless there are preschool children in the home. This is one reason why the National Welfare Rights Organization opposed the FAP. But the NWRO seemed to overstate the penalty for refusing to work, which was not the loss of all benefits, but the loss, in effect, of the refusing parent's share. Assistance in behalf of the children would still be provided. But the penalty was more than nominal.

Family assistance payments under the plan would be administered at the national level by the Social Security Administration, and separate from social services. States and localities could supplement these payments, if necessary, through existing social welfare departments; or they could contract with the Social Security Administration to administer these payments as well. Since the latter is the more probable outcome, we have said in Table 5-2 that the FAP would "probably" separate transfers from services.

The Family Assistance Plan, then, would have been an improvement in most respects, a step backward in a few. But in spite of a great deal of talk about radical reform, it would have done little to change the fundamental character of poor people's welfare in America. Congress' failure to enact even these changes demonstrates how far the United States is from meaningful welfare reform.

REFERENCES

For two approaches to a statement of income strategy, see A. Dale Tussing, "Anti-Poverty Policy for the Seventies," in Robert B. Carson, ed., *The American Economy in Conflict* (Lexington, Mass.: Heath, 1971); and the congressional testimony of Daniel P. Moynihan, reprinted in *New York Times Magazine* (February 5, 1967). The quotes on pp. 146-47 are from Leonard Goodwin, *Do the Poor Want to Work?* (Washington, D.C.: Brookings Institution, 1972). See also the *Summary Reports, The New Jersey Graduated Work Incentive Experiment* (Washington, D.C.: U.S. Department of Health, Education and Welfare, 1973).

Much of our discussion of public assistance is taken from reviews found in the President's Commission on Income Maintenance Programs, *Background Papers* (Washington, D.C.: Government Printing Office, c. 1969). Data are also taken from various issues of *Social Security Bulletin* and *Welfare in Review*. Another extremely valuable source, especially as regards the history of policy, is Gilbert Y. Steiner, *The State of Welfare* (Washington, D.C.: Brookings Institution, 1971). Chapter 5 relies heavily on Steiner's work. See also Steiner's earlier work, *Social Insecurity: The Politics of Welfare* (Chicago: Rand McNally, 1966).

The proposal for urban land reform is found in, and some of the language is taken from, A. Dale Tussing, "No Vacancy in the Little Boxes," *Nickel Review* (October 9-22, 1968). Permission to reprint this material is gratefully acknowledged.

The Kerner Commission Report's formal title is National Advisory Commission on Civil Disorders, *Report*. The Bantam edition, with an introduction by Tom Wicker, appeared in 1968.

Milton Friedman first proposed his negative income tax in *Capitalism and Freedom* (Chicago: University of Chicago Press, 1962). Theobald's version of the guaranteed income plan appears in *Guaranteed Income: Next Step in Economic Evolution* (New York: Doubleday, 1965). For a thorough and scholarly review of these and other proposals, see Christopher Green, *Negative Taxes and the Poverty Problem* (Washington, D.C.: Brookings Institution, 1967).

The income-maintenance proposals discussed in the latter part of the chapter, including Alvin Schorr's version of children's allowances, are based on versions in Theodore R. Marmor, ed., *Poverty Policy* (Chicago: Aldine, 1971). This is an excellent compendium of major income-maintenance proposals.

An interesting, if somewhat self-serving, account of the origins, development, and ultimate defeat of President Nixon's Family Assistance Plan appears in Daniel P. Moynihan's *The Politics of a Guaranteed Income* (New York: Random House, 1973). Moynihan, nominally a Democrat, was the principal author and proponent of the bill within the Nixon administration.

6

Antipoverty Action

There are a number of ways of categorizing antipoverty strategies. There is, first, a distinction, discussed in previous chapters, between preventative policies, concerned with keeping the nonpoor from becoming poor, and curative policies, concerned with helping make poor people nonpoor. Preventative policies have already been discussed.

Curative policies, to succeed, must increase the incomes of the poor, generally through income transfers or new employment opportunities. Thus they can be further categorized as *income strategies* or *employment strategies*.

Almost all approaches to fighting poverty fit into one of these two categories. For instance, *educational strategies* that seek to raise the incomes of the poor by making them more employable and raising their market value are basically a form of employment strategy.

The major antipoverty strategies are listed in Table 6-1. As we have noted in previous chapters, the primary social device for keeping individual, family, and social calamities from creating vicious circles of poverty is the welfare system, broadly conceived. And as we have also seen earlier, there exists not only a vicious circle of poverty, but also a "benign circle of nonpoverty" perpetuated by superior educational opportunities, better health facilities, greater political power, and more even-handed treatment by the legal system. Thus there are essentially two strategies for preventing poverty from developing among the nonpoor: the establishment of a welfare system and the reinforcement of existing benign cycles of causation.

In this chapter, however, our concern is with curing rather than preventing poverty. Since income strategies have already been discussed in Chapter 5, we shall concentrate here on the remaining, nonwelfare

TABLE 6 - 1

Antipoverty Strategies

Preventative strategies
    Establishment of a welfare system
    Reinforcement of benign cycles of causation
Curative strategies
    Income strategies (income transfers)
    Employment strategies
        Direct (job-creation strategies such as increasing
            employment opportunities through a tight full-employment
            policy, government employment, or subsidized
            private employment)
        Indirect (strategies for increasing the employability,
            productivity, etc. of the poor)
            Educational programs
            Relocation programs
            Health and nutrition programs
            Child-care programs
            Minimum wage laws
    Organizing strategies

.approaches. We shall focus, in particular, on direct-employment strategies, or *job-creation strategies*; on education and training; and on organizing strategies. This last group of strategies, as the name suggests, entails efforts to organize the poor. They are not really an alternative to income or employment strategies, but an adjunct to them. They are treated separately mainly because the means employed to achieve various goals are different.

Before turning to a discussion of specific antipoverty strategies, we shall look briefly at two prior issues: the implications of the vicious-circle concept for antipoverty policy and the implications of the four main elements in Chapter 3's social model (class structure, isolation, individualism, and racism) with respect to that policy.

VICIOUS CIRCLES AND ANTIPOVERTY POLICY

The fact that chronic poverty involves a cycle of cumulative causation means that the distinctions between causes and effects, or symptoms and fundamental causes, are often blurred. Chains of causation are likely to be complex, with many interdependent elements. Because of the large number of elements involved in vicious circles—income, motivation, education, health, crime, racial prejudice, and the like—they can be very hard to break, particularly where poverty has persisted for a long time. It is extremely unlikely that a change in any one variable, except possibly income itself, will interrupt the cycle of poverty for a substantial number of today's poor. Because of this, antipoverty programs that attack only one problem at a time are much less likely to succeed than those that attack a large number of interrelated problems.

THE SOCIAL MODEL REVISITED

In Chapter 3, we developed a social model to explain not only whether and why a society will produce a chronically poor subgroup, but also what forms poverty will take and how the society's welfare system will develop. The model is not really intended as a basis for policy recommendations, since, to a large extent, policy is endogenous. It reflects and contributes to conditions in the model. The existence of a given type of class structure, an ideology of individualism, and prejudice, in particular, influences the kinds of policies adopted. The isolation of certain groups also affects social policies, but not, as a rule, so strongly. Let us look again, however, at these four elements, this time to determine when, if ever, they are likely to be affected by, rather than affect, government policy.

CLASS STRUCTURE

It is unusual in the extreme for a government seriously to undertake, as a policy objective, a change in the fundamental class structure of a nation. Government policies generally *reflect* the existing class structure. Some policies may inadvertently influence the social order, but there are few circumstances in which the government is likely to mount an attack on the status quo. Sweeping changes might, of course, be instituted immediately after a revolution, when those represented by the new government have political and military power but have not yet gained a socioeconomic upper hand. Or, a political party representing a minority faction that has come to power by gaining a plurality in a multiparty election may seek to convert its temporary political control into a more permanent power base.

INDIVIDUALISM

Like class structure, the individualist ideology—or, for that matter, *any* dominant social ideology that affects the distribution of income and the socioeconomic order—is hard to change by official fiat. It is hard to imagine any government deliberately attempting to alter the dominant ideology of a nation except, as we have noted, during the aftermath of a revolution or during a temporary period of political ascendancy of a normally weak subgroup. What is more, such an effort at state thought-control and official indoctrination would be objectionable on many grounds.

When an ideology is a hindrance to social progress, when it is largely a myth, or when it is obsolete (i.e., when it relates to *past* needs and problems), it may be more appropriate for dissenters, rather than the government, to attempt to bring about ideological change. In such a case, educational efforts on two fronts are indicated. Members of subordinate groups—the poor, racial minorities, and the like—may need help to overcome such problems as group self-hatred, self-blame, and self-pity that are byproducts of the dominant ideology. Members of dominant groups will need to be shown the myths, fallacies, and obsolete elements in the current philosophy.

PREJUDICE

Like class structure and individualism, prejudice, where it is dominant, will be reflected in the fundamental structure of social and economic relationships. It has come to be official policy in the United States, at virtually all levels of government, that racism is wrong and that its manifestations are to be eradicated. This official policy is reflected both in court decisions and in legislation. Civil rights decisions and legislation—particularly those relating to discrimination in employment—constitute antipoverty action as well. This is because, to the extent that discrimination contributes to poverty, civil rights action fights poverty.

It is not impossible, then, for public policy to eliminate some of the surface manifestations of prejudice. But it is less likely that policy can or will deal with the sort of unconscious and rationalized racism that seems to lie just below the surface in discussions of busing, quality education, law and order, and the like. President Nixon's statements about busing, for example, indicate that although the government may oppose, as a matter of policy, such open and official forms of racism as dual school systems, it is unlikely to act counter to the wishes of the dominant group in the electorate with respect to less official manifestations of racism.

ISOLATION

Of the four major elements in our model, isolation is probably the most amenable to change by official action. It is the least attitudinal element and the least tied to fundamental power balances and economic relationships. Wiping out pockets of isolation is not a revolutionary action in the sense that changing the class structure, the fundamental ideology, or the racial views of a nation would be. But the problems of isolation are often profound and difficult to overcome.

In the United States economic problems due to geographic and economic isolation exist largely in "depressed areas" and among reservation Indians. Remarkably similar controversies have developed over what sort of action the government should take in each case.

The key question in both cases is whether an effort should be made to revitalize the area, to attract industry, to improve transportation, and so on or whether, instead, an effort should be made to retrain the population and relocate it in more economically viable regions.

In both cases, when economic considerations alone are weighed, it is probably better to move people out than to try to bring industry in. In the case of depressed areas, the general rule is to consider efforts to revitalize the region only if it contains some natural resources or reasonably good capital facilities. The term *capital facilities* includes not only factories and manufacturing equipment, but also homes, schools, churches, sewers, and the like. If these facilities are in good shape, it may be wise to make an effort to revitalize the region; moving the population out, after all, would require building such facilities elsewhere. In most depressed areas, however, these facilities are run down and need replacing anyway.

In the case of Indian reservations, economic analysts are not optimistic about revitalization. Most reservations were never economically viable. They are remote from markets and services, they lack adequate transportation facilities and natural resources, and some Indian institutions such as common ownership of land (which makes it hard to get mortgage loans) do not match non-Indian institutions and hence create legal and credit problems. The fact that most reservations are remote and bereft of needed resources should hardly be surprising, since the Indians have, historically, been placed on land that, in most cases, no one else wanted. When Indian land turned out to be valuable, it was taken away.

But although narrow economic considerations point to moving people out, there are other considerations that militate in the opposite direction. To give up on the economic development of an area and to attempt to relocate its population elsewhere is in effect to abandon a part of the nation that has an identity and a history. Sometimes doing so means leaving the land scarred and damaged, as it has been by strip mining and clear-cut lumbering. Relocating the entire population of an Indian reservation can mean the death of a nation, a culture, a language, and a heritage reaching back for hundreds or thousands of years. Many Indians put the survival of their nation ahead of economic development and have no wish to see the reservations broken up.

There are also political considerations in dealing with poor areas. Congressmen, state legislators, governors, and other elected officials do not like to see their constituents moved out and their region pronounced mortally ill. Senators and representatives get plenty of credit for new industry and government spending in their district; they get no plaudits for population declines (which, through reapportionment, may even lose them their districts). The same may be true of tribal presidents, chiefs, and councils, whose power and status are likely to be increased by influxes of industry and money and reduced by the loss of population.

Three federal programs aimed at solving the problems of isolated areas are the Economic Development Administration (EDA), a successor to the Area Redevelopment Administration (ARA); the Employment Assistance Program of the Bureau of Indian Affairs (BIA); and the Appalachian Regional Development Program.

Of the three, the oldest is the Employment Assistance Program, which dates back to 1952 and is the BIA's second most costly program. (The first is an education program.) Some 10,000 Indian families a year are helped by this program, which is basically a relocation effort. It provides counseling for Indians at the reservation, gives them vocational training, provides them with transportation, gives them a subsistence income in their new homes, helps them to get a job, and provides counseling after relocation. Between one-quarter and one-half of these families ultimately return to the reservation, but even the returnees seem to earn more than they would have without the program.

It is perhaps significant that the only major program dedicated to moving people out rather than industry in is directed at American Indians, who have a long history of involuntary relocation.

The EDA was established in 1965, to replace the ARA, established in 1961. Both were created to attract new industry and permanent jobs to areas with high unemployment or chronically low incomes. In some cases Indian reservations are eligible for help from the EDA. Hence poverty on the reservation is being attacked both by moving people out and by trying to move jobs in.

In order to attract industry to depressed areas, the government provides low-interest, and often high-risk, loans; it trains and retrains local workers to meet industry's needs; it provides some technical assistance; and it sometimes gives priority on government contracts to new or expanded firms in these areas. Unfortunately, the program has had very few unqualified successes. In many cases, plants that opened with government assistance or contract priorities closed down once the government funds ran out or the contract was completed.

The EDA differs somewhat from the old ARA in that it introduces regional planning and cooperation through multistate commissions. One region, Appalachia, has its own separate legislation, the Appalachia Regional Development Act (1965). In Appalachia, about 60 percent of the expenditures have been on highway development, a fact that testifies to the importance of isolation in explaining the region's poverty, at least in the eyes of economic policy-makers.

The most powerful and dependable way of overcoming regional depression and isolation is to maintain full employment in the nation as a whole, something the United States has generally failed to do for two decades. Without action to expand the total amount of employment in the nation, programs such as those just discussed can only try to shift jobs from prosperous areas to slack ones. Such a task is not only difficult, but of questionable value. Shifting unemployment and poverty from one area to another hardly seems an appropriate national goal.

THE PRINCIPAL ANTIPOVERTY STRATEGIES

We now turn to an examination of the major curative strategies, other than income strategies. We will concentrate on job-creation strategies, educational strategies, and organizing strategies, though several other approaches will also be covered briefly.

JOB-CREATION STRATEGIES

Few antipoverty policies can be successful in a slack economy, where there is substantial unemployment. And although many programs may seem successful in a buoyant, full-employment economy, it is often the underlying growth and prosperity, rather than the antipoverty programs, that are responsible for the reduction of poverty. Hence the adoption of a full-employment policy is the most important single action that can be taken against poverty.

It is for this reason that war has traditionally been an occasion for the rapid reduction of poverty in America. It is not military hostilities themselves, but the tight labor markets associated with war, that have this effect. World War II in particular, World War I, and to some extent the Korean War were associated with large movements of the rural, mainly Southern poor, both black and white, into expanding urban, industrial areas; with significant improvements in the occupational status of these groups; and with rapid reductions in poverty. The Vietnam War, by contrast, caused a boom only during the early years of rapid military buildup (roughly 1965-68). For the remainder of the war, the United States had a slack economy, with unemployment rates remaining above 5 percent. As Figure 1-1 showed, poverty declined fairly rapidly during the first of these two periods, and not at all from 1968 through 1971.

Virtually all poverty is explained by employment problems of one kind or another. "Employment problems," in this context, include unemployment, intermittent employment, part-time employment, employment at poverty-level wages, and a failure on the part of some people even to seek work because of prolonged and seemingly hopeless unemployment (the "discouraged worker" syndrome).

Employment problems are, in general, the result of either *aggregate-demand* factors or *structural* factors. This distinction between the root causes of unemployment is fundamental and important. Unemployment is said to be caused by aggregate-demand factors when total spending by all parts of the economy—households, businesses, and government—is not sufficient to generate jobs for all the people who want to work. It is said to be due to structural factors when the number of job openings equals or exceeds the number of unemployed persons. Structural unemployment may exist for any one of a number of reasons: because the unemployed don't know about the jobs that are available; because they live too far away from where the jobs are; because they lack the skills, abilities, or academic credentials required by employers;

because the wages offered by employers are lower than the unemployed are willing or able (because of minimum wage laws, union contracts, etc.) to accept; and so on.

There is a relationship between these two types of unemployment and the two sets of theories of poverty discussed in Chapter 3. Generic explanations of poverty, it will be recalled, involve *economywide* problems, because of which the economy fails to provide nonpoverty incomes to all its members. Inadequate aggregate demand is the chief generic explanation of poverty in industrialized, developed economies.

Case poverty and structural unemployment are also closely linked. Case poverty results from characteristics of the poor that make it impossible for them to hold regular, nonpoverty jobs or to receive adequate incomes from other sources, even though there is no overall deficiency in demand. Structural unemployment can be a cause, then, of case poverty.

Obviously, the type of policy needed to combat employment problems will vary depending on whether they are caused by demand or structural problems. In general, one deals with aggregate-demand problems by creating jobs and with structural problems by finding ways to match available workers with open jobs (through placement programs, relocation, education and training, etc.).

Structural explanations of unemployment and other employment problems seem to be quite popular, particularly among those who are not economists. Moreover, the lack of an adequate education, a leading structural explanation of unemployment, also appears to be a favorite explanation of poverty itself. This accounts for the fact that the vast majority of federal antipoverty programs stress education.

In spite of its popularity, we should be skeptical of the structural explanation, for three reasons.

First, it attributes employment problems to defects in the unemployed. This is not, of course, altogether impossible. But when, in the past, a significant amount of unemployment was blamed on the unemployed, this explanation frequently turned out to be incorrect. It may be hard to believe today, but even the massive unemployment of the 1930s was once blamed on the inadequacies of the unemployed.

Second, structural explanations tend to be self-serving when they are offered by educators, manpower specialists, and the like. Not only do such theories make jobs for these people, but they make them feel socially important and useful.

And third, structural explanations have had relatively little support among professional economists, who tend, to a greater or lesser degree, to be aggregationists (supporters of the "inadequate-aggregate-demand" theory) rather than structuralists. Indeed, the major controversy among economists has been between the fiscalists (neo-Keynesians) and the neomonetarists (Friedmanites), who represent competing schools of thought among aggregationists, rather than between structuralists and aggregationists. There are, however, a number of structuralists among competent economists.

The operation of the labor market should make structural unemployment a short-term problem at most. The market has, after all, two sides. Employers do not set job requirements in a vacuum, but are influenced by the skills, abilities, and location of workers.

This is not to say that everyone who wants to be, for instance, a schoolteacher can expect to have a claim on that particular job. It would be too much to ask of any labor market that anyone could have whatever job he or she wanted, irrespective of what goods society wanted and of the state of technology. But the existence of a surplus of schoolteachers sets off forces that change the skills required for other occupations and provide other employment for the erstwhile schoolteachers. It also sets off other forces that reduce the number of future would-be schoolteachers.

For short periods of a year or two, a structural disequilibrium, and hence unemployment, may exist in particular occupations. Redundant electronics engineers released from aerospace firms may not be able to adapt their skills readily to other jobs. But this problem is likely to affect those with narrow fields of specialization, not those who are undereducated and unskilled.

Whenever labor has been truly scarce in the United States, as in wartime, employers have hired the unskilled and trained them. This approach has an advantage over antipoverty manpower training programs in that workers are trained for actual jobs and equipped with skills that are actually needed.

The relative frequency of aggregate and structural causes of unemployment is unsettled, because it is hard to tell them apart in practice. When large numbers of unfilled jobs exist in economies where unemployment is also high, one would infer that structural problems exist. But it is virtually impossible to measure—or even to define adequately—"unfilled jobs." So many employers have positions they would fill if the "right man" came along, or if they could get a certain contract, or if other conditions obtained that the notion of unfilled jobs is very fuzzy indeed. There are a few usually reliable rules of thumb, however, which can help us decide the aggregate vs. structural question.

—*Relatively high levels of unemployment (5 percent or above) usually mean an aggregate-demand problem.* Since the United States has experienced such high levels more or less continuously since 1957 (with the exception of the Vietnam-buildup years, 1965-68), one would have to conclude that the country has something of a chronic aggregate-demand problem.

—*Unemployment and inflation together imply some degree of structural problems.* But the structural problems may be only transitional. For example, when there are rapid shifts in the *kinds* of goods produced in an economy (such as at the start or end of a war), the inability of businesses and workers to adjust as fast as spending is able to shift can account for both unemployment and inflation.

An expansionary fiscal policy (more government spending, perhaps combined with lower taxes to encourage more private spending) can help to overcome aggregate-demand problems. So, too, can an expansionary monetary policy (increasing the money supply, which usually means lower interest rates and generally easier borrowing terms), though perhaps less dependably. In both cases, the goal is to increase aggregate demand. It is *also* possible to overcome structural problems in this way, but it will take longer than overcoming aggregate-demand problems and may result in more inflation.

On the other hand, it is *impossible* for structural solutions (such as education and training programs) to overcome aggregate-demand problems. This point must be emphasized because of a common confusion. When a recession or chronic slack periods throw people out of work, the unemployed are likely to be mainly those with the least education. For this reason, many people are tempted to blame unemployment on inadequate education and call for new education and training programs. They confuse the factors explaining the *distribution* of unemployment with those explaining unemployment.

Direct government employment of the unemployed can deal equally effectively with both kinds of unemployment. It can create jobs when there are not enough jobs because of aggregate-demand problems. And although it cannot match unemployed workers with job openings when, for structural reasons, the two do not match, it can at least make other jobs for people.

Structural techniques are best adapted to dealing with the unemployment that remains in a high-demand, full-employment economy. One illustration of a structural program that worked much better in a buoyant than in a slack economy is JOBS, or Job Opportunities in the Business Sector. Under this program, hard-core unemployed poor persons are hired by private firms and given on-the-job training (OJT) and work experience. The firms, in return, may receive a federal subsidy. (See Table 6-2, later in the chapter, for a list of federally funded or subsidized training programs.)

JOBS was introduced in 1968, when the unemployment rate was at a fifteen-year low (3.6 percent). In that year and the next (when unemployment hit 3.5 percent), there was a labor shortage in many areas and employers gladly hired and trained the hard-core unemployed, especially when federal subsidies were available. Enrollments peaked in 1970, when unemployment began to rise, and fell steadily during 1971, when unemployment rose to 5.9 percent. A structural program, it could not contend with inadequate aggregate demand.

One of the most vigorous advocates of a tight full-employment policy is Professor Hyman Minsky, who wants an excess demand for workers. According to Minsky,

the war against poverty cannot be taken seriously as long as the Administration and the Congress tolerate a five percent unemployment rate. . . . Only if there are more jobs than available workers over a broad spectrum of occupations and locations can we hope to make a dent on poverty by way of income from employment. . . . The war against poverty must not depend solely, or even primarily, upon changing people, but it must be directed toward changing the system. However, the changes required are not those that the traditional radicals envisage. Rather they involve a commitment to the maintenance of tight full employment and the adjustment of institutions, so that the gains from full employment are not offset by undue inflation and the perpetuation of obsolete practices. . . .

Tight full employment not only will eliminate that poverty which is solely due to unemployment, but, by setting off market processes which tend to raise low wages faster than high wages, it will in time greatly diminish the poverty due to low incomes from jobs. In addition, by drawing additional workers into the labor force, tight full employment will increase the number of families with more than one worker. As a result, families now in or close to poverty will move well away from it.

One could draw up an impressive list of benefits that would accrue from a policy of tight full employment. Not all of them are limited to poor people alone. For example:

—The unemployed would get jobs, total output (GNP) would increase, public assistance and unemployment rolls would decline, and standards of living would rise.
—Employers, if they could not find exactly the skills and capacities they sought in employees, would either tailor the jobs to match the people available or provide on-the-job training.
—Job rationing via the denial of work to those who, for example, had arrest records or did not have high school diplomas would break down, and only criteria related to the work to be done would be used as a basis for hiring.
—Wage rates would rise in the lowest-wage industries, where pay rates are currently held down by the weak bargaining position of the workers.
—People could move out of poor, isolated areas into prosperous ones. More employers would send personnel people out on recruiting trips and help with relocation.
—Fewer families would break up because of the prolonged unemployment of the father.
—Mothers who wished to do so could go to work as second earners, possibly raising the family income beyond the point where poverty is imminent.
—The availability of jobs for qualified persons would motivate some children to work harder in school. On the other hand, no one who did not want to continue school would be forced by a lack of job opportunities to do so.
—More responsible positions would become available to women, youth, racial minorities, and older people. People who today feel useless and a burden on society would instead feel needed.
—Fewer persons would turn to crime for income, status, and a chance of

advancement. This would be especially true in the case of ex-convicts, whose inability to find jobs is the major reason so many return to crime.

The foregoing is not mere speculation. Precisely such results occurred in wartime tight labor markets. During wartime, of course, the absorption into the armed services of several million men, primarily nonpoor (since the poor had extremely high failure rates on physical and mental examinations), caused a dramatic reduction in the civilian labor force. The peacetime effects of full employment would be slightly less dramatic, but even so, powerful and permanent.

Various beneficial side effects might also occur. The attitudes of many workers, both union and non-union and in all regions, are influenced by the fear, sometimes unconscious but always present, of unemployment. This fear influences their attitudes toward reduced defense spending and deescalation of the cold war; toward antipollution efforts, especially if businesses threaten to shut down when faced with orders to stop polluting; and toward programs to train and employ teenagers, the poor, and the otherwise disadvantaged. The long-run consequences of eliminating the fear of unemployment could profoundly alter America.

Of course, a full-employment policy would not be decisive in all these areas; its contribution would be large in some cases, small in others. But any policy or program that can be expected to make, at one time, a significant contribution to lowering unemployment, increasing GNP, reducing poverty, undermining "credentialism" and other dysfunctional employment tests, increasing family mobility, reducing the number of broken homes, advancing civil rights and women's liberation, reducing recidivism, slowing the arms race, and conserving the ecology is certainly remarkable.

If, in fact, a tight full-employment policy can have all these benefits, why haven't administrations and Congressmen pressed for its adoption?

The answer is that such a policy does have a cost, and the cost is inflation. Experience indicates that an unemployment rate of 2 to 3 percent is associated with an annual increase in the price level of more than 6 percent per year.

In 1959, Professors Paul Samuelson and Robert Solow modified and adapted to the United States the "Phillips Curve," named for Professor A. W. Phillips of Great Britain, who offered the first version of it. The *Phillips-Samuelson-Solow (or PSS) curve* shows the average historical relationship between price level changes (inflation or deflation) and unemployment. According to Samuelson and Solow, in the United States during the 1930s, 1940s, and 1950s, price stability was obtained only with an average unemployment rate of 5 1/2 percent and full employment (defined as an unemployment rate of 3 percent) was achieved only with an average price level increase of 4 1/2 percent per year. Their PSS curve suggested that the U.S. economy did not, as a rule, achieve price stability and full employment together but rather had to choose between them.

In Figure 6-1, Samuelson and Solow's figures have been updated, and the depression and war years omitted. The resulting PSS curve is even worse than the original. The "cost" of price stability turns out to be an unemployment rate of around 6 1/2 percent, while the "cost" of full employment may be an inflation rate as high as 9 percent! One might well

FIGURE 6 - 1

**A PSS Curve Showing Unemployment Rates and Changes
in the Consumer Price Index from 1949 to 1972**

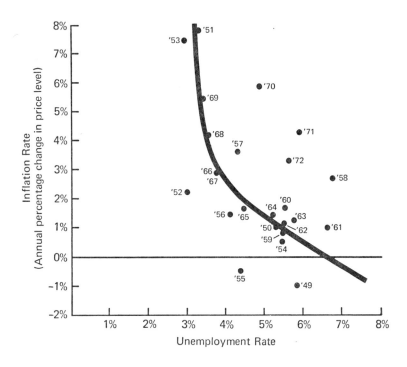

conclude, in spite of the impressive benefits to be derived from a full-employment policy, that it is simply not a viable option. The PSS curve in Figure 6-1, however, does not tell the entire story. It does not, for example, purport to be an economic law. It merely describes and summarizes what has happened, in the past. Moreover, the existence of a number of points off the curve underlines the fact that there is nothing controlling about the relationship.

A second point to be considered is that not all full-employment policies are equally inflationary. A somewhat exaggerated illustration will help make the point. Suppose that the unemployment rate is 6 percent and that getting it down to 3 percent would involve finding jobs for 2.5 million workers. The 2.5 million unemployed persons are, for the most part, hard-to-employ persons of low or uncertain productivity, older persons with obsolete skills, the unskilled and undereducated poor, school dropouts, and various new entrants into the labor force. Government officials can ponder two ways to lower the unemployment rate.

The first is via general fiscal and monetary techniques such as a general tax cut, which would affect primarily the employed and those with substantial incomes. Although the initial beneficiaries of this action are not the unemployed, there is what is called a *multiplier effect*. The initial beneficiaries of the tax cut will probably spend the major part of their increased after-tax income. Those who sell goods and services to them will also, for the most part, spend most of what they receive. This second round of spending will generate a third, and so on. The increase in demand caused by all this spending should raise prices and expand profit opportunities; hopefully, the resultant boom will be strong enough, ultimately, to create jobs for the 2.5 million hard-to-employ workers. But the process of getting these people employed will also involve bidding workers from one job to another; competition for scarce natural resources and other factors of production; and a considerable shifting of resources in the economy. The entire process will be inflationary.

The second approach the government can consider is to provide more directly for the employment of the 2.5 million unemployed. This could be done through government employment or through inducements to industry to hire unemployed persons. As an alternative, tax cuts and greater spending could be concentrated in the areas of where unemployment and poverty are greatest. The total pressure on the economy required to get the unemployed employed would be much less than in the case of a general tax cut because the expansion would be selective. The process will still raise prices, but not as much. For example, suppose that all the unemployment is on the West Coast. (This is an extreme oversimplification and would probably not happen in the real world, but it will serve to make the point.) The government could get rid of most of this by injecting funds into the region through various expenditure programs. It could also get rid of West Coast unemployment by spending money only on the East Coast, if it spent enough money and waited long enough. But the latter policy would be vastly more inflationary.

The Public Employment Program (PEP), created by the Emergency Employment Act of 1971, is a good example of a program that follows this second approach. In periods of high unemployment, federal funds are made available to state and local governments to hire unemployed and underemployed workers—though not necessarily the chronically unemployed or the poor. The jobs provided must be "transitional"—that is, they must lead to permanent public- or private-sector positions. A few poor people have been helped, but PEP is viewed as an antiunemployment program rather than an antipoverty program, and the percentage of participants who are poor is small.

Some inflation is almost certain to occur as a transitional byproduct of shifting to a full-employment policy. To an extent, this inflation will result from the increase in wages in low-wage industries (vegetables and fruits will cost more, for instance, if farm workers receive above-poverty wages), as well as from the higher costs inherent in employing workers whose productivity is low. As time goes by, however, as wages in even the lowest-wage industries stabilize at a decent level and experience increases the productivity of the formerly unemployed, the upward pressure on prices should dissipate. Prices will not fall to their prior level, of course, but the inflation should abate somewhat.

In short, although there are ways to minimize the inflationary consequences of a tight full-employment policy, and although some of the remaining inflation will be only transitional, it is unlikely that full employment can be achieved with no inflation at all. Some inflation will remain—though certainly nothing like 6 or 9 percent. Fortunately, there are ways of making inflation more tolerable. Social Security benefits and other government pensions, for example, can be tied to the price level; the federal government could issue "purchasing-power bonds" whose redemption value was tied to the price level, both for individual savers and private pension funds; and international monetary changes could insulate the balance of payments somewhat from the harmful effects of small but persistent price-level increases.

There are basically only two ways of eliminating poverty. One is to provide poor people with above-poverty incomes through the welfare system. The other is to employ them at above-poverty wages and salaries. In almost all circumstances, the latter strategy requires a job-creation program of some kind. There is simply no getting around that fact. As for structural techniques such as education, training, relocation, and job placement programs, although they cannot solve aggregate-demand problems and hence cannot increase the total number of jobs, they do have a role to play. They can raise productivity and hence wages, and, by making the unemployed easier to employ, they can reduce the inflationary consequences of a tight full-employment policy. Preparing people for and helping them look for jobs that do not exist can at times be worse than doing nothing at all; but, obviously, the same criticisms do not apply when there are vacancies.

THE EDUCATION STRATEGY

From casual comments, one discerns that education (including skill training) is the favorite "solution" to poverty of the man or woman in the street. Judging from the programs brought into being under the "War on Poverty" rubric, or at least related to it, this opinion has been shared by those in government, at least during Lyndon Johnson's administration. Operation Head Start was initiated to deal with the special needs of preschool children from poor families. Programs for the disadvantaged were emphasized in the Elementary and Secondary Education Act of 1965, for in-school youth. The Job Corps and the Neighborhood Youth Corps programs, among others, focused on youth outside of school. New manpower programs for adults were developed. A number of programs that antedated the "poverty program," such as the Manpower Development Training Administration, Adult Basic Education, and federal aid to vocational training, were reoriented and made, at least in large part, poverty programs. Though antipoverty programs in the area of education were concentrated in the federal government's Office of Economic Opportunity, Office of Education, and Department of Labor, other departments, such as Health, Education and Welfare (which had the "WIN" program discussed in Chapters 4 and 5) and even Defense (which had "Project 100,000," a scheme to draft and provide Army training for 100,000 disadvantaged young men), were called upon to make contributions.

The Nixon administration put less emphasis on education for the poor. "Career Education," its major new effort in the education area, seems to emphasize the poor and disadvantaged, however, and the administration seems to have accepted the theory of poverty on which the education strategy is implicitly based. In this section, we will review the major federal programs in the area of education. We will then look at the successes and failures of these programs. Where there have been failures, we will inquire as to the possible reasons.

Federal education and training programs divide logically—and chronologically, when enrollees' ages are considered—into three categories: programs for preschool children; programs for those in grades K-12, including career and vocational education and Title I aid programs; and, finally, manpower programs for young people and adults.

Federal Programs for Early Childhood Development. Pressures are building for a greatly expanded program of preschool child care and development. They arise from at least four sources. One is a desire to use preschool education to break the cycle of poverty, cultural deprivation, and low learning potentials. The second is a desire on the part of educators and parents of nonpoor children to take advantage of the considerable learning abilities of preschool children and to give them more educational, recreational, and socialization opportunities than they would have at home. The third is the fact that many persons view the availability of adequate numbers of professionally staffed day-care facilities, which would permit mothers of young children to work, as a way of eliminating poverty and dependency. (Day-care will be discussed more fully later.) Finally, there are pressures arising from the women's liberation movement, which has called for day-care facilities for all children. Pressures from these four sources are not always focused on the same kind of early childhood development program, but they do point to some kind of expanded program in the 1970s.

Operation Head Start, which was created in 1965, provides summer and year-round preschool experiences to children of the poor. The program has been extremely popular with participants, staff members, and voters, but its effect on the cycle of poverty is a matter of dispute. Indeed, there has probably been more controversy over evaluations of Head Start than over the program itself. However, several points can be made with a fair amount of assurance.

One is that short programs (for two months or less), such as summer-only programs, have almost no effect on the cycle at all. Another is that, where Head Start or similar programs have raised IQs, the effects have "decayed" quickly when the children were placed in unchanged elementary school classes. These two points are consistent with our understanding of vicious-circle poverty, which implies that what is needed are strong, secure, continuing programs rather than quick, one-shot, crash efforts. For these reasons, emphasis has shifted from summer-only to year-round programs. And a follow-through program to provide continuing compensatory aid to Head Start graduates has been created to supplement school experiences in after-school hours.

Head Start has had important health and nutritional consequences. As Professors Marshall S. Smith and Joan S. Bissell point out,

despite the controversy about the "overall" effectiveness of Head Start, there is striking evidence that both summer and full-year centers have been successful in at least one area: large numbers of children who might otherwise have gone unattended have received medical and dental care through the Head Start Centers.

They note, moreover, that

a fact sheet released by the Office of Economic Opportunity in March, 1967, reported the following accomplishments of the medical program:
98,000 children with eye defects were discovered and treated;
90,000 children with bone and joint disorders were discovered and referred for special treatment;
900,000 dental cases were discovered, with an average of five cavities per child;
740,000 children were discovered without vaccinations against polio and were immunized through Head Start; [and]
more than 1,000,000 children were found not to be vaccinated against the measles, and were immunized through Head Start.

The Office of Child Development, which administers the Head Start program, is building upon these health-care achievements in a demonstration program called "Health Start," begun in 1971, whose purpose is to provide medical and dental screening and services to preschool poor children. Laudable as they are, however, these efforts constitute only one more patch in America's patchwork welfare system. The need that prompts them reflects once again the serious health-care deficit of America's poor.

Federal Programs for Grades K-12.   Three federal programs require discussion here: the Career Education and Vocational Education programs and Title I of the Elementary and Secondary Education Act (ESEA) of 1965.

Career Education is the newest and least well-defined of the three programs. Sidney P. Marland, Jr., then Commissioner of Education and later appointed to the newly created position of Assistant Secretary for Education in the Department of Health, Education and Welfare, declared in 1971 that his highest priority mission was to ensure that every pupil completing high school in the United States had either a ticket to college or a marketable skill. Accomplishing this involves more than a heavier emphasis on vocational education. It involves virtually doing away with the "general" curriculum (as opposed to college-prep and vocational curricula), which has been an educational and economic dead-end for so many poor children. The federal government now funds a number of research and demonstration projects and encourages school districts to emphasize career education. However, it will be a long time before it will be possible to evaluate this program.

The federal government contributes handsomely to vocational education (or voc-ed) programs in secondary schools, paying 23 percent of the costs. But the quality of voc-ed programs continues to vary widely, partly because the U.S. Office of Education (USOE), in administering federal aid, does little to monitor its use. Consequently, too many voc-ed programs continue to constitute the bottom track in the schools in which they are found, or even a largely custodial dumping ground for lower-class children; and too many shop courses make do with obsolete, donated equipment. Yet vocational curricula are typically better than the general program mentioned above.

The ESEA is a landmark piece of legislation—the culmination of over a decade of debate about federal aid to K-12 education. Title I solved an impasse over the distribution of federal funds by capitalizing on the mid-1960s concern with poverty, distributing funds among school districts according to the incidence of poverty and focusing within school districts on schools serving poor neighborhoods. Within the schools, funds were to be used for "educationally deprived" children, most of whom are presumably poor.

The most common criticism of Title I, however, is that the funds are often used for purposes other than special programs for the disadvantaged—a charge that has frequently been borne out by audits. In many instances, federal funds were treated as general aid. The NAACP has charged that there have been serious violations of law in state administration of the program. These charges have brought some changes in the USOE's monitoring policy but no legislative changes.

Federal Manpower Programs.   The size, character, and purposes of the main federal manpower programs in existence in 1972 are shown in Table 6-2. Beginning in 1974, the Comprehensive Employment and Training Act (CETA) replaced many of these programs, including the Manpower Development Training Administration (MDTA), with a form of ''manpower revenue sharing,'' under which the federal government provides states and localities with cash grants, and the latter conduct training programs. In spite of the shift of responsibility from federal to state and local governments, the purposes and methods of the programs, as well as their clientele, are expected to continue much as before.

The WIN program, a revised public employment program, and the Job Corps will continue as Federal programs.

The first important manpower program was MDTA, created in 1962 to deal not with poverty but with unemployment that was attributed to automation and related causes. In the mid-1960s, MDTA became in large part a poverty program with 65 percent of its slots reserved for disadvantaged workers.

Garth L. Mangum, perhaps the nation's leading authority on manpower programs, sums up the contribution of the MDTA in the following way.

Although MDTA has to its credit numerous accomplishments which more than justify their cost, its original goal is not among them. The Act was passed primarily on the assumption that widespread job vacancies existed and that unemployment could be reduced by training the unemployed to fill them. Tens of thousands of persons trained under the Act are employed more steadily or have higher earnings than could have been expected if they had not participated in the program. The annual *Manpower Report of the President*, required by the Act, has raised manpower policy to a visibility and a status second only to fiscal and monetary policy in the hierarchy of economic policy-

TABLE 6 – 2

Federal Manpower Programs in Existence in 1972

(Total Enrollment 649,000)

Name	Functions	Persons Eligible
MDTA institutional program (43,500 enrollees)	Trains or retrains unemployed workers, emphasizing skills needed by local employers. Trainees receive allowances equal to unemployment compensation. Some supplementary classroom education in basic skills (reading, writing) and work habits is given.	Unemployed, underemployed, and poorly paid workers
JOBS *a* and other OJT programs (104,600 enrollees)	Works with National Alliance of Businessmen (NAB) to get private-sector jobs for the hard-core unemployed. Federal government pays a subsidy of up to $3,000 per worker.	"Disadvantaged" workers only
Neighborhood Youth Corps in-school and summer programs (104,100 enrollees) *b*	Provides part-time and summer work for pay and experience, and to discourage dropping out, in recreation facilities, hospitals, and community agencies.	High-school youth from poor families (variable income line)
Neighborhood Youth Corps out-of-school programs (42,100 enrollees)	Provides work experience, remedial education, and other aid to school dropouts and makes an effort to get them back in school.	Dropouts 14 – 18 years old from poor families (variable income line)
Operation Mainstream (28,600 enrollees)	Creates jobs and provides training for chronically unemployed and disadvantaged adults and senior citizens in rural areas.	Rural adults chronically unemployed or disadvantaged

Name	Functions	Persons Eligible
Public Service Careers Program (20,700 enrollees)	Provides on-the-job training and supportive services in entry-level positions in federal, state, and local government and nonprofit agencies; also attempts to stimulate upgrading other employees.	Disadvantaged persons
Public Employment Program (142,300 enrollees)	Creates federally financed jobs in state and local government when the national unemployment rate exceeds 4½ percent or a local rate exceeds 6 percent for three consecutive months.	Unemployed or underemployed workers
Concentrated Employment Program (30,000 enrollees)	Provides training and supportive services in urban and rural neighborhoods with particularly high rates of unemployment and poverty.	Unemployed and disadvantaged workers
Job Corps (22,200 enrollees)	Provides work training, remedial basic education, and other services in 65 Job Corps Centers throughout the U.S.	Disadvantaged youth
Work Incentive Program (WIN) (111,000 enrollees)	Requires all but specifically exempted adults receiving AFDC to register for employment or training to keep their AFDC eligibility; discussed in Chapter 5.	Eligible AFDC recipients

SOURCE: Most of the information in the table is from the *Manpower Report of the President, 1972* (Washington, D.C.: U.S. Government Printing Office). For other sources, consult the reference sections at the end of Chapters 4, 5, and 6.

[a] JOBS enrollees hired by employers who do not receive federal subsidies are not included.
[b] This figure reflects the November 1972 enrollment. The August figure was nearly 700,000.

making. Federal, state, and local governments are engaged in various forms of manpower planning. MDTA's experimental and demonstration projects developed new tools for serving the disadvantaged, which were to become basic strategies in the "war against poverty." These innovations and the earmarking of federal funds to such purposes have provided leverage to pressure lethargic institutions into serving population groups unfamiliar to them in new ways. The Act's research funds have uncovered new information and relationships, but, more important, they have played a major role in shifting the attention of academic labor economists from industrial relations to manpower problems. It is even possible that lower levels of unemployment may be achievable, with a given degree of price stability, than would have been the case without MDTA and related programs. However, *there is no evidence that the unemployment rate is appreciably lower than it would have been had the program never existed.* [Emphasis added—A.D.T.]

To see what lies behind Mangum's statement, we must examine the successes and failures not only of manpower programs, but of the entire education strategy.

Successes and Failures.   How successful has the education strategy been? There are three possible *levels* of success for these—and many other, noneducational—antipoverty programs. Too many people, including some who should know better, tend to confuse these three types of success.

First, there is the programs' *educational* success, however one wants to measure it. Have compensatory education programs succeeded in improving the school performance, raising the IQ scores, or increasing the skills and knowledge of the economically disadvantaged?

Second, there is the programs' *economic* impact on *individuals*. If educational programs have economic goals, as all those mentioned do, then they can be evaluated in economic terms. Have they resulted in lower unemployment rates and higher incomes for enrollees?

It is worth pointing out that educational programs can contribute to economic success without necessarily being an educational success. People who learn nothing useful in school but nonetheless receive diplomas (or who only attend and receive no academic credentials) can still go on to earn more as a result of their educational experiences. It is worth pointing out, also, that educational success is no guarantee of economic success. However much people tend to confuse the two, they are frequently separate and distinct.

And third, there is the programs' *economic* impact on *society* as a whole. Have they reduced *overall* unemployment rates or *overall* poverty, as opposed to merely redistributing unemployment and poverty? Confusion between a program's effect on individuals and its macroeconomic (societywide) success is even more common than confusion between the educational and economic results. For example, if those who complete a manpower training program have lower unemployment rates or higher incomes than a control group of similar persons, there is a tendency to conclude that the program is a success. But the unanswered question is whether *other* people *failed* to get nonpoverty jobs because the enrollees got them. In other words, is there any way that educational programs can increase the total number of nonpoverty jobs; or do they only influence who gets them, by moving their enrollees toward the front of the line?

Unfortunately, educational programs have not been terribly successful at any of the three levels.

Educational Success.   There is no consistent evidence of educational success in compensatory education programs run by school systems. This is true, specifically, in the case of Head Start and ESEA Title I, according to official evaluation studies. Subsequent research has not invalidated the finding of the famous Coleman Report of 1966, that differences in educational resources do not seem to explain differences in educational outcomes among the poor—that dollars do not seem to matter.

Indeed, after enormous expenditures on experimental and demonstration programs and on evaluation studies, we know very little about what makes for educational success. A massive RAND Corporation survey of *all* current research bearing on the determinants of educational effectiveness reached the following conclusions:

1. Research has not identified a variant of the existing system that is consistently related to students' educational outcomes. . . . We are not suggesting that nothing makes a difference, or that nothing "works." Rather, we are saying that research has found nothing that consistently and unambiguously makes a difference in student outcomes.

2. Research suggests that the larger the school system, the less likely it is to display innovation, responsiveness, and adaptation and the more likely it is to depend upon exogenous shocks to the system.
3. Research tentatively suggests that improvement in student outcomes . . . *may* require sweeping changes in the organization, structure, and conduct of educational experience.

In another massive survey, the American Institutes for Research in the Behavioral Sciences reviewed *all* available evaluation studies and reports of precollege compensatory programs for disadvantaged children in the United States. Of over 1,200 evaluation reports reviewed, 422 provided follow-up on the programs, and 326 provided detailed evaluation on information that met the study's standards. Of the 326 programs reviewed in this fashion, only ten met the majority of the project's criteria for success. The remaining 316 did not necessarily fail educationally. In most cases, the "evaluation methodology was so inadequate that a conclusion about [their] success or failure could not be drawn." The consistent failure to provide for adequate data collection and evaluation in demonstration or exemplary programs is a major reason why we are still in the dark about how to design educationally successful compensatory programs.

Why have there been so few educational successes? Some writers attribute the lack of success to defects in the children; others attribute it to defects in the schools.

Psychologist Arthur R. Jensen, in one of the most controversial studies of recent times, argues that differences in intelligence and abstract learning ability are largely genetic, or inherited. He further argues that lower-class children (whose measured IQs tend to be lower than those of other children) and black children (whose measured IQs also independently tend to be lower) are less intelligent because they have inherited less intelligence. Jensen appears to be arguing for statistical support for the notion of racial inferiority, although he uses his results to "explain" the failure of compensatory education.

Of course, Jensen's findings have not gone unchallenged. There are scholars who dispute his interpretation of the data. Indeed, there are scholars who argue that virtually *all* differences in intelligence are explained by environmental factors (including health, nutrition, and prenatal care) rather than heredity. There are many documented cases of significant increases in measured intelligence associated with educational programs, improved health and nutrition, and even increased incomes. One of the most dramatic examples is that of the Osage Indians, whose scores on IQ tests were once among the lowest in America, well below those of blacks and other deprived groups. After oil was discovered on their reservation, raising their incomes suddenly and significantly, and incidentally providing a test of the income strategy, their test IQs rose to equal the national norms!

In Chapter 2, we noted that illness, malnutrition, lead poisoning, and cultural deprivation can have profound and sometimes permanent effects on intelligence. Although preschool programs like Head Start may be able to offset some of the effects of cultural deprivation (though there is no strong evidence that they do), there is *no* way of overcoming permanent organic damage through education. Pouring additional resources into education will do little for the child with permanent brain damage from eating leaded paint chips or from his mother's and his own chronic malnutrition.

As we have seen, the RAND Corporation study concludes that a drastic shakeup of the U.S. school system may be necessary in order to improve educational outcomes. This seems to be particularly true with regard to poor children and members of racial minorities, who to a very large extent have been failed by the schools. Accounts of individual experiences and impressions, such as Jonathan Kozol's *Death at an Early Age* or Charles Silberman's *Crisis in the Classroom*, reveal systematic patterns of prejudice, lack of concern, and lack of effort in the direction of poor children. And horror stories such as Kozol's do not seem to be exceptional cases; they are consistent with detailed studies, such as Patricia Cayo Sexton's *Education and Income*, and with statistical evidence on the treatment of poor people in school systems.

Consequently, a substantial reform of the American school system seems to be a prerequisite to successful use of the schools as a vehicle for antipoverty strategy. It is undoubtedly for this reason that the Office of Economic Opportunity (OEO) has sponsored a number of school-reform experiments, such as having a school district in effect hire a private firm to run the schools and pay the firm according to the degree of pupil achievement, as measured by test scores ("performance contracting") and giving families "vouchers" that can be used to pay tuition for their children at the school of their choice, so that schools are led to compete with each other. Some federal policy-makers have even suggested that Career Education, mentioned earlier, is a vehicle for reforming schools and school systems. The U.S. Office of Education and the National Institute for Education, who are in charge of Career Education, are federal agencies, as is OEO, but education decisions are made predominantly at the state and local level. Moreover, entrenched bureaucracies such as the American school system are exceedingly difficult to change, no matter what level of government does the trying.

Perhaps an answer to the failure of compensatory education is that we expect too much of the schools. There is a tradition that schools have, in the past, been important in eliminating poverty, particularly among immigrants in big cities. Colin Greer, in an impressively documented study called *The Great School Legend*, shows that this tradition is almost entirely a myth. High failure and dropout rates and delinquency are an old story for America's inner-city schools. Moreover, these problems existed even when the inner cities were all white.

Individual Economic Success. When the criterion of success for educational programs is their impact on the economic position of individuals, the results are just as discouraging. The two main evaluative techniques used by economists—benefit-cost analysis and rate-of-return analysis—have shown very poor results. The benefit-cost ratio is a popular tool of economic analysis, particularly in evaluating public-expenditure programs. All the economic benefits of a program are estimated (in the case of educational programs, these are mainly increases in lifetime earnings), as are all the economic costs. If either benefits or costs will occur in the future, they are "discounted," using an appropriate interest rate, on the theory that future dollars are worth less than present dollars. The ratio of benefits to costs is an index of a program's success. (The higher it is, of course, the better.) Thomas Ribich, in a Brookings Institution study, calculated benefit-cost ratios for several poverty-oriented educational programs conducted both through and outside the regular school system. In general (with one exception, to be noted later), the programs Ribich examined had benefit-cost ratios of less than one. They did not, in other words, return their cost. According to these studies, it would have been more economical simply to have given the money to the poor than to have spent it on the compensatory education programs analyzed. In rate-of-return analysis, expenditures on education are treated as an "investment," and increases in income as the "return." A rate of return is then calculated, as on any investment. Studies indicate that rates of return are much lower for poor children and for racial minorities than for nonpoor and for white children, often close to nil. Jobs are made for those who work in the schools or other educational programs, but the poor who are the intended targets of the programs receive no significant, measurable economic benefit.

Similar conclusions are reached by Christopher Jencks and his associates at the Center for Educational Policy Research in their important and controversial book, *Inequality*. These researchers find that variations in educational attainment do not have, very much to do with income distribution:

> The primary reason some people end up richer than others is not that they have more adequate cognitive skills. While children who read well, get the right answers to arithmetic problems, and articulate their thoughts clearly are somewhat more likely than others to get ahead, there are many other equally important factors involved. Thus there is almost as much economic inequality among those who score high on standardized tests as in the general population. Equalizing everyone's reading scores would not appreciably reduce the number of economic "failures."

There is one exception to this dismal finding. Ribich and others find consistently high benefit-cost ratios for manpower training programs; and those using other methods of evaluation find frequent success, measured in individual economic terms. Ribich, for instance, reports on three programs with benefit-cost ratios averaging about ten to one—$10 in benefits for every $1 of outlay. Even in this regard, though, not every program is equally successful. Of the programs listed in Table 6-2, the MDTA program and JOBS seem the most successful at this level. The most doubtful programs, according to the evidence and the analysts, are the Work Incentive Program, the Concentrated Employment Program, the Neighborhood Youth Corps, and the Job Corps.

Societywide Economic Success. If educational programs do not succeed in significantly reducing poverty or unemployment at the individual level among enrollees, they cannot succeed in reducing them nationwide. And even if programs do succeed at the individual level, there is no assurance that they will succeed nationally. When a previously unemployed enrollee gets a job or a previously employed enrollee gets a better job, there is no assurance that that job was not, in effect, taken from someone else.

It is extremely difficult to ascertain the success or failure of a program at this all-important national level. Graduates of programs who get jobs are easier to locate and count than nongraduates who fail to get them. Such evidence as is available suggests that most of the manpower programs that are successful at the individual level are not successful in a larger sense. D. O. Sewell, whose study of benefits and costs of training the poor is probably the most thorough and methodologically careful yet, shows that the increase in earnings of trainees noted in previous studies—including Ribich's—consisted entirely of increases due to reduced unemployment, rather than to higher average hourly earnings. He presents convincing evidence that reduced unemployment of trainees is offset by increased unemployment of other poor people. Consequently, programs that are successful from an individual economic standpoint are failures from a societywide perspective. Jobs are merely redistributed among the poor. But Sewell then proceeds to find, in his own study of a rural North Carolina training program, *both* increased hourly earnings and reduced unemployment, which he takes to mean that the trainees' productivity actually increased; and he finds "true" benefit-cost ratios averaging around three to one. There is, then, at least one apparent MDTA success.

As we saw in Chapter 2, economist Lester Thurow has attacked the notion that those with the most education have the most income mainly because of the skills they have learned or the capacities they have developed in school. He argues that the distribution of income depends on the distribution of job opportunities in the economy—that there are high-wage jobs and low-wage jobs, that skills are taught informally on the job, and that employers prefer to hire persons with more schooling not because they are already skilled but because they are thought to be trainable. The difference may seem slight, but it is all-important. If schooling provides people with skills and raises their productivity, then more schooling for the poor can increase their productivity and raise their incomes, without lowering anyone else's income. But if schooling only improves access to better jobs, and the actual training takes place on the job, then more schooling for the poor would give them access to jobs that would otherwise go to others, and any increase in the incomes of the one group would be at the expense of the other. The incidence of poverty among certain groups would change, but the total amount of poverty would remain the same.

If Thurow's argument is correct, programs that appear successful at the individual level would all be failures at the societywide level. This would be true even for the one manpower program found by Sewell to be an apparent success. Since manpower programs make a special effort to place their graduates in good jobs, and since many employers presumably favor program graduates over otherwise similar persons who have not taken manpower training courses, it should not be surprising that graduates have not only lower unemployment rates but also better jobs, at higher wages. This does not mean that there has been any overall gain in income and output, or any overall reduction in poverty.

It is for this reason that Garth Mangum, in the statement quoted earlier, admits that there is no evidence that the MDTA has lowered the unemployment rate at all. But Mangum believes, nonetheless, that the MDTA has been a success, not a failure, from a social as well as an individual standpoint, because it has increased equality of opportunity. He and John Walsh, in a history of the MDTA, present the following argument:

> But who expected manpower training to reduce general levels of unemployment? That could be achieved only by (1) speeding the rate of economic growth and job creation, (2) adding to the efficiency of the labor market to reduce the average duration of unemployment, or (3) reducing the size of the labor force. A training program does none of these. . . .
>
> Is there justification for expenditures of funds wrested from taxpayers in order to supply skills which can only increase competition for existing jobs? . . . The long-term objective of the American society has been the expansion of individual freedoms, achievable in a concrete sense only by broadening the range of choices available to each individual. If that can be accomplished by increasing the total supply of opportunity, so much the better. If not, each individual should have his choices expanded, even if by doing so, he forces others to face greater competition in attaining their choices. . . .
>
> MDTA is best evaluated in this context. It would be well to know whether by training A, we make him capable of winning a job in preference to B who would have otherwise obtained it. . . . But MDTA's role is a simple one: to identify individuals who, as defined by public policy, have limited opportunities and to expand those opportunities by training the individuals to enable them to compete more effectively for existing jobs. Demonstration of the program's ability to achieve these objectives requires only determination that most of the enrolled achieved improvements in their employment

stability and earnings substantially beyond that which would have
occurred in the absence of the program.

One needn't disagree with the spirit of Mangum and Walsh's statement
to note three important problems.

1. Their statement seems to concede that the MDTA is not successful *as
   an antipoverty program*, since it does not reduce total poverty.
2. If, as they suggest, the MDTA helps graduates compete more effectively with workers who are not disadvantaged, so that everyone has a
   more equal chance at success, then the program can be called successful in that sense. It is more likely, however, that manpower program
   graduates are moved ahead of *other poor people* in the competition for
   jobs. Some disadvantaged adults may be made more able to compete,
   but others may be made less able to compete.
3. Whenever a program tends to make poor, disadvantaged, and workers, especially those from minority groups, more able to compete with
   nonpoor, advantaged, white workers, one may confidently predict that
   the latter will strongly resist the program. This statement applies not
   only to training programs, but to civil rights programs, apprenticeship
   schemes, and placement programs as well. This is one reason manpower programs have stayed clear of occupations in which there are
   powerful unions or other entrenched groups. And this is, in fact, one
   reason so many white workers remain hostile to racial minorities and to
   any government program to increase opportunities for the racial
   minorities. They fear the competition.

Programs that merely reshuffle existing opportunities, then, tend
either to victimize other poor people or to increase intergroup hostility, or
both, without reducing overall poverty or unemployment. All of this,
meanwhile, costs the government billions of dollars that could have been
used to create jobs directly.

The Organizing Strategy

The organizing strategy entails the formation of community, interest,
or pressure groups, trade-union-type organizations, and the like by poor
people, to demand and support antipoverty programs and policies.
Those who advocate this approach argue that poor people stand to

achieve not only the specific goals they seek, but other advantages as well. For one thing, the gains achieved, having been sought by the poor themselves, would reflect their own estimates of their needs rather than well-meaning but biased middle-class notions of what poor people want. For another, organizing would give the poor vital institutional and political experience. Finally, and perhaps most important, organizing would give poor people a sense of power—a feeling that they could, to an extent, control their own lives and influence programs and agencies that affected them. This sense of power becomes extremely important when we recall that the poverty of the poor may be measured in terms of powerlessness. Those who advocate this strategy strongly favor the interpretation of poverty as a form of powerlessness.

Unfortunately, there are some built-in barriers to the effective organization of poor people. They lack both the financial resources upon which to build an organization and, often, the self-confidence needed to create a strong organization.

Second, it is difficult to organize people on the basis of characteristics they feel are undesirable or of which they may be ashamed. This accounts for the reluctance to join groups labeled "poor people's organizations" or "welfare clients' organizations." Neighborhood groups or groups formed to support particular policies are more likely to attract members.

And third, poor people who successfully challenge their condition do not remain poor and are unlikely to continue to feel solidarity with the poor or to want to retain membership in poor people's organizations. Thus such organizations tend to continually lose their best members. Once again, this suggests using some organizing principle other than poverty.

Of the dozens of approaches to organizing the poor, we will discuss the four most important: the Alinsky approach, welfare rights, Community Action Programs (CAPs) sponsored by the Office of Economic Opportunity (OEO), and the community control movement.

The Alinsky Approach. The late Saul Alinsky, who until his death in 1972 was Executive Director of the Industrial Areas Foundation, attempted to apply the techniques of militant industrial unionism, particularly those associated with the CIO in the 1930s, to the problems of the poor. Alinsky-organized or Alinsky-inspired organizations in Chicago, Kansas City, Oakland, Rochester, Syracuse, and elsewhere have met with mixed success. The Woodlawn Organization (TWO) in Chicago,

Alinsky's home base, is the largest and most successful of these groups, and has lasted the longest. The Community Action Training Corps (CATC) in Syracuse, N.Y., by contrast, had a brief (though hardly quiet) existence. Since its funds came not from the community (an Alinsky rule) but from the U.S. Office of Economic Opportunity, CATC was too vulnerable from the beginning to create problems for the local power establishment.

Alinsky's organizations are based on the following premises: that the chronic and pathological characteristics of poverty are associated more with powerlessness than with moneylessness; that this powerlessness not only makes people feel helpless, but makes them present-oriented (shortens their time horizon), making it unlikely that they will plan ahead or save; and that, even with no increase in income, these psychological dimensions of poverty can be attacked through organizing. In the words of Alinsky protégé Warren Haggstrom, who headed the Syracuse CATC, "when income remains constant, but persons in a neighborhood of poverty become involved in successful social action on important issues in their own behalf, their psychological orientation does extend over a greater period of time, their feeling of helplessness does lessen, [and] their skills and activities do gradually change."

Alinsky had at least two other organizing principles. One was that poor people must demand and take gains through power. Gains that are granted by the power structure through charity or for some other motive apart from responses to poor people's pressure can just as easily be taken away. The second is that making such gains through pressure and power inevitably involves conflict. Alinsky groups use such nonviolent techniques as rent strikes and sit-ins, as well as picketing and voter registration campaigns, in this conflict.

The ideal method of applying pressure, according to Alinsky, is to start with a strongly felt and easily attainable close-to-home demand (such as an added school crossing guard at a hazardous street corner), because it is essential that the first experience of poor people with organizing be both personally meaningful and, more important, successful.

There are divided opinions as to the success of the Alinsky organizations. Obviously, no quantitative test, such as benefit-cost analysis, is possible. It is not even clear exactly how, other than impressionistically, one can discern success from failure. TWO has won a number of struggles in Chicago, including political contests with the Daley machine;

critics say that it has not won enough. FIGHT in Rochester has won concessions from business; critics say, again, that the concessions are not enough. The same can be said of the gains of most such groups.

Clearly, from a national as opposed to a local standpoint, the critics are right; organizing successes in a few cities, with no general or national impact, is not sufficient to make this kind of grass-roots organizing a viable instrument against American poverty, whether it is defined in terms of moneylessness or powerlessness.

Welfare Rights Organizations. The only national welfare client group is the National Welfare Rights Organization (NWRO). It, too, is patterned on the model of trade unions, but in a more traditional way. It negotiates collectively for its welfare-recipient members, to win economic benefits for them. The NWRO is not above occasional non-violent civil disobedience, mainly sit-ins. It also tends to use the courts or the ballot box to gain its ends.

The NWRO has had a number of purposes. Professors Richard Clo-ward and Francis Fox Piven of New York University's School of Social Work first proposed such an organization in 1966, as a novel way of achieving a guaranteed income. According to Cloward and Piven, the amount of money the poor were eligible to receive from public assistance vastly exceeded the amounts actually paid, both because many who were eligible did not receive any assistance and because many of those who did received less than the full amount to which they were entitled. If poor people around the country organized to demand everything they were entitled to, they argued, the current inadequate, inefficient, and degrad-ing welfare system would collapse; and it would be necessary for the federal government to establish a new guaranteed income program. Although this strategy has been sharply criticized, it is too soon to claim that it has failed. It *is* true that NWRO activities have helped increase aggregate public assistance payments, and it *is* true that the Nixon administration did sponsor a welfare reform bill that many regarded as a step in the direction of a guaranteed income (although the Nixon ap-proach to welfare reform was opposed by the NWRO).

If the NWRO is really trying to destroy the public assistance system, that fact is not apparent from their activities. NWRO does advocate a guaranteed income program that would provide $6,500 for a family of four. But most of the activities of local chapters are directed not at obtaining the passage of national legislation, but at getting local or state welfare departments, or local or state legislators, to see their point of view on bread-and-butter issues. The NWRO was organized by the late Dr. George Wiley, who left a promising career as a chemistry professor at Syracuse University to work full-time first in CORE and then in the area of poverty rights. Wiley had just lost a national power struggle within CORE (an organization which NWRO went on to eclipse). On a shoestring, Wiley and his associates organized the NWRO, which by 1972 was unquestionably the premier national poor people's organization, in spite of the fact that it had faced the organizational problems mentioned earlier. Its constituency is inherently politically weak and by definition possessed of only meager financial resources. Nonetheless, the NWRO insists that all members pay dues and intends, ultimately, to be entirely self-supporting. The organizing principle—the receipt of public assistance—is one many people find demeaning. Yet one purpose of the NWRO is to raise the self-esteem of recipients. And the most aggressive and ambitious welfare recipients, one would guess, cease to be recipients and become self-sufficient rather than becoming leaders of the movement. Yet the NWRO leadership has been dynamic and aggressive.

The NWRO is hardly a mass movement. Only around 2 percent of all recipients are members. But its strength is concentrated in crucial areas such as New York City and is used effectively. If the organization continues to grow in numbers and in power, it will become a force to be reckoned with nationally as well as locally.

Significantly, at his death, Wiley was attempting to organize a national body called the Movement for Economic Justice, which would draw its membership from a broader group of the poor and the near-poor than did the NWRO, and which would not suffer as much from the organizational handicaps of poor people's groups.

Community Action Programs. Anomalously and, apparently, accidentally, when the Economic Opportunity Act of 1964 was passed, federal antipoverty funds were provided to a few local agencies to create Alinsky-type, conflict-oriented organizations of poor people to fight local government and other parts of the power establishment.

The act provided federal financing of local Community Action Programs (CAPs), whose purpose was to marshall and coordinate existing community resources and agencies and to attack poverty in ways over which the local community had discretion. It also provided for the "maximum feasible participation" of the poor themselves in running the programs.

Community Action Agencies (CAAs) running CAPs could be part of local government, or they could be independent, nonprofit agencies. Since an effort was made to establish the programs in a hurry, since each interpreted its mission somewhat differently, since some CAAs were tied directly to city hall and others were wholly independent of the local power structure, and since perceived needs varied widely from locality to locality, the variation in results was vast. In some cases, CAAs added to the patronage power of city hall. In other cases, they saw it as their mission to fight city hall. Though CAAs of the latter type were never very numerous and were by no means less successful than other CAAs in terms of the number of conventional missions accomplished, they did get the most publicity, all of it unfavorable from the standpoint of Congress.

One result was the shutting down of some programs, such as Syracuse's CATC, mentioned earlier. Another was a change in the legislation placing all the CAAs under the control of local governments. Today's CAAs tend not to be based on the organizing strategy; instead, they are "umbrella agencies" set up to receive federal funds, distribute them among various programs from Head Start to services to the elderly, and provide some degree of supervision of these programs.

Daniel P. Moynihan, who has been more critical than anyone else of the early Alinsky-type orientation of the CAAs, sees considerable value in them, nonetheless:

> Very possibly, the most important long run impact of the community action programs of the 1960s will prove to have been the formation of an urban Negro leadership echelon at just the time when the Negro masses and other minorities were verging towards extensive commitments to urban politics. Tammany at its best (or worst) would have envied the political apprenticeship provided the neighborhood coordinators of the antipoverty program.

The Community Control Movement. Finally, the community control movement, which came to prominence when controversy flared over schools in New York City (in the Ocean Hill-Brownsville area of Brooklyn) and over the police in Berkeley, California, relates in an important sense to the organizing strategy.

The main theme of the community control movement is that poor people and minority groups are unrepresented or underrepresented by those who make public policy and that they should at least control public services in their own neighborhoods. Attention has been concentrated on services that poor people and minorities feel are administered in ways hostile to their interests (such as police services) and those they believe have failed them (such as the school system).

The goals of community control groups are similar to those of poor people's organizing. There is the immediate goal of improved services. There is the goal of giving neighborhood people a voice in matters affecting them. And, finally, there is the goal of providing experience in working through an organization, face to face with leaders of government, industry, and labor.

Thus far, no community control effort has had substantial success. The two groups opposing it—policemen, schoolteachers, and others whose services are involved on the one hand, and the dominant, white majority on the other—are politically potent and unlikely to surrender their power without a struggle.

OTHER STRATEGIES AND TACTICS

Finally, there are a number of other actual or proposed strategies for combating poverty, as well as some tactics that are part of other strategies which still need to be discussed. These include (1) child care, minimum wages, and programs for improving health and nutrition, all of which are indirect employment-strategy programs, and (2) the provision of legal services and the use of violence, which are—in quite different ways —related to the organizing strategy.

Child Care. Those who advocate child care as a way of reducing poverty seem, usually, to be more concerned with reducing the AFDC rolls than poverty, though of course it is possible for policies to do both. They point to the large percentage of poor families headed by women (or the even larger percentage of AFDC families headed by women) and reason that if these women did not have to care for their children, they could go to work and "get off welfare."

There are important weaknesses in this approach. For one thing, it costs about $1,000 per year to provide after-school and summer care for school-age children and about $2,000 per year to provide care for preschool children (even more if special educational, health, and other services are to be provided the children). Thus for society to "break even" on child care (i.e., for the benefit-cost ratio to be at least one), it would be necessary for the head of an average family of four—the mother, a preschool child, and two school-age children—to earn $4,000, plus enough to cover train or bus fare and the other expenses of working. Most AFDC mothers lack the skills needed to earn that much, and training them would cost even more.

This is not to say that publicly supported day-care should not be made available. Day-care, especially when it is combined with a full-employment policy, can make it possible for many women to lead more rewarding lives. It may even permit some to escape poverty. But no one should expect miracles. This is a policy we can expect to cost money, not save it.

One suspects that the day-care strategy is often proposed by those who, consciously or unconsciously, object to public assistance on moral rather than economic grounds. A person who adhered to the individualist ideology described in Chapter 3 might be quite willing to put mothers of AFDC children to work, even if it cost tax money to do so. Yet even if a mother of three could earn $4,000 a year or so, she would still be poor. "Getting off welfare" and escaping poverty are not necessarily the same thing.

Publicly supported child-care facilities are more likely to fight poverty among the working poor than among AFDC families. Enabling a woman whose husband is present and working to go to work *as a second earner* can mean the difference between being poor and not being poor, especially for black families. In such cases, the wife's earnings add to the family's total income, instead of merely substituting for public assistance. The cut-off income for eligibility for child care should therefore be high enough to include the working poor.

Minimum Wages. Minimum wage laws, first passed in 1938, are among America's oldest antipoverty strategies. The idea, of course, is that placing a floor under the wages of the lowest-income workers ensures that anyone who works for a living will not be poor.

There are two problems with the minimum wage strategy.

First, as we saw in Chapter 4, minimum wage laws have never been universal. Moreover, those occupations excluded have always been those with the greatest concentrations of poor people.

And second, many economists believe that minimum wages cause unemployment. Their reasoning is as follows. Suppose there is a universal minimum wage of $2.00 per hour. Is it not likely, then, that anyone whose value to his or her employer is less than $2.50 an hour or so (allowing 50 cents an hour to cover such items as employer OASDHI taxes and other labor costs) will not be hired at all? Those hardest hit by the minimum wage laws are thought to be teenagers, especially those from poor and minority-group families.

Some people take the position that even if minimum wages do create short-term unemployment, their long-run effects are beneficial. Suppose an industry has traditionally been exempted from minimum wage laws, and that its wages are very low—below the poverty level. If the industry is then brought under the minimum wage laws, they argue two things will happen. First, production techniques will be changed, to use more capital and less labor. And, second, the price of the industry's products will rise somewhat. Sales will probably fall somewhat, thereby reducing still further the need for labor. The remaining workers will receive a wage above the poverty level, and those unemployed will eventually find better jobs elsewhere. Thus, in the long run they will actually benefit from being "forced out" of their jobs.

There are circumstances in which a minimum wage law could clearly be desirable, not as a major antipoverty strategy, but as part of a larger strategy, such as a full-employment policy. In the long run, a full-employment strategy would raise wages in low-wage industries anyway; a minimum wage law would speed up the process, and workers forced out of one industry would be absorbed elsewhere in the economy.

A minimum wage law would also facilitate a comprehensive welfare program or guaranteed income system that included an incentive element (an effective tax rate of less than 100 percent). With such a welfare program, the working poor would get partial assistance. Where their bargaining position was weak, employers might give them lower wages, keeping their total income at just about the same level as they were before. Just as a tax on businesses is sometimes shifted to consumers, so too welfare payments may be "shifted" in this way to employers. A minimum wage, in conjunction with the welfare program, could prevent this from happening.

Health and Nutrition Programs.   There is a substantial body of opinion to the effect that many problems of the poor, from lower intelligence and learning ability to apathy and low productivity, stem directly from poor health and malnutrition. We have noted in Chapter 2, in this chapter, and elsewhere that lead poisoning, vitamin deficiencies in pregnant mothers, poor nutrition during a person's early years, and inadequate health care for young children can cause irreversible brain damage, as well as physiological weaknesses.

Although there are medical and nutrition programs for the poor (notably Medicaid, the surplus commodities program, and food stamps), school lunch and even breakfast programs for the poor, and a federally assisted campaign against lead poisoning, the intensity and breadth of these efforts do not seem equal to the size of the problem. Much of the damage done, especially by lead poisoning and malnutrition, is preventable. But once it has occurred, there is no cure: No amount of education, no full-employment program, and no neighborhood organizing can reverse it.

A massive program of prevention seems, clearly, to be a necessary part of any really serious antipoverty campaign.

Legal and Consumer Protection Programs. As we noted in Chapter 2, poor people are vulnerable to all kinds of victimization and are often dealt with arbitrarily by public agencies over whom they have little control. One way of reducing their vulnerability is through consumer protection legislation and programs, through the Neighborhood Legal Services offices established through the OEO, and through the "law clinics" run for poor people by law schools and others.

Unfortunately, most existing consumer protection legislation is based on the disclosure principle—truth in lending, truth in packaging, and so on—and does not help those who are too unsophisticated to benefit from the facts disclosed. These laws reflect another unconscious bias of the dual economy. What is needed is tougher regulatory (as opposed to disclosure) statutes, together with a greater focus on consumer education of the poor.

Legal services for the poor have been important, not only in dealing with unscrupulous businesses, but also in challenging the actions of welfare departments and other public agencies. Much of the case law liberalizing welfare regulations and increasing the certainty of welfare payments has been written in courts where recipient plaintiffs were represented by, or at some time advised by, legal services organizations.

Riots. There is a disposition on the part of some people to consider the ghetto riots—the "civil disturbances"—that flared up in 1964 and raged for a number of years thereafter, peaking in 1968 after the assassination of Martin Luther King, Jr., as a kind of antipoverty, antiracist strategy aimed at "persuading" the business community and civic leaders to come through with new jobs, housing, and other programs.

It now seems clear that (1) the riots that did occur were not part of any grand strategy and (2) from a tactical standpoint, they didn't work. What the riots really were is too complex a subject to deal with here. They represented an explosion, a way of releasing tension that had become unbearable. They may have been psychologically useful, for rioters and the community alike, though that is far from certain. But to call them a strategy is to create an *ex post* rationalization of the facts.

As for their tactical results, one can point to occasional programs and policies created in response to the riots. There was definitely an increase in summer employment programs for youth. However, most of these were temporary and *ad hoc*, and made no lasting imprint. And more riots would not have made them permanent; more riots would only have brought more repressive security measures. Proposals for permanent policy changes—notably by the Kerner Commission—went wholly unheeded.

The riots had a substantial negative effect too. Businesses are less willing, now, to open in ghetto areas, reducing both employment opportunities and shopping alternatives for the poor. Insurance is harder to get. And the increased fear of poor, black people among middle-class whites has led to more resistance to school integration and a faster flight to the suburbs.

CONCLUSION: CAN WE HAVE A UNIFIED ECONOMY?

The American economy at present is a dual economy. Poor people must live with a consumption technology, an educational system, and a price structure designed to serve the nonpoor, to their further disadvantage. There is a dual labor market, which provides low-wage, irregular, and dead-end jobs to the poor. There is a dual welfare system, whose nature not only discriminates against the poor but whose characteristics often tend to keep them poor. There is a dual housing system, a dual health care system, and a double standard that affects everything from morals to social experiments.

Since much of this dualism is neither malicious nor conscious, the first step in changing it is to increase our consciousness of it. We have only recently begun to realize, as our unconscious biases have been pointed out to us by blacks, by other racial minorities, by women, and even by children, how fast our level of consciousness can rise. Where poor people are concerned, the new consciousness still has a long way to go.

The obvious place to begin to unify the American dual economy is in our social welfare programs, where duality arises out of a deliberate policy choice and not as a byproduct of an advancing consumption technology, the price structure, or the like. In other developed countries, though there tends to be a persistent debate between the advocates of "universal" and "selective" social welfare programs, the former win out far more frequently than they do in the United States, where virtually every welfare, health, housing, and employment program is designed specifically for either the poor or the nonpoor.

This dual approach is harmful, as we have seen. Separate programs for the poor are typically inferior; they involve demoralizing stigmata, and they tend to be built on the assumptions that poverty is attributable to defects in the poor, with demoralizing consequences.

Perhaps worst of all, this segregation of social welfare programs has separated, or seemed to separate, the interests of the poor from the interests of the rest of society. This separation has helped to foster a mutual hostility between the poor and lower-income nonpoor, notably the working class, which has been enormously destructive to the interests of both. It is hard to believe that much progress can be made against poverty in America while this separation and hostility persist.

REFERENCES

For a study of the economic problems of American Indians, see Alan L. Sorkin, *American Indians and Federal Aid* (Washington, D.C.: Brookings Institution, 1971); and the President's Commission on Income Maintenance Programs, *Background Papers* (Washington, D.C.: Government Printing Office, 1968). For Hyman Minsky's views, see his *Poverty: The Aggregate Demand Solution and Other Non-Welfare Approaches*, mimeographed (Los Angeles: UCLA Institute of Government and Public Affairs, 1965); or his article "The Role of Employment Policy," in Margaret S. Gordon, ed., *Poverty in America* (San Francisco: Chandler, 1965). The quotation in the text is from the latter source. The Samuelson and Solow version of the Phillips curve appears in their article, "Analytical Aspects of Anti-Inflation Policy," *American Economic Review*, 50 (May 1960). Information on the manpower programs discussed in this chapter can be found in the *Manpower Report of the President, 1973* (Washington, D.C.: Government Printing Office).

The RAND survey cited is Harvey A. Averch *et al.*'s *How Effective Is Schooling? A Critical Review and Synthesis of Research Findings* (Santa Monica, Calif.: The RAND Corporation). The survey was prepared for the President's Commission on School Finance. Also mentioned was Michael J. Wargo, Peggie L. Campeau, and G. Kesten Tallmadge's *Further Examination of Exemplary Programs for Educating Disadvantaged Children* (Palo Alto, Calif.: American Institutes for Research in the Behavioral Sciences, 1971). This survey was prepared for the U.S. Office of Education.

Benefit-cost analyses of a number of educational programs for the poor are reported in Thomas I. Ribich's *Education and Poverty* (Washington, D.C.. Brookings Institution, 1968). See also Bennett Harrison, "Education and Under-employment in the Urban Ghetto," *American Economic Review* (December 1972); Christopher Jencks *et al.*, *Inequality* (New York: Basic Books, 1972); and D. O. Sewell, *Training the Poor: A Benefit-Cost Analysis of Manpower Programs in the U.S. Anti-Poverty Program* (Kingston, Ontario: Industrial Relations Centre, Queen's University, 1971). The quote on p. 205 is from *Inequality*.

Arthur R. Jensen's long (117 pages plus references) and controversial theory is presented in his "How Much Can We Boost IQ and Scholastic Achievement?" *Harvard Educational Review*, 39 (Winter 1969). Jensen is a professor at the University of California, Berkeley. For separate comments on Jensen's article, see also J. M. Hunt, James Crow, Carl Bereiter, David Elkind, and Lee Cronbach, *Harvard Educational Review*, 39 (Spring 1969); and Rodger Hurley, *Poverty and Mental Retardation, A Causal Relationship* (New York: Random House, 1969).

Colin Greer, senior editor of *Social Policy*, is the author of *The Great School Legend* (New York: Basic Books, 1972). Lester Thurow's article "Education and Economic Equality," *Public Interest* (Summer 1972), was also discussed in Chapter 2. Charles Silberman's *Crisis in the Classroom* (New York: Random House, 1970) and Jonathan Kozol's *Death at an Early Age* (Boston: Houghton Mifflin, 1967), mentioned on p. 203, were both best sellers.

For a sample of the controversy over Head Start evaluations, see Marshall S. Smith and Joan S. Bissell, "Report Analysis: The Impact of Head Start," *Harvard Educational Review*, 40 (February 1970), from which the quotes on p. 195 are taken, and, in the same issue, Victor G. Cicirelli, John W. Evans, and Jeffry Schiller, "A Reply to the Report Analysis." Other sources are discussed in two papers from the Office of Child Development of the Department of Health, Education and Welfare: Lois-ellin Datta's "A Report on Evaluation Studies of Project Head Start," a paper presented at the 1969 Convention of the American Psychological Association; and *Review of Research 1965 to 1969 of Project Head*

Start (1969). The new program is discussed in Nancy Perlman, "What Is Health Start? Profiles of Selected Projects" (Washington, D.C.: Urban Institute, 1972).

For data on "Career Education," see the Office of Education of the Department of Health, Education and Welfare's *Career Education, A Handbook for Implementation* (Washington, D.C.: Government Printing Office, 1972).

The most publicized charges against Title I appear in Martin and McClure's "Title I of ESEA: Is It Helping Poor Children?" published by the Washington Research Project and the NAACP Legal Defense Fund (1969). For a survey and bibliography of studies, together with additional analyses, see the National Advisory Council on the Education of Disadvantaged Children's *The 1971 Annual Report to the President and Congress—Title I, ESEA—The Weakest Link, The Children of the Poor* (Washington, D.C.: 1971).

The quotation from Garth L. Mangum is from his book, *MDTA—Foundation of Federal Manpower Policy* (Baltimore: Johns Hopkins Press, 1968). The quotation from Mangum and John Walsh is from *A Decade of Manpower Development and Training* (Salt Lake City, Utah: Olympus, 1973). See also Joseph A. Kershaw's *Government Against Poverty* (Washington, D.C.: Brookings Institution, 1970); and Sar A. Levitan and Robert Taggart III's *Social Experimentation and Manpower Policy: The Rhetoric and the Reality* (Baltimore: Johns Hopkins Press, 1971).

Two articles on Saul Alinsky in Herman P. Miller's *Poverty, American Style* (Belmont, Calif.: Wadsworth, 1966) are especially useful. One, from which our quotation is taken, is Warren Haggstrom's "[Poverty] Perspectives from . . . [a] Psychologist"; the other, a reprinted newspaper article on the Syracuse CATC, is Erwin Knoll and Jules Witcover's "Organizing the Poor." For a critique of Alinsky, see Frank Riessman's *Strategies Against Poverty* (New York: Random House, 1969). An objective but sympathetic account of the development of the NWRO, from which our quotation is taken, is Gilbert Y. Steiner's *The State of Welfare* (Washington, D.C.: Brookings Institution, 1971). See also Richard Cloward and Francis Fox Piven's "A Strategy to End Poverty," *The Nation* (May 2, 1966). For information on the CAPs, see Kershaw, *op. cit.*, and Daniel P. Moynihan, *Maximum Feasible Misunderstanding* (New York: Macmillan, 1969).

For a discussion of minimum wages, see Jacob J. Kaufman and Terry G. Foran's "The Minimum Wage and Poverty," in Sar A. Levitan, Wilbur J. Cohen, and Robert J. Lampman, eds., *Towards Freedom from Want* (Madison, Wis.: Industrial Relations Research Association, 1967), reprinted in James G. Scoville, *Perspectives on Poverty and Income Distribution* (Lexington, Mass.: Heath, 1971).

Index

About the Author

A. Dale Tussing is Professor of Economics at Syracuse University and Senior Research Fellow at the Educational Policy Research Center at Syracuse. He received his Ph.D. at Syracuse and has taught at Washington State University. His books and articles have been in the fields of the economics of education, poverty, and employment problems, as well as public finance and related fields.

1 2 3 4 5 6 7 8 9 10 11 12 13 14 15   88 87 86 85 84 83 82 81 80 79 78 77 76 75